Communication and Culture

A Reading-Writing Text

Communication and Culture

A Reading-Writing Text

Fourth Edition

Joan Young Gregg
*New York City Technical College
of the City of New York*

Heinle & Heinle Publishers
*A Division of Wadsworth, Inc.
Boston, Massachusetts 02116 USA*

English Editor: Angela Gantner
Editorial Assistant: Tricia Schumacher
Production: Ruth Cottrell
Print Buyer: Diana Spence
Designer: John Edeen
Copy Editor: Beverly Cory
Cover: Lois Stanfield
Compositor: Graphic World, Inc.
Printer: Malloy Lithographing, Inc.

Photo credits: Serena Nanda: pages 1, 55, 125, 139, 197, 246, and 267; Joan Gregg: pages 18, 23, 165, and 170; United Nations: pages 29, 48, and 153; International Ladies Garment Workers' Union: page 83; Richard Kenefick: pages 108 and 247; Ravinder Nanda: page 109, left and right; Catherine Clark-Nelson: page 109, middle; Bianca Baar: page 175; Steve Girardi/NYCTC Media Service: page 187; John Gregg: page 204; Robert P. O'Rourk: page 221.

Manufactured in the United States of America.

Heinle & Heinle Publishers is a division of Wadsworth, Inc.

Library of Congress Cataloging-in-Publication Data

Gregg, Joan Young,
    Communication and culture : a reading-writing text / Joan Young
Gregg. —4th ed.
      p.   cm.
    ISBN 0-8384-50504
    1. English language—Textbooks for foreign speakers. 2. Culture—
—Problems, exercises, etc. 3. Intercultural communication.
4. English language—Rhetoric. 5. Reading comprehension.
6. Readers—Culture. 7. College readers. I. Title.
PE1128.G659   1992
808'.0427—dc20   92-20530
                                                  CIP

10 9 8 7 6 5 4 3 2 1

To Aunt Lee, with love

Preface

Communication and Culture has been successfully used in advanced English as a Second Language/Dialect reading and writing skills courses (both credit and noncredit) in community and four-year colleges over the past several years. It provides instruction for a minimum of ninety semester hours.

This Fourth Edition reflects the insights I have gained from two experiences in recent years. One is that of teaching advanced ESL composition in a different branch of the university, utilizing *Communication and Culture* with a new group of students and conducting classroom observations and consensus composition evaluation sessions in a new setting. This experience provided me with a refreshing perspective on the text and several ideas about how to improve it. The second experience that brought me fresh insights about second language acquisition, particularly in regard to academic reading and writing, was a recent sabbatical leave, which I spent working in French libraries and studying Italian, particularly museum publications. I hope that the fruits of these experiences will be discernible in this Fourth Edition.

The text still integrates reading, writing, and composing skills with rich content material from a well-known freshman anthropology textbook. The broad subject of human culture has proved stimulating and relevant to both students and instructors, and it provides a useful springboard for classroom discussion and college-level expository writing. Now more than ever, with the focus on pluralism and multicultural activities in every realm of our social and political lives, it is vital for students to understand the real meaning of these terms and develop an *informed* opinion about the various, often controversial issues that pluralism and multiculturalism raise.

To further this aim, the Fourth Edition adds a new Chapter Ten, which applies the cross-cultural concepts of the previous chapters to the pluralistic culture of the Caribbean and one of that region's most interesting subcultures, the Rastafarians.

Appendix A, "The Composition Process," Appendix B, "Basic Terminology for English Language Study," and Appendix C, a list of irregular verbs with their basic parts, have been found useful in fostering student independence in editing their written work and are retained in full; improvements have been made in the "Useful Signal Expressions for Coherence," a part of Appendix B that I have found increasingly more important in the ESL teaching of both reading and composition.

Organization and Use of the Text

The organization of the text has been significantly revised for this Fourth Edition, as the new chapter divisions indicate. It has been my aim to simplify the layout and rubrics of the text and make it more compact without eliminating those targets and exercises that have proven useful in past editions.

Chapter Opening

The use of each chapter's opening photograph as a subject for discussion and writing has been retained. In addition, a new feature, termed "Freewrite," stimulates students to write freely and informally on a theme related to that of the topic, but in a mode that emphasizes personal expression, fluency, and concrete detail rather than the more formal logic of the expository essay. The material elicited from students in this Freewrite may later serve as part of the content base for their more formal compositions, or it may simply be treated as a challenging personal exercise in the expression of feelings and ideas in English.

Vocabulary in Context

"Vocabulary in Context" is a new preliminary exercise that directs attention to approximately a dozen key words, highlighted with bold type in the text, that are important for literal comprehension of the reading passage. Students should be alerted not only to complete this exercise carefully before proceeding to the passage, but also to study the words on their own so that they will be able to mentally fill in the meaning as they read, without interrupting their pace to go to a dictionary.

Reading Passages

Reading passages range from about 1,000 words in the first chapter to more than 2,000 in the last. Each reading includes examples of the writing and composing items treated in the chapter's "Writing Exercises" and "Composition Development" sections; thus, selected passages can serve the student as a guide to writing in an academic style. The reading passages also use the target vocabulary items in natural academic contexts that can provide a model for the student's oral or written vocabulary development.

The content of the reading passages is excerpted from one of the most widely used introductory anthropology texts. This text, used in colleges nationwide and abroad, has been praised for its clarity of language and accessibility of conceptually complex materials appropriate for college freshmen. The text lends itself to use in content-skills bridge courses, and students may be appropriately tested on their comprehension of its content through examinations taken from the "Reading Comprehension" section, or through instructor-made multiple-choice quizzes or essay examinations.

Even when the text is being utilized only for a composition class, it is important that students read the passage before going on to the writing and composing material, as each chapter's reading material is the basis for the contextualized work in those sections.

Key Concepts

Students should review the key terms or themes from the reading passage before beginning to read, to ensure that they understand the literal meanings of the words employed. The instructor may wish to hold brief oral discussion of the terms, illustrating them with examples from students' own life experiences, before assigning the reading.

Reading Comprehension

This section has been redesigned and expanded. It contains a variety of questions designed to focus attention on the main ideas, significant details, relevant illustrations, expressions of coherence, and organizational patterns of paragraphs. The exercises are text-based, directing the students back to the reading passages for information and inferences.

The first "Reading Comprehension" exercise is generally a true–false quiz that requires critical thinking as well as comprehension of information. Review of student responses to this first exercise will indicate the extent to which students have grasped the basic facts and inferences of the reading passage.

The second comprehension item, "Reading Review," is a new exercise that contains thought questions requiring open-ended responses, preferably in written form. There is no better test of students' comprehension of academic material than whether they can answer, completely and precisely, and in comprehensible English, such questions as these. In addition, chalkboard presentation of student responses for peer critiquing is an invaluable aid to the improvement of both syntax and coherence of written work. Such open-ended questions as these also provide practice in the type of response often required on quizzes or short-essay examinations in credit courses.

The third comprehension section, "Analyzing the Text," focuses on function words, signal expressions, paragraph patterns, and similar types of material, related to the organization rather than the content of the reading passage.

In the fourth section, attention is focused on a particular reading target such as summarizing, paraphrasing, skimming, or scanning. These are discrete skills that transfer to students' reading assignments in their credit courses and provide students with a firm basis for academic success, regardless of their major.

Vocabulary Study

This section has been substantially revised to include more lexical items from the reading passages that may be unfamiliar to students and to better integrate the application of word forms. A mix of contextualized and non-contextualized items allows for the different vocabulary abilities of students, the former presenting greater conceptual challenges than the latter. While every instructor will have his or her own favorite method for students to acquire new vocabulary beyond the limits of this section, the new title word "Study" indicates my belief that concentrated, disciplined, and frequent review of new words is required for students to increase their receptive and productive vocabulary. Instructors should encourage students to apply their new vocabulary in their written work.

As in previous editions, the "Word Form Table" and "Word Formation" exercises focus on root, prefix, and suffix elements that aid students in building their vocabularies by semantic clusters.

Writing Exercises

Revisions have been made in this section of each chapter to sharpen the focus of the targets, simplify their presentation, and expand the number of exercises that require sustained sentence writing. At this level of composition, it is presumed that students have been formally exposed to the basics of English grammar, and it is not the aim of this section to reteach these items. Rather, the purpose of "Writing Exercises" is to provide coherent review of some of the points of syntax that students continue to have difficulty applying, even at the advanced level of ESL. Once again, the chalkboard presentation of student writing for peer critiquing is an invaluable aid to progress in English composition.

The sentences included in these exercises are, like those in the "Vocabulary Study" section, a mix of contextualized items related to the chapter themes and discrete items relating to everyday life, the former presenting a greater challenge conceptually and semantically than some students may be capable of handling. When students are ready to apply syntactic structures to text-based material, this should be encouraged, but students who are not ready for this more difficult application should be directed to apply the grammatical targets while writing about experiences from their everyday lives.

Students should do all written work in this section (either in the text or on separate paper, as directed) with careful attention to items such as punctuation, capitalization, subject–verb agreement, word forms, and spelling, as well as the particular target structure. This section is enriched with sentence-combining exercises, which develop skills in manipulating language for coherence and effect, and with focused paragraph-length writing tasks for the application of specific items of language.

Small Group Assignment

Each chapter except the last includes one or more activities especially designed for small group collaboration. These assignments help build oral/aural skills and provide practice in analyzing and applying abstract ideas.

Composition Development

In this section, students will learn how to develop, organize, and express their views on selected topics in a substantial and coherent manner. The reading passages and additional paragraphs on the same theme provide examples of the particular composing skill in each chapter, so that students have a sufficient selection of focused, self-contained models of academic writing.

While the focus of this section continues to be the most important rhetorical items required for writing the pre-Freshman Composition or Writing Proficiency Examinations that are in effect in many colleges, the material has been extensively revised to regroup the targets more logically, reduce extraneous information, clarify explanations, illustrate more targets from the reading passage content, and require a more sustained composition for practice.

Prewriting activities such as brainstorming and outlining are included throughout the text in this section, and the instructor is encouraged to apply these strategies before each major writing session. It is presumed that students will be writing a minimum of one formal composition per week and revising and editing these weekly pieces before starting the next composition. The rewriting process, with its attendant activities, will be structured differently by each instructor depending on the time available and other factors, but it should be incorporated on a systematic basis throughout the term.

Composition Topics

The suggested topics for composition in this section have been revised for clarity and to more closely conform to the type of writing proficiency assignments students may be given as an exit from their ESL programs. Instructors may wish to engage in class discussion and outlining of one or both topics before setting students to their composition task, or they may wish to use one topic for that purpose and assign the other without such prewriting activities as a simulated examination activity.

Appendix A: The Composition Process

This section includes information about the general requirements of expository writing; a form for composition review, which poses a series of questions for students to consider after writing their first draft of a paper; and a sheet of editing symbols, which allows the instructor to locate and identify errors for the student without correcting them.

Appendix B: Basic Terminology for English Language Study

This section identifies and explains the basic terms used in the "Writing Exercises" and "Composition Development" sections. Student comprehension of this material is essential for the self-correction process and is requisite for mastering the concepts involved in language learning. The appendix includes a verb summary that students should use to correct verb errors pointed out by the instructor. It also includes a chart of signal expressions to which students may refer for improving the coherence of their written expression.

Appendix C: List of Common Irregular Verbs with Their Basic, Simple Past, and Past Participle Forms

This section provides the present, past, and past participle forms of irregular verbs. It should be referred to by students for the correction of verb errors in their written work.

Acknowledgments

It gives me great pleasure to acknowledge the many different contributions of my friends and colleagues to this text. First, I wish to express my gratitude to Serena Nanda, whose engaging and sensitive anthropology textbook, *Cultural Anthropology,* provides the content base for this book. I would also like to thank anthropologist William Lewis, who provided me with his research on the Rastafarians as a content base for Chapter Ten. I am grateful to my colleagues at New York City Technical College, College English as a Second Language Program, for their continued support and valuable insights, and to my colleagues in the field at other institutions who have been so generous in sharing their expertise with me. I particularly want to express my admiration for our ESL students, whose persistence and progress in mastering English as a second language at the postsecondary level has earned my deepest respect. I would like to thank Ruth Cottrell, who handled the production for this edition, and Beverly Cory, the copy editor. For their most welcome and constructive reviews of the manuscript, I thank Kathryn Butcher, University of New Orleans; Donna Capowich, Sacred Heart University; O. Dean Gregory, University of Kansas; Gillian Kitrick, Chapman College; and Sharon G. Sunico, Kings River College.

To Raj Nanda, the first in our new generation to carry on our commitment to the art of teaching, this book is affectionately dedicated.

Contents

6

The Cultural Patterning of Space   *139*

7

The Arts in a Cultural Context   *165*

A

The Composition Process   *277*

B

Basic Terminology for English Language Study   *281*

C

List of Common Irregular Verbs with The Basic, Simple Past, and Past Participle Forms   *297*

Culture and Human Behavior

Every society teaches its children the traditions and values it wants to pass on to new generations. In American culture, with its emphasis on individuality, a child's birthday is an occasion for extra attention, a personalized cake, special gifts, a birthday song, and a secret wish while blowing out the candles.

Freewrite

Freewrite about a birthday or another event in a child's life that teaches a tradition or value of your culture. You may want to compose your Freewrite as a personal memory from your own childhood.

Vocabulary in Context

You will need to know the meanings of the following words to fully comprehend the reading passage. Use your dictionary as necessary. Choose words from these lists to complete each sentence below.

Verbs	Nouns	Adjectives	Adverbs
distinguish	heredity	isolated	genetically
investigate	participation	infinite	apathetically
restrict	potential	immoral	
		indifferent	
		exceptional	

1. People who are color-blind cannot _____ red from green.

2. A pacifist would consider all wars to be wrong and _____ . Instead of _____ in the armed forces, he or she might choose useful work in a hospital.

3. Most religions _____ the kind of clothing people can wear in their house of worship.

4. Some elderly people become _____ from society because they cannot walk, drive, or use public transportation.

5. There are an _____ number of stars in the universe; astronomers can _____ only a few of these through their telescopes.

6. The color of one's eyes, hair, and skin is _____, not culturally, transmitted.

7. Caged animals often become _____ to their surroundings and merely sit _____ on a rock, staring at the bars of their cage.

8. In the United States, athletes with _____ ability may earn a higher income than the president of the nation.

9. If a child demonstrates great musical ability at an early age, he or she may have the _____ to become a professional musician.

10. When the police _____ a crime, they consider such factors as motive and opportunity.

11. Culture, not _____, is responsible for transmitting such social traits as marriage customs and religious beliefs.

Reading: Culture and Human Behavior

Key Concepts
- *Culture*
- *Sociocultural system*
- *Cultural restrictions as the basis for human development*

[1]   What does the term *culture* mean throughout this book? As used by anthropologists, *culture* means any human behavior that is learned rather than **genetically** transmitted. The South African bushman's method of hunting game, the Navajo's belief in certain medical ceremonies, and the middle-class American's high school senior prom   5
are all elements of culture. All of the significant parts of a culture are passed on to different generations not through biological **heredity** but through "tradition" or social learning. From this standpoint, all human groups have a culture. Culture exists in agricultural as well as in industrialized societies. Culture is not necessarily high or low; it exists in any   10
type or stage of civilization. Ideally, culture is satisfying to both the individual member and the society to which he or she belongs. There are many types of culture, as well as an **infinite** variety of cultural elements. The cultural patterns that are typical of a certain group communicate the essence of that group. Culture distinguishes one group of   15
people from another.

[2]   Culture is necessary for the survival and existence of human beings as human beings. Practically everything humans know, think, value, feel, and do is learned through **participation** in a sociocultural system. The few well-documented cases of children who are **isolated**   20
from society in their early years support this statement. One of these cases, that of the "wild boy of Aveyron," is of **exceptional** interest. In

1799, a boy of about twelve was found in a forest near Aveyron, France. He was brought to Paris, where he attracted huge crowds who expected to see the "noble savage" of romantic eighteenth century philosophy.* Instead they found a boy whose

... eyes were unsteady, expressionless, wandering vaguely from one object to another. . . . [they were] so little trained by the sense of touch, they could never **distinguish** an object in relief ** from one in a picture. His . . . hearing was insensible to the loudest noises and to . . . music. His voice was reduced to a state of complete muteness and only a guttural sound escaped him . . . he was equally **indifferent** to the odor of perfume and the fetid exhalation of the dirt with which his bed was filled. . . . [His] touch was **restricted** to the mechanical grasping of an object. . . . [He] had a tendency to trot and gallop . . . [and] an obstinate habit of smelling at anything given to him . . . he chewed like a rodent with a sudden action of the incisors† . . . [and] showed no sensitivity to cold or heat and could seize hot coals from the fire without flinching or lay half naked upon the wet ground for hours in the wintertime. . . . He was incapable of attention and spent his time rocking **apathetically** backwards and forwards like the animals in the zoo.‡

This description of the wild boy of Aveyron is provided by Jean-Marc-Gaspard Itard, a young psychologist who undertook the education of the boy, whom he called Victor. He believed that Victor appeared subnormal not because of mental disease or retardation but because Victor had not participated in normal human society.

[3]   There is another case of children growing up apart from human society that also makes fascinating reading, although this case is not as well documented as that of the wild boy. Its meaning is the same, however: Participation in human culture is necessary for the development of human characteristics. In the province of Midnapore in India, the director of an orphanage was told by local villagers that there were "ghosts" in the forest. Upon **investigating,** the director found that two children, one about eight years old and the other about six years old, appeared to have been living with a pack of wolves in the forest. These

*In this philosophy, primitive people were believed to be more innocent, and therefore nobler, than highly civilized people.

**An object in relief is one that is raised above its background surface, such as the pictures and words on coins.

†Incisors are the pointed, front-cutting teeth.

‡From Jean-Marc-Gaspard Itard, *The Wild Boy of Aveyron*, trans. by George and Muriel Humphrey. Englewood Cliffs, N.J.: Prentice-Hall, 1962. Reprinted by permission.

children, part of a wolf pack with two cubs, were the ghosts described by the local people. In his diary, the director describes his first view of Kamala (as the older child was named) and Amala (the name given to the younger child): 60

[Kamala was] a hideous looking being . . . the head a big ball of
something covering the shoulders and the upper portion of the
bust. . . . Close at its heels there came another awful creature exactly
like the first, but smaller in size. Their eyes were bright and piercing,
unlike human eyes. . . . They were covered with a peculiar kind of 65
sore all over the body. These sores . . . had developed from walking
on all fours. . . . [They were] very fond of raw meat and raw
milk. . . . They could not stand erect . . . [they were] able to move
about a little, crawling on feet and hands. . . . Gradually, as they got
stronger, they commenced going on all fours, and afterwards began to 70
run on all fours . . . just like squirrels.*

Many of the other details in the orphanage director's diary about the "wolf-children" are similar to those told about Victor. The wolf-children seemed to be continually looking for the cubs and the wolves with which they had been raised. They were shy and would not play 75 with the other children in the orphanage. Even when the other children would laugh, play, or chat in their presence, the wolf-children would sit **apathetically** in a corner facing the wall, indifferent to all that was going on. While the other children were active during the day, the wolf-children often slept, and at night they prowled around the orphanage, 80 lapping up with their tongues the food and water left for them. They became friendly with only one child, a one-year-old who was just learning to crawl. But they must have sensed that he was different, because one day they bit and scratched him roughly. Apparently, without early human contact, human beings will not develop a "human nature" that 85 allows them to feel comfortable with others of their species.

[4] People have always been interested in how human beings would develop in a "culture-free" setting. Today it is considered **immoral** to isolate individuals at birth for experimental reasons, but such experimentation was attempted in the past. The Egyptian pharaoh 90 Psammetichus tried to discover what language children would "naturally" speak if they were reared where they could hear no human voice. He ordered two infants isolated from society and had them brought up without the sound of any human speech. He assumed that they would "naturally" talk in the language of their ancestors, and to his ears, their 95

*From Robert Zingg and J. Singh, *Wolf Children and Feral Man.* New York: Harper & Row, 1942.

babbling sounded like Phrygian, an ancient Mediterranean tongue. In the fifteenth century, King James IV of Scotland tried a similar experiment and claimed his two infants spoke in Hebrew, the language of the Old Testament of the Bible. Both monarchs were mistaken, of course. As the cases of Victor, the wild boy, and Kamala and Amala demonstrate,   100 children learn human language in the same way they learn other kinds of human development—by participation in a cultural community. They learn a *specific* human language as well as *specific* kinds of human behavior through their membership in a *specific* cultural community. The cases of Victor and the wolf-children make fascinating reading. But   105 more important, they emphasize that we as human beings can only develop our human **potential** through growing up in close association with other human beings. Although culture restricts us to certain kinds of values, thoughts, and behavior, culture is also what allows us to develop our human qualities and abilities. The price that we pay for being   110 human is that we become human in a culturally specific way.

Reading Comprehension

1. True–False

After each statement write *T* for true, *F* for false, or *NI* for no information, according to the information given in the reading passage.

a. Culture refers only to the high art and classical music of a particular society. _____

b. The essence of American culture is the high value placed on individuality. _____

c. The case of the "wild boy" of Aveyron is well supported by historical evidence. _____

d. The Parisian crowds found the "wild boy" to be noble and gentle in his behavior. _____

e. The passage suggests that learning language is an element of culture. _____

f. Amala and Kamala were raised in a forest by ghosts. _____

g. Amala and Kamala learned to speak the language of southern India. _____

h. An Egyptian pharaoh and a Scottish king both experimented with the cultural development of infants. _____

i. Children brought up in isolation will automatically speak the language of their ancestors. _____

j. Human beings can only develop human abilities if they are raised by their biological parents. _____

2. *Reading Review*

In oral discussion or in writing, respond to the following questions based on information in the reading passage.

a. Define the term *culture.*
b. Briefly describe the "wild boy" in your own words.
c. According to Dr. Itard, why did the wild boy appear to be below normal in intelligence and behavior?
d. Who were the "ghosts" of the Midnapore forest seen by the local villagers?
e. In what way(s) were the wild boy and the wolf-children similar?
f. How do we know the details about the existence of the wolf-children?
g. What concept about human nature is shown by the cases of the wild boy and the wolf-children?
h. Why do people consider it immoral to isolate infants from society?
i. What was the point of the experiments with infants tried by the Egyptian pharaoh Psammetichus and King James IV of Scotland?
j. What does "culturally specific" mean?

3. *Analyzing the Text*

What is the thought relationship of the following pairs of statements: (a) reason-result, (b) contrast, (c) example, (d) condition, (e) sequence, (f) addition? Circle the word or phrase that signals the relationship.

a. (1) . . . the significant parts of a culture are passed on to different generations not through biological heredity
   (2) but through "tradition" or social learning.
b. (1) There are many types of culture
   (2) as well as an infinite variety of cultural elements.
c. (1) [Dr. Itard] believed that Victor appeared subnormal not because of mental disease or retardation
   (2) but because Victor had not participated in normal human society.
d. (1) There is another case . . . that makes fascinating reading,
   (2) although this case is not as well documented.

e. (1) While the other children were active during the day,
    (2) the wolf-children often slept. . . .

f. (1) [The wolf-children] must have sensed that [another child] was different
    (2) because one day they bit and scratched him roughly.

g. (1) . . . Psammetichus tried to discover what language children would "naturally" speak
    (2) if they were reared [without hearing a] human voice.

h. (1) Although culture restricts individuals,
    (2) . . . our participation in a sociocultural system . . . allows us to become human.

4. Summarizing

Summarizing, which integrates reading and writing, is an essential skill for success in academic work. For example, summaries are useful for reviewing class notes or text chapters in preparation for an exam. A **summary** is a condensation of a passage *in your own words* that expresses the passage's purpose, its overall central idea, some important secondary ideas, and some of the major pieces of support for the passage.

Summarize the reading for Chapter One by using the following guide:

a. State the purpose or central idea of the entire passage.

b. Skim paragraph [2] for its main idea. State it in your own words. You may introduce your statement as follows:
    The author states that
    According to the text,

c. Skim paragraphs [2] and [3] to determine the kind of evidence the author uses to support the main idea. Write two or three sentences of your own that describe this evidence.

d. Skim paragraph [4] for its main idea. Your last summary sentence(s) should be a paraphrase of the author's conclusions. You may wish to use one of the following:
    The author concludes that
    The author's illustrations/examples show that

Vocabulary Study

1. Words That Describe

Adjectives are words that describe nouns. Adjectives provide interesting, specific details about people, places, and things. Use your dictionary as necessary to obtain the meaning of the following adjectives from the reading passage. Then use each adjective in a meaningful sentence of your own.

a. industrialized societies
b. obstinate habit
c. fascinating reading
d. peculiar kind

e. guttural sound
f. huge crowds
g. hideous human being
h. shy children

Adverbs often describe the way in which verb action is done. Write a synonym for each of these adverbs from the reading passage. Then choose one adverb from the list to complete each sentence below.

biologically	apathetically
vaguely	gradually
roughly	continually

i. Children are usually taught not to play _____ with others, not to fight, and not to take others' toys.

j. As you _____ study the anthropology readings in this text throughout the semester, you will begin to understand the main concepts and methods of investigation used in this discipline.

k. General body size is _____ inherited from one's parents, but nutrition may also play an important role.

l. Without my reading glasses, I can only _____ see things and people at a distance.

m. In too many classrooms students are just sitting _____ , not actively participating in discussions or taking notes on the lectures.

2. *Word Form Table*

Fill in the following table with the appropriate forms of the given words. Some nouns or adjectives may have two forms. The xxx indicates that there is no common form.

	Verbs	*Nouns*	*Adjectives*	*Adverbs*
a.	restrict	_____	_____	_____
b.	_____	participation	_____	xxx
c.	_____	_____	specific	_____
d.	_____	_____	apparent	_____
e.	continue	_____	_____	_____

Use the correct form(s) from each lettered line in the table to complete the same lettered sentence(s) below. The first one is done for you.

a. Landlords cannot _restrict_____ their rentals on the basis of race, religion, or ethnic origin. Such _____ are against the law.

b. Research shows that students who actively _____ in class discussions earn better grades than those who don't.

c. Doctors _____ warn us against the dangers of smoking. Even cigarette packages state _____ that smoking is harmful to your health.

d. In ancient Greek mythology, the gods and goddesses _____ as jealous, excitable, and disloyal, just like human beings. It is _____ that the Greeks viewed their divine beings as similar to human beings in personality.

3. *Word Formation*

Suffix *al:* frequent adjective ending meaning "belonging to" or "having the character of."

agricultural	guttural	psychological
anthropological	logical	social
biological	mechanical	special
cultural	medical	typical
exceptional	mental	
factual	musical	

To make the adverb form of these words, add *ly* to the adjective ending: *logically*.

Write a brief paragraph about a person or people you know who have special or interesting skills and abilities. Try to use at least five adjectives and two adverbs from the above list.

Writing Exercises

Structures for Description

Adjectives
Adjectives make writing more detailed and concrete by providing descrip-

tions of people, places, and things. In the reading passage in this chapter, for example, the author wants the reader to clearly see the condition of the wild boy and the wolf-children. She uses adjectives to make their appearance and behavior clear to us.

Adjectives answer the question: *What kind of (noun/pronoun)?* Adjectives are commonly used in two grammatical patterns.

[1] Adjective—Noun Combinations. These may occur in any part of a sentence. The use of two or even three adjectives in front of a noun is not uncommon in English.

> **Victor, the *wild* boy, made *strange, low, guttural* sounds**
> (adj.-noun)   (adj.)   (adj.)   (adj.)   (noun)
>
> **like an animal.**

[2] Subject + Linking Verb + Adjective. The most common linking verbs in English are *to be, to feel, to seem, to become,* and *to appear.*

> **Kamala and Amala *appeared apathetic* during the day, but**
> (subject)   (l.v.)   (adj.)
>
> **they *became active* and *alert* at night.**
> (l.v.)   (adj.)   (adj.)

1. Composing a Paragraph with Adjective—Noun Combinations

Turn to the photograph at the front of this chapter. Make a list of all the adjective—noun combinations that the photograph suggests. You may use two adjectives in front of a noun in a series: *seven lighted candles.*

Write a brief paragraph about birthday celebrations in your culture. Use adjective—noun combinations to describe aspects of the food, clothing, games, music, and the like that are part of the birthday party.

2. Sentence Composition

Write one sentence in pattern [2]—subject + linking verb + adjective— to describe how a person might *be, feel, seem, become,* or *appear* in each of the following situations. Vary your subjects. Choose an appropriate adjective from the list for each sentence.

> **I was very excited to see my old friend Mary, who was my college roommate.**

a.	received a B+ on an exam	thrilled	proud
b.	won a lottery	happy	depressed
c.	failed an exam	excited	anxious
d.	saw an old friend	downcast	upset
e.	read about some difficulties in his or her native country		
f.	figured out how to solve a math problem		

Participial Adjectives (Adjectives Formed from Verbs)

Many common English adjectives are formed from either the **present participle** (—*ing*) or the **past participle** (–*ed* in regular verbs; check Appendix C for irregular verbs) of a verb.

to pour	**pouring**	The "wild boy" always slept outside in the *pouring* rain. (What kind of rain? *Pouring* rain.)
to paint	**painted**	The "wild boy" could not distinguish between painted and carved objects. (What kind of objects? *Painted* and *carved* objects.)

Present and Past Participial Adjectives: Confusing Sets

The meanings of adjectives made from the present and past participles of the same verb are sometimes confused. Study the following lists.

Present participial adjectives often suggest (a) an ongoing process or (b) a quality that has an effect *on* people—it does something *to* people.

exciting	causes excitement
surprising	causes a surprise
boring	causes boredom
disgusting	causes disgust
interesting	causes interest
frightening	causes fright
troubling	causes trouble
puzzling/confusing	causes puzzlement or confusion
boiling	cooking or heating at a boil (212°F, 100°C)
divorcing	in the process of getting a divorce
growing (up)	in the process of becoming an adult

Past participial adjectives usually suggest (a) the emotion that a person feels or (b) a completed action.

to be excited	feel excitement
to be surprised	feel surprise
to be bored	feel boredom
to be disgusted	feel disgust
to be interested	feel interest in someone or something
to be frightened	feel fright
to be troubled	feel trouble
to be puzzled/confused	feel puzzlement/confusion
to be boiled	cooked by boiling
to be married	united or joined by marriage
to be divorced	separated by a divorce action
to be grown	having become an adult

1. Using Participial Adjectives

Respond to the following items in a complete sentence. Use an appropriate participial adjective based on the verb in parentheses. Use the noun in parentheses when given. Write your sentences on a separate sheet of paper.

a. (fascinate) Does the study of anthropology interest you?

Anthropology is a fascinating subject to me.

b. (bore) Why do some students drop out of school?

c. (disgust/creatures) Rats and cockroaches live in filth and garbage.

d. (disappoint/grades) I received a C in biology and a D in math last semester.

e. (marry) Who has a better life: a single person or one with a spouse and children?

f. (boil/water) How can you avoid stomach trouble in an area with poor sanitation?

g. (frighten) The film I saw last night was full of violence.

h. (frustrate) When does a parent commonly feel a sense of frustration in bringing up a child?

i. (confuse) Why were you so late in filling out your financial aid application?

2. Composing Diary Entries with Adjectives

Over a number of days compose several diary entries in which you record your observations, thoughts, and feelings about your daily college experience. Use concrete adjectives to make your entries as precise as possible. Try to use at least three present participial adjectives and three past participial adjectives from the lists given.

March 3–

Today I attended an interesting class in human biology. Our instructor told us some surprising things about the brain. Most of the students looked bored, but I thought it was fascinating.

Nouns as Adjectives

There are many words in English that we ordinarily think of as nouns, yet they may function in a sentence as adjectives. That is, they are not used for the names of things; they are used to describe things, to tell what kind of things they are.

noun: pioneer; child   Arnold Gesell was a *pioneer* in the field of psychology. He studied how the mind of a *child* develops.

adjective: pioneer work; child psychology

Arnold Gesell did *pioneer work* in the field of *child psychology*. (What kind of work? *Pioneer* work. What kind of psychology? *Child* psychology.)

1. Sentence Composition

Use each of the following words as a noun in one sentence and as an adjective in another sentence.

army, school, college, equal, model, human, potential, individual, savage

Adjective Clauses

Adjective clauses are dependent clauses that describe a preceding noun in the main clause. They are introduced by one of the following connectors:

who (for people), *which* or *that* (for things), *whose* (for possession), or *where* (for place). An adjective clause should follow the noun it describes as closely as possible.

If the noun being described is already quite specific and the adjective clause is providing extra, *nonessential* description, it is set off by commas (and it uses *which* for things). If the adjective clause is *essential* to identify the noun and for the sentence to make sense, it is not set off by commas (and it uses *that* for things).

The verb of the adjective clause is either singular or plural, depending on whether the noun described is singular or plural.

An adjective clause may be used in the middle of a sentence between the main clause subject and its verb, or it may conclude a sentence.

Victor, *who grew up in a forest,* behaved like a wild animal. (specific noun) (person; nonessential—commas)

The problems *that "wild children" experience* are both physical (general noun) (thing; essential—no commas) and psychological.

Victor's behavior, *which resembled an animal's,* caused others (specific noun) (thing; nonessential—commas) to fear him.

The orphanage *where Kamala and Amala were taken* was in Midnapore. (general noun) (place; essential—no commas)

The wolf-children, *whose health was poor,* died at a young age. (specific noun) (possession; essential—no commas)

---

1. *Sentence Revision with Adjective Clauses*

Read the following conditional statements about child development. Then rewrite each sentence using an adjective clause structure. Keep your sentences singular or plural as they are given.

If children live with criticism, they may learn to be critical.

Children *who live with criticism* may learn to be critical.

(adj. clause)

---

a. If children live with hostility, they may learn to be aggressive.
b. If a child lives with ridicule, he or she may learn to be shy.
c. If children live with jealousy, they may learn to feel guilty.
d. If a child lives with tolerance, he or she may learn to like himself or herself and other people.
e. If children live with praise, they may learn to be appreciative.
f. If a child lives with security, he or she may learn to be confident.
g. If children live with approval, they may learn to like themselves.
h. If children live with acceptance and friendship, they may learn to find love in the world.

2. *Sentence Composing*

Now compose ten sentences of your own about child development using the adjective clause structure. You may want to use some of the adjectives listed below. Use your dictionary for their meanings as necessary.

Positive Adjectives

beautiful	generous	loving	affectionate
peaceful	creative	loyal	curious
kind	respectful	playful	reasonable

Negative Adjectives

aggressive	timid	arrogant	anxious
apathetic	lazy	bored	unkind
jealous	intolerant	indifferent	hostile

3. *Sentence Combining with Adjective Clauses*

Combine each of the following sets of sentences into one sentence using one or more adjective clauses as necessary. Put your adjective clause as close as possible to the noun that it is describing. Write your complete new sentences on a separate sheet of paper.

a. Culture is a term. It describes learned human behavior.

Culture is a term that describes learned human behavior.

b. Culture exists among all human groups. It is necessary for survival.
c. Jean-Marc Itard educated the "wild boy." Jean-Marc Itard was a psychologist. The "wild boy" grew up in a forest.
d. The "wild boy" had sharp teeth. He used these teeth like a rodent.
e. Amala and Kamala were called "wolf-children." Their "family" was a pack of wolves.

f. In the orphanage, Amala and Kamala acted differently from the other orphans. They were taken there.

g. The orphanage director kept a valuable diary. The diary was read by Arnold Gesell. Arnold Gesell was a well-known American psychologist.

h. Children grow up speaking French naturally. Their parents speak French.

i. The color of one's hair is genetically transmitted. It cannot be changed by social traditions.

j. A senior prom is a special dance. It celebrates the end of high school.

k. Walking erect is unique to human beings. This allows our hands to be free for toolmaking and grasping things.

l. People live in tropical climates. The weather is warm and humid there. These people develop ways to keep cool.

Small Group Assignment

Schools teach children cultural elements directly through such subjects as history, language, and science. But they also teach children indirectly; they implant the values of their specific culture by what they require children to do or not do. If Victor, the wild boy, were to be educated in a modern French elementary school, he might have an educational experience similar to the one described in the following passage. Think about the values of French culture that he might be learning in school.

Form small groups. Have different members of your group read aloud a paragraph from the selection while the others follow in the text. Then discuss some or all of the questions that follow the passage, as directed by your instructor. One person should serve as recorder of the group's answers in note form.

Elementary School in France

Until quite recently, the French educational system was quite different from the American. It was directed by the central government, and the basic curriculum was the same throughout the country. In French towns and cities, most small children attended school in their immediate neighborhood. They entered school on their fourth birthday and were grouped with others of their age. They wore a uniform coat of a special color to indicate their grade.

The American ideal of paying special attention to the individual needs of each child was not a primary value in the French school system. For example, there were few special classes either for brighter children or for those who needed extra help in their subjects. If students did not complete their grade's work satisfactorily, they had to repeat the grade. Children were given more difficult tasks in French primary schools than in American schools. At four years of age, for instance, the French pupil began to learn writing in script; printing was not taught as an easy first step. French pupils

The French school system teaches children to appreciate their national artistic heritage. Here, schoolchildren in a provincial art museum discuss paintings with their teacher.

were taught to draw by copying an object set up before them. If they did not copy the object accurately enough, the teacher may have marked an **X** through their paper and had them try again. Artwork was not given to the children to take home and show their parents each day. It was collected for a folder that was given back to them at the end of the term.

The routines and discipline of the French primary school were also more rigid than those in an American school. School began at 8:30 A.M. when a bell rang for the children to line up and enter as a class. If it was raining, each child had to wipe his or her boots on a doormat under the eye of the teacher standing at the door. Each child had to say "good morning" to the teacher and promptly and quietly take his or her seat. (The teacher was called "teacher." Personal names were not used.) Each subject taught was allotted a certain period of time and followed a specific sequence nationwide. At 11:30 there was a two-hour break for lunch, when most children went home. Those children who could not go home for lunch were served a meal in school. When they finished their main course completely, their plates were turned over, and the shallow, dishlike part on the bottom was used for serving the dessert. School ended at 4:30. There were few after-school programs for young children who had no one to pick them up at 4:30.

The enforcement of the school's rules lay with the principal and the teachers. If children were noisy or inattentive in class, the teacher sometimes punished them by making them stand facing the wall in different corners of the room. Students may have been tugged by an ear or pulled by the hand to correct their behavior. Parents may have come to the school to speak with the teacher or the principal about their child, but there was no "open school" period when they could sit in and observe their child's class. There were no Parent–Teachers Associations in French elementary schools. The pupils were expected to meet the expectations of the schools, not the reverse, and it was the child, not the school, who bent if this situation could not be achieved.

The French school system, like many other European educational systems, is currently becoming more relaxed in its rules and standards. Although some of the observations in the above passage are still true, in some respects the French classroom is discarding its more rigid educational principles.

Discussion Questions

Answer the questions in brief note form.

1. Where did the authority in a French school seem to be: with the parents, the children, or the staff? Support your answer by reference to the text. What attitudes about authority do you think a French child acquired in school?
2. How do you learn from the text that the French were careful about the use of material things, things that cost money?
3. Emphasis in American schools is on the individuality and self-expression of the child. From your analysis of the text, did the French seem to share this value? Explain your answer.
4. Current American educational philosophy emphasizes the importance of a child's *feelings*—the child's psychological and emotional needs. To what extent did concern for a child's feelings seem to exist in the French school? Did the discipline of the French school seem reasonable or unreasonable to you? Explain.
5. What does the schedule of the French school tell you about French family life? Compare the French schedule to that of an elementary school in your own country.
6. Discuss and then write about the following subject.

    French schools have been strict or traditional. American schools tend to be lenient or permissive. What are the advantages and disadvantages of each type of system? Which type of school do you have in your native culture? Which type of system do you think is better for children? Why?

Role Playing

Imagine that you are an American parent with a child in a traditional French elementary school. In class your child drew a bowl of fruit that did not faithfully copy the shape, composition, and color of the model. The teacher marked an X across the paper. Your child angrily crumpled up the drawing and threw it on the floor. The teacher yanked your child by the arm and put her in the corner for fifteen minutes. After your child tells you about this episode, you come to the school for a meeting with the teacher and the principal.

Choose group members to play the parts of the parent(s), the child, the teacher, and the principal. Then enact the meeting that might take place. Discuss this issue with your group or class.

Composition Development

Topic Statements

Although there are many different ways to develop paragraphs and essays, these various patterns are all based on their relationship to a main idea, or topic statement, which controls your details and information. A topic statement offers a generalization or an assertion (opinion) about your subject. It provides a focus for the paragraph or essay that follows.

Study the topic statement analyses of the following paragraphs.

(1) Among the Trobriand Islanders of the South Pacific, *kula,* or shell trading, has many psychological purposes. (2) It provides prestige if the people involved behave generously. (3) It provides an opportunity for people to display their wealth. (4) It provides an opportunity for social contact.

Topic: Trobriand Island *kula,* or shell trading
Main Idea: *Kula* has many psychological purposes.
Topic Statement: Sentence 1

(1) Among the Arapesh of New Guinea, women are not allowed to join the *tamberan* cult, because the tamberan is the patron or god of adult men. (2) Arapesh women are not allowed to see the tamberan god-figure or even think about what it looks like. (3) This custom of repressing spiritual and intellectual thoughts has become habitual among Arapesh women, and their personalities have become more passive than those of their neighbors.

Topic: The personalities of Arapesh women
Main Idea: Arapesh women have more passive personalities than their neighbors.
Topic Statement: Sentence 3

A topic statement is sometimes formed by only one sentence. In other cases the topic statement may be formed by several sentences or sentence parts.

With your class, review paragraph (1) of the main reading passage. Underline the topic statement.

Review paragraph (2). Underline the sentence(s) that form the topic statement. Do the same for paragraph (3).

Review paragraph (4). Underline the sentence(s) or sentence parts that form the topic statement. Rewrite a topic statement for paragraph (4) in your own words.

1. *Composing Topic Statements*

Consider each list of specific details that follows and decide on a topic that covers all of the given items. Then write a topic statement for each set. A topic statement is always written in the form of a *complete sentence,* even in an outline, so that its controlling idea or point of view is clear.

a. **(1)** North Americans value punctuality and careful planning of time.
(2) Latin Americans value sociability above punctuality.
(3) Sioux Indians do not even have a word for "late."
(4) The Hindu view of an infinite future is quite different from the Navajo skepticism about the future.

Topic: _____

Topic Statement: _____

b. **(1)** Trains allow people to see many parts of the country as they travel.
(2) Planes cover long distances in the shortest amount of time.
(3) Buses are the cheapest, but slowest, means of transportation.
(4) Automobiles allow people to go and stop where they want.

Topic: _____

Topic Statement: _____

c. **(1)** In past generations, most mothers didn't work outside the home.
(2) In past generations, mothers spent most of their time taking care of their homes and children.
(3) In past generations, mothers belonged to few outside organizations.
(4) Today, many mothers work at outside jobs.
(5) Modern working mothers place their children with baby-sitters or in day care.
(6) Modern working mothers often belong to social or political groups.

Topic: _____

Topic Statement: _____

d. **(1)** A dictionary usually shows how to divide a word into syllables.
(2) A dictionary usually offers several definitions of a word.

(3) A dictionary sometimes gives the origin and development of a word.

(4) A dictionary sometimes shows model sentences that use the word.

Topic: _____

Topic Statement: _____

e. **(1)** The wild boy of Aveyron chewed his food like a rodent.

(2) The wild boy of Aveyron galloped like a four-footed creature.

(3) The wild boy of Aveyron could only utter guttural sounds.

(4) The wild boy of Aveyron could expose himself to rain and cold without feeling uncomfortable.

Topic: _____

Topic Statement: _____

f. **(1)** African masks and sculpture are appreciated by people who do not know African languages.

(2) East Indian music has become popular in the United States, even though most Americans do not understand the words.

(3) German and Italian operas attract large audiences of people who do not understand these languages.

(4) Dance communicates across language barriers.

Topic: _____

Topic Statement: _____

2. *Developing Paragraphs*

In each of the following items there is an assertion or topic statement about the culture of college in the United States. Discuss each assertion in one paragraph that uses your actual college classroom and student group to illustrate your point of view. Before you begin to write, take three minutes to list all the details you have observed about the class and your fellow students. Then take a few more minutes to select and arrange your details for your paragraph development.

a. *Most human institutions try to provide their members with suitable places in which to live, work, and study. Our college, for example, offers us classrooms that are comfortable for learning.* (What kind of lighting does your classroom have? Can the teacher and other students be easily heard? What kind of furniture does the classroom have? Is the room large enough or too large?)

b. *The dress of American college students suggests some important values of the American culture such as informality, a high standard of living, and individuality.* (Consider the kinds of shirts and pants students are wearing. Are the women wearing skirts or slacks? What kind of footwear are they wearing? Does their clothing appear worn or new? Out of date or fashionable? The same in color and cut as the clothing of others or different? Do the students have possessions such as radios or sports equipment with them?)

3. *Developing Your Own Topic Statement*

Look out the window of your classroom. Take three minutes to note down as many concrete details of the view as you can. Review your details. What overall feeling or general impression or idea do they suggest to you? Use this feeling, impression, or idea as the basis for a topic statement for a paragraph.

Human cultural knowledge is passed down from older to younger generations. Here the son of an Italian glassblower helps his father keep alive the traditional art of glassblowing. Discuss some skills or special knowledge that you have learned from an older family member, friend, or colleague at work.

> *City views present an interesting variety of architectural detail.*
>
> *The peaceful campus of a small town American college is a fine place to study.*

Now write a short paragraph that accurately describes the scene to others and supports your main idea or topic statement with specific information.

Keep your topic statement in mind as you write. Do not include details that do not relate to your topic statement and do not include details that contradict it.

4. *Paragraph Combining*

The following sentences were originally part of a paragraph written by a student at a college in the downtown area of a large American city. Her complete sentences have been broken up into small details. Combine the details into logical, interesting, and grammatically correct sentences. The directions in parentheses will guide the fluency of your paragraph. Rewrite your complete paragraph on a separate sheet of paper.

(1) A view is typical of space.
(2) The view is interesting.
(3) The view is varied.
(4) The space is urban.

(5) From my window I see many buildings.   (Use a phrase to introduce your example.)
(6) The window is in my classroom.

(7) The classroom is in my college.
(8) My college is in Brooklyn.
(9) The part of Brooklyn is downtown.
(10) The buildings are of different types.
(11) The buildings have different functions.

(12) Some buildings are factories.   (Join with an adjective clause.)
(13) Some buildings are more than 50 years old.
(14) Some buildings are more than 100 years old.

(15) Some buildings are tall.

(16) They have more than twenty-five stories.

(17) Others are smaller.   (Use a signal word of con-

(18) They have less than six stories.   trast.)

(19) There is air around these buildings.

(20) The air is _____ (use a past participial adjective from the verb *to pollute*).

(21) The pollution is from the smoke.

(22) The smoke is from the chimneys.   {(Use a noun as an adjective.)

(23) The chimneys belong to the factories.

(24) The _____ air has changed the buildings (insert an adjective).

(25) The change is to a color.

(26) The color is dark.

(27) The color is sooty.   (Use a signal word of contrast.)

(28) The buildings have carvings.

(29) The carvings are of stone.

(30) The carvings are fascinating.

(31) The carvings are above the entrance.

(32) The carvings are above the windows.

(33) There are apartment buildings.   (Use a signal to show addition.)

(34) The buildings are high rises.

(35) The buildings are modern.   (Add your own prepositional
phrase such as *in this neigh-
borhood* to show place.)

(36) The buildings are many.

(37) High-rise buildings are popular here.

(38) The area is populated.   (Signal cause and effect.)

(39) The population is dense.

(40) A few college buildings are located here.   (Use a word to show addition.)

(41) The college buildings are new.

(42) The college buildings are clean.   (Use an adjective clause to

(43) The college buildings are made of white brick.   describe *buildings*.)

(44) The college buildings present a contrast.
(45) The contrast is to the older buildings.

(46) There are only a few houses.
(47) The houses are one family.
(48) The houses are wooden.

(49) The houses look _____ (use a past participial adjective of the verb *to lose*).
(50) The houses look (use a past participial adjective of the verb *to abandon*).
(51) The houses are among the bigger buildings.

Answer the following questions when you have finished revising your paragraph.

1. Find three nouns that are functioning as adjectives and underscore them in the paragraph.
2. Have you used more than one adjective in front of a noun? Check their order and punctuation.
3. Review your adjective clause sentences. Draw an arrow from each adjective clause marker *(who, which, that, whose, where)* to the noun it describes. Are both the verbs in the main and the adjective clause either singular or plural to agree with the noun they describe?
4. Which of your complete new sentences is the topic statement of your paragraph? Explain.

Composition Topics

1. The well-known anthropologist Margaret Mead stated that the culture of the United States does not value highly enough people who are aged sixty-five and older. Mead asserts that many elderly people have the wisdom, energy, and interest in life to make significant contributions to their families, neighborhoods, and larger communities.

Compose an essay of about 300 words in which you support Mead's view. Use as your illustration a real older person whom you personally know. Provide some introductory physical details to bring this person to life for your reader. Present some of his or her most admirable characteristics and/or actions. Compose a suitable conclusion that restates your idea on the topic in a different way from your introduction. Use paragraphs [2] and [3] of the reading selection as a guide.

2. At certain times in our lives we come under the influence of a person who affects us in important and beneficial ways. Write an essay of 200–300 words in which you identify such a person in your own life. Explain how that person came to influence your life. Give a clear and detailed illustration of some specific change(s) that resulted because of that person's influence on you.

Culture and Food Habits

In most of the world, as in this Egyptian market, food distribution patterns depend on such factors as local growing conditions, distance between farm and market, speed of transportation, perishability of produce, and availability of refrigeration. Discuss the extent to which supermarkets, small grocery stores, or open-air stalls such as this one are typical in your native culture.

Freewrite

"Mom's apple pie" not only is one of America's typical dishes but also suggests care and nurturing. Freewrite about some special food that is typical of your culture. What events, activities, or values are associated with this food?

Vocabulary in Context

You will need to know the meaning of the following words to fully comprehend the reading passage. Use your dictionary as necessary.

Verbs	Nouns	Adjectives	Adverbs
generate	taboo	ritual (also n.)	primarily
deprive	aversion	edible	
rely	adaptation	detrimental	
maintain	component		

Circle the letter of the answer that best completes the given statement.

1. The *edible* part of an apple is
   (a) the stem.
   (b) the flesh.
   (c) the seeds.
   (d) the blossom.
2. Because of my *aversion* to onions, I
   (a) eat them every day.
   (b) eat them only in restaurants.
   (c) eat them in any form.
   (d) never eat them.
3. If children are *deprived* of nutritious food,
   (a) they will have strong teeth and bones.
   (b) they will be successful in school.
   (c) they will suffer from physical weakness.
   (d) they will become cannibalistic.
4. The proposal to put a fast-food restaurant on the quiet street *generated* conflict; arguments were
   (a) started.
   (b) avoided.
   (c) forbidden.
   (d) resolved.
5. A child has probably made a good *adaptation* to school if he or she
   (a) runs away.
   (b) spends time working on assignments.
   (c) doesn't make any close friends.
   (d) has an aversion to the food.

6. Smoking is *detrimental* to health because
   (a) it makes people less tense.
   (b) taxes on cigarettes are high.
   (c) tar and nicotine help cause cancer.
   (d) it's a social custom in the United States.

7. A *taboo* on eating pork would
   (a) encourage people to eat pork.
   (b) prevent people from eating pork.
   (c) suggest recipes for eating pork.
   (d) reserve eating pork for holidays.

8. A new immigrant to the United States would be interested *primarily* in
   (a) buying fashionable clothing.
   (b) learning a new sport.
   (c) improving English language skills.
   (d) visiting sight-seeing attractions.

9. One is most likely to *rely* on one's parents when
   (a) one is elderly.
   (b) one is an infant.
   (c) one is educated.
   (d) one is wealthy.

10. An important *component* of a democratic society is
   (a) a secret police.
   (b) a capitalistic economy.
   (c) mass education.
   (d) a controlled news system.

11. If your apartment building is well *maintained*, it will have
   (a) a good security system.
   (b) a faulty boiler.
   (c) poor ventilation.
   (d) infrequent garbage pickup.

12. A high school senior prom may be called an American *ritual* because
   (a) it is held in urban high schools.
   (b) it is held at the same time of the year all over the country.
   (c) it is enjoyed by most high school seniors.
   (d) it requires buying new clothes.

Reading: Culture and Food Habits

Key Concepts
- *Food taboos*
- *Ecological adaptation*
- *Cultural patterns of getting food: hunting/ gathering; pastoralism; agriculture*

[1]   All individuals must eat to survive—but what people eat, when they eat, and the manner in which they eat are all patterned by culture. No society views everything in its environment that is **edible** and might provide nourishment as food: Certain edibles are ignored, others are tabooed. These food **taboos** may be so strong that just the   5
thought of eating forbidden foods can cause an individual to feel ill. A Hindu vegetarian would feel this way about eating any kind of meat, an American about eating dogs, and a Moslem or orthodox Jew about eating pork. The taboo on eating human flesh is probably the most universal of all food taboos. Although some societies in the past practiced   10
ritual cannibalism, members of most modern societies have resorted to cannibalism only under the most desperate of circumstances. The cases of cannibalism by the Donner Pass party (trapped in the Sierra Nevada mountains in the winter of 1846) and recently by a South American soccer team (whose plane crashed in the Andes) caused a great furor.   15
Human flesh may be a source of protein, but it is not one that most humans are willing to use.

[2]   The ways in which human beings obtain their food is one of culture's most fascinating stories. Food getting has gone through several stages of development in the hundreds of thousands of years of human-   20
ity's existence on earth. For most of this time on earth, people have supported themselves with the pattern called *hunting and gathering.* This pattern **relies** on food that is naturally available in the environment. It includes the hunting of large and small game animals, fishing, and the collecting of various plant foods. It does not include producing   25
food either by planting or by keeping domesticated animals for their milk or meat. Today, only about 30,000 of the world's people live solely by hunting and gathering.

[3]   Another ancient pattern of obtaining food is *pastoralism,* which is the raising of domesticated herd animals such as goats, sheep,   30
camels, or cattle, all of which produce both milk and meat. Pastoralism is a specialized **adaptation** to a harsh or mountainous environment that is not productive enough to support a large human population through agriculture. The major areas of pastoralism are found in East Africa, where cattle are raised; North Africa, where camels are raised; Southwest   35
Asia, where sheep and goats are raised; and the sub-Arctic, where caribou and reindeer are domesticated and herded. Pastoralism alone cannot support a human population, so additional food grain must either be produced or purchased by trade with other groups.

[4]   The third major type of acquiring food is through *agriculture,*   40
or the planting, raising, and harvesting of crops from the land. Agriculture, which is only about 10,000 years old, may range from simple, nonmechanized horticulture to farming with the help of animal-drawn plows, to the extensively mechanized agriculture of industrialized na-

tions. Anthropologists generally agree that it was the gradual transition   45
from hunting and gathering to agriculture that opened up new possibilities for cultural development.

[5]   Cultural patterns of getting food are **generated primarily**
by the natural, or physical, environment of the group. All human groups,
like other animal communities, have developed special ways of making   50
their environment nurture and support them. Where several groups
share the same environment, they use it in different ways, so they can
live harmoniously with each other. In a study of northern Pakistan, for
example, Kohistanis, Pathans, and Gujars inhabit the same mountainous
area. These three groups are able to coexist peacefully because each   55
utilizes a different aspect of the land. The Pathans are farmers, using
the valley regions for raising wheat, corn, and rice. The Kohistanis live
in the colder mountainous regions, herding sheep, goats, cattle, and water
buffalo and raising millet and corn. The Gujars are full-time herders
and use marginal areas not used by the Kohistanis. The Gujars provide   60
milk and meat products to the Pathan farmers and also work as agricultural laborers during the busy seasons. These patterns of specialized
and harmonious relationships among different cultures in a local environment are typical of pastoral, or herding, people.

[6]   Some food-getting patterns or food habits are not so easy   65
to understand as those described. The origins of many culturally patterned food habits still puzzle anthropologists. Some of these food habits appear on the surface to be irrational and **detrimental** to the
existence of the group. For example, consider the Hindu taboo on
eating beef despite the widespread poverty and periodic famine in   70
that country. Yet anthropologist Marvin Harris views this Hindu taboo
as an *ecological adaptation*—that is, as an adjustment to a specific
environmental condition. Harris states that cows are important in India
not because they can be eaten but because they give birth to bullocks,
the essential farming animals that pull plows and carts. If a family   75
were to eat its cows during a famine, it would **deprive** itself of the
source of its bullocks and could not continue farming. Thus the religious taboo on eating beef strengthens the ability of the society to
maintain itself in the long run.

[7]   It is also possible that there is a biological **component** to the   80
avoidance of certain foods in specific cultures. The Chinese **aversion**
to milk, for example, may be caused by the fact that lactase, an enzyme
that helps digest the sugar lactose in milk, is missing in many Mongoloid
populations. As a result, the milk sugar, lactose, cannot be digested, and
drinking milk frequently causes intestinal distress. Evidence to support   85
biological reasons for food taboos is scarce, however, and at this point
it seems safest to say that it is primarily culture that tells us which foods
are edible and which are not.

Reading Comprehension

1   Matching Concepts

In each blank space in column A, write the number of the item from column B that best corresponds.

A	B
hunting and gathering _____	1. tropical climate; wet, swampy terrain
sub-Arctic _____	2. good digestion of milk
herding of domestic animals _____	3. Russia
ecological adaptation _____	4. hoes; digging sticks
pastoral environment _____	5. cannibalism
lactase _____	6. pastoralism
horticulture _____	7. early human societies
mechanized agriculture _____	8. dry climate; rocky land; infertile soil
	9. domesticated reindeer
	10. Hindus not eating beef

2.   Reading Review

In oral discussion or in writing, answer the following questions based on the reading passage.

a. What is a food taboo? Which food taboo is almost universal in human societies?

b. Psychosomatic illness is the name for physical pain that originates in the psyche, or mind. What are some examples of psychosomatic illness mentioned in the reading passage?

c What point is made by the example of the Donner Pass party?

d. Explain the terms *hunting/gathering* and *pastoralism*.

e. What are some regions of the world where pastoralism is found?

f. Which of the three major methods of providing food is the basis for highly developed societies? Why do you think this is so?

g. In paragraph [5], what does the example of the Kohistanis, Pathans, and Gujars of northern Pakistan demonstrate?

h. What would happen if an Indian family ate its cows during a famine?

i. Why is it difficult for many societies of Mongoloid origin to digest milk? What effect has this had on their food patterns?

3.   Analyzing the Text

(1) The main idea of the chapter is the second sentence in paragraph (1). Which of these sentences would best follow the main idea sentence?

a. In some societies, for example, eating human flesh was practiced in a ritual context.

b. North Americans, for instance, do not eat insects, although they are available and edible.

c. Anthropologists living in foreign cultures frequently have intestinal problems from eating unfamiliar foods.

d. Two famous cases of cannibalism have occurred in recent history.

(2) Understanding the noun referents of pronouns is important when reading for comprehension. For each of the following sentences, write which word or phrase the italicized pronoun has replaced.

a. Most Americans shudder at eating insects, although *this* is a common practice in many parts of the world. _____

b. In societies where cannibalism is strongly tabooed, the taboo against *it* is rarely overcome. _____

c. If an Indian family were to eat *its* cow during a famine, *it* would deprive itself of the source of bullocks. _____

d. No society views everything in *its* environment that is edible and might provide nourishment as food. _____

e. All human groups, like other animal communities, have developed special ways of making *their* environment nurture and support *them.*

_____

(3) What is the thought relationship of the following pairs of statements to each other: (a) reason-result, (b) contrast or contradiction, (c) example, (d) condition? Circle the word or expression that signals the relationship.

a. **(1)** Food taboos may be so strong that just the thought of eating forbidden foods causes individuals to feel sick.

   (2) A Hindu vegetarian would feel this way about eating beef, for example.

b. **(1)** Although in most societies cannibalism occasionally occurs under special conditions,

   (2) there have been a few societies in which human flesh was simply another source of protein.

c. **(1)** Cows are important in India because they provide bullocks for farming.

   (2) Therefore, killing cows for beef would endanger the Indian agricultural process.

d. **(1)** Even though eating insects or dogs is not physiologically harmful,

   (2) the American culture has tabooed eating such creatures.

e. **(1)** It is possible that there is a biological component in certain food avoidances.

(2) The Chinese, for instance, may have an aversion to milk because they lack an enzyme to digest it.

f. **(1)** Pastoralism alone cannot support a large human population

(2) so food grain supplements must either be produced by the pastoralists or purchased by trade with other groups.

g. **(1)** Where several groups share the same environment, they must use it in different ways

(2) if they are to live harmoniously with each other.

h. **(1)** . . . lactase, an enzyme that helps digest the sugar, lactose, in milk is missing in many Mongoloid populations.

(2) As a result, the milk sugar, lactose, cannot be digested . . . .

4. *Outlining Reading Passages*

An outline of a reading passage states the main idea sentence and lists significant supporting facts, details, or examples in brief note form.

a. The following paragraph is an explanation of cultural response to the environment. Fill in the outline for the paragraph by stating the main idea in a sentence of your own words. Then complete the list of significant details that support the main idea.

Human cultures have developed in response to specific natural environments. Every culture transmits patterns of behavior that help it to survive in its specific ecological setting. Technology, economic systems, political organizations, and social values all develop in response to a specific natural environment. Hindus, for example, have a taboo on eating cows, which are also their farm animals. If they ate their cows, there would be no young bullocks to pull their plows the next season. Perhaps, as another illustration, we might look at the Jews and Moslems, who both have a prohibition on eating pork. These two groups originated in the desert, an environment in which it would be difficult to raise pigs; the pig, furthermore, is an animal that may easily get the disease trichinosis, which can make its meat unfit for humans. Another instance of how the ecology may have influenced the human diet is the case of the Aztecs of Mexico, who had a meat-poor diet because the harsh soil of their environment did not permit them to raise sufficient cattle. Did their ritual cannibalism arise as a way for them to obtain protein by eating human flesh on certain occasions?

Outline
Main idea sentence:

a. List supporting details. (The first one is done for you.)

 Hindus not eating their cows

b. Outline paragraphs (2), (3), and (4) of the reading selection. Write a complete main idea sentence in your own words and list the important supporting details in brief note form.

Vocabulary Study

1. Additional Vocabulary: Words in Context

In reading academic material, you cannot stop to look up every word that you do not know. The general meaning of some words must be guessed at in the context, or background, of the sentence. If you can understand the information and ideas that surround a word you are not sure of, you can underscore or circle the word and look up its meaning in the dictionary after you have finished the reading passage.

Review the chapter reading to find the words in the following list. Without using a dictionary, write your own brief definition or explanation for each. Then discuss your meanings with the class. Finally, consult a dictionary and revise any of your definitions that were incorrect or too vague.

a. desperate (paragraph 1)
b. unsuitable (paragraph 3)
c. transition (paragraph 4)
d. inhabit (paragraph 5)
e. avoidance (paragraph 7)
f. intestinal (paragraph 7)
g. furor (paragraph 1)
h. domesticated (paragraph 3)
i. marginal (paragraph 5)
j. harmonious (paragraph 5)
k. famine (paragraph 6)

2. Word Form Table

Fill in the following table with the appropriate forms of the given words. Some nouns or adjectives may have two forms.

	Verbs	Nouns	Adjectives	Adverbs
a.	deprive			xxx
b.	produce			
c.			ritual	
d.	xxx			primarily
e.	rely			

Some of the following sentences contain an error in word form. Use your table as a guide to make the necessary corrections in the lettered sentences corresponding to the table.

a. Poor teeth, frequent illness, and constant tiredness are evidence of a nutritionally deprivation child.

b. Different kinds of agricultural productive come from different natural environments.

c. A ritualistic that Americans follow at birthday parties is to have a cake with candles that are blown out by the person having the birth day.

d. The primarily reason for the terrible famine was corruption in the distribution of food.

e. Chefs, waiters, and other restaurant help must be reliably, for without them, the restaurant cannot function.

3. *Word Formation*

Suffix *ible/able:* syllable attached to the end of a root, forms an adjective meaning "able to" or "able to be."

accountable/unaccountable	reliable/unreliable
avoidable/unavoidable	responsible/irresponsible
credible/incredible	sensible/insensible
digestible/indigestible	suitable/unsuitable
edible/inedible	tolerable/intolerable

Construct a meaningful sentence for each of the following sets of words. You may change the order of the words, but not their forms.

a. taboos/edible

b. furor/avoidable

c. intestinal problems/digestible

d. politicians/responsible

e. harmonious living/sensible

f. aversion/understandable

g. humidity/intolerable

h. chef/incredible

Writing Exercises

Structures for Generalizing

Subjects

In forming general statements that define, explain, or assert opinions, the following types of sentence subjects are useful.

   [1] Uncountable Nouns.   These are **mass items** (such as *furniture*) that cannot be divided into individual units and **abstract nouns** (such as *honesty*) that name qualities, activities, or other aspects of life that are not made specific by descriptive phrases, for example, *the furniture in my room.* Uncountable nouns are treated as singular.

Primitive *agriculture does* not involve the use of power

(mass noun)   (sing. verb)

machinery.

The primitive *agriculture* of *certain South American*

(article   +   mass noun   +   descriptive prepositional phrase)

***peoples does* not provide them with sufficient**

(sing. verb)

nourishment.

---

[2] Gerunds. Gerunds, *–ing* forms of verbs used as nouns, and gerund phrases are frequently used as subjects in generalizations. These are *not* preceded by articles unless they are made specific by descriptive phrases. Gerunds function as singular subjects.

***Hunting for food* is not essential in industrialized**

(gerund subject)   (sing. verb)

societies.

The *gathering of wild plants* is sometimes called foraging.

(article + gerund subject + descriptive prepositional phrase)   (sing. verb)

---

[3] Individuals Representative of a Class. A single person, place, or thing may define or represent a class or type. Such singular subjects are preceded by an article.

A *vegetarian* can obtain *his or her* protein from a variety

(article + sing. subject)   (sing. pronoun)

of foods.

---

[4] Pluralized Countable Nouns. These refer to several members of a class of persons, places, or things. Pluralized countable nouns are *not* preceded by an article unless they are made specific by descriptive phrases. They take plural verbs and pronouns.

> **Traditional cooking *utensils have their* place in every**
> (plural noun) (plural verb) (plural pronoun)
> **Chinese household.**

> **The methods of agriculture in developed nations are**
> (article + plural noun + descriptive prepositional phrase)
> **highly mechanized.**

1. Composing Generalizations

Review some of your reading material in your academic courses. Write ten to twenty definitions, explanations, or general statements based on important topics in your other college courses. Try to use the four different structures for generalizing presented above.

> *Researching a library paper requires a knowledge of the library's computer catalogue.*

Verbs

Three verb forms are useful in the construction of general statements: simple present tense, present perfect tense, and modals. When using either the present or the present perfect tense, **agreement in number** between the subject and its verb is essential. Modals are always followed by the basic form of the main verb; they do not show number.

1. Paragraph Revision for Subject-Verb Agreement

Read the following paragraph about the Dani people of western New Guinea. Then follow the directions for revising it to the singular. Finally, review your revised sentences for agreement among subject, verb, pronoun, and other words relating to the subject.

(1) The Dani people live in the central mountains of western New Guinea above the tropical jungles of the coast. (2) Few wild animals live in the tropical forest. (3) Although a few wild foods are collected from the

forests and the fields, these do not play an important role in the Dani diet. (4) Basically the Dani people rely on the products from their gardens and on their domesticated pigs for most of their food. (5) The main item of the Dani diet is the sweet potato. (6) Other cultivated plants include taro, banana, ginger, sugar cane, and greens. (7) For ordinary meals, sweet potatoes are merely cooked and eaten; ceremonial meals consist of steamed vegetables and pork. (8) The Dani people cultivate three garden areas: the valley floor, hill slope gardens, and small plots behind their homes. (9) In these gardens, a typical round of horticultural activities takes place. (10) The fields are cleared of brush and trees, and the cleared vegetation is burned. (11) The clods of earth are turned with digging sticks. (12) Sweet potatoes are planted with vine cuttings from other gardens. (13) A few months later the gardens are weeded, and about seven months later the harvesting begins.

Directions
a. Keep the first sentence as it is given.
b. Throughout the passage, change the plural subject *Dani people* to *the Dani farmer*. Make all other necessary changes in number.
c. In sentence 2 change *few wild animals* to *little animal life*.
d. In sentence 6 change *other cultivated plants* to *other cultivated food*.
e. In sentence 7 change the plural subjects of both clauses to an individual representative of a class.
f. In sentence 9 change *a typical round* to *typical horticultural activities*.
g. In sentence 10 change the subject to *each field;* change *vegetation* to *weeds and roots*.
h. In sentence 12 change the plural subject to an individual representative of a class.
i. In sentence 13 change *harvesting* to *harvesting activities*.

2. *Simple Present: Rewriting Generalizations*

The following generalizations in the simple present tense are derived from Chapters One and Two. Revise each statement as directed, making all the necessary singular/plural changes. The first one has been done.

a. Practically everything *humans* perceive, know, and believe is learned through participation in a specific culture. (Change the italicized subject to the singular.)

Practically everything a human perceives, knows, and believes is . . .

b. *The Navajo's belief* in certain healing ceremonies is an aspect of culture. (Change the italicized subject to the plural.)

_____

_____

   c. *Each aspect* of culture is an outgrowth of the collective activity of a specific people. (Change the italicized subject to the plural.)

_____

_____

   d. *Every individual* must eat to survive, and *every group* reproduces its membership or *it* dies. (Change the italicized subjects to plural.)

_____

_____

   e. *Hindu vegetarians* become ill at the thought of eating beef, *Moslems* at the idea of consuming pork, and *Americans* at the thought of eating dog—these are examples of food taboos. (Change the italicized subjects to singular.)

_____

_____

   f. *All human groups* exploit their environment in ways that will nurture and support them. (Change the italicized subject to the singular.)

_____

_____

   g. *Facts* supporting the biological basis for certain food aversions are scarce. (Change the italicized subject to a singular countable noun synonymous with the word *facts*.)

_____

_____

3. *Present Perfect for Assertions*

Read the following paragraph, which offers many strong statements, or assertions, about the American interest in various ethnic foods. Because the paragraph is written in the simple past tense, it sounds as if the change in American dining patterns is finished—that it is no longer true now, in the present.

Review the present perfect tense in the "Verb Summary," Appendix B. Then follow the directions given to revise the paragraph. Pay particular attention to subject–verb agreement.

(1) Eating various ethnic foods became a favorite pastime of Americans about two decades ago. (2) It is true that the first American settlers ate

with relish the corn and squash of Native American neighbors; later, in the nineteenth century, Americans became tremendous consumers of the peanut, introduced by African–Americans. (3) Still later, as each new immigrant group entered the United States, it brought its native foods with it. (4) Americans learned to appreciate Italian pasta in its many forms: spaghetti, linguini, and macaroni. (5) The frankfurter became such a popular American food that it practically lost its original German associations. (6) Then the dark breads of Eastern Europe found a place in many American supermarkets, and Mexican dishes became available in packaged, canned, or frozen form not only in the Southwest but all over the country. (7) By the 1960s, Middle Easterners had introduced falafel, and the Hispanic population had added such tropical delicacies as mangoes and papayas. (8) Greeks opened restaurants in many large cities, and Americans enjoyed the spinach pie, shish kebab, and honeyed desserts of this culture. (9) By the 1970s, Caribbean, Filipino, and East Indian restaurants and markets had opened in some large cities; these offered many new products to the adventurous diner. (10) Americans in the major cities have always had French and Chinese restaurants to enjoy, but in the late 1960s and 1970s, numerous authentic French and Chinese restaurants opened in small cities, suburbs, and even small towns across the country. (11) It is not an exaggeration to state that American dining patterns underwent a significant change in the last third of this century.

Directions
Make the changes indicated. Note agreement of time expressions with present perfect tense.
a. Begin sentence 1 with the expression *In the past two decades;* use present perfect.
b. Begin sentence 3 with *Recently;* use present perfect.
c. Change the verb tenses in sentences 4, 5, and 6 to conform with the change in sentence 3.
d. Begin sentence 7 with *Since the 1960s;* use present perfect.
e. Change the verb tense in sentence 8 to conform to the details in sentence 7.
f. Begin sentence 9 with *More recently;* use present perfect.
g. Change sentence 10 from *In the late 1960s and 70s* to *Since the late 1960s and 70s;* change the verb to conform to the new time expression.
h. Change sentence 11 to a present perfect time frame to indicate that the change in dining patterns is still continuing today.

Discuss
Why must sentence 2 remain in the simple past tense?

4. *Tense Choice*

Fill in the blank spaces in each of the following paragraphs with the correct tense of the verb in parentheses. Use the various time expressions as a guide to tense choice.

a. Last semester I (read) (1) _____ about the different food production activities of the Baffin Island Eskimos and the African Temne, and how these activities (influence) (2) _____ the space perception skills of these peoples. Recently, other anthropological studies (show) (3) _____ how, in the past, food production activities (lead) (4) _____ to the development of different personality types among farmers and herders in Africa. In 1971, anthropologist John Whiting (study) (5) _____ four African tribes, two of which (be) (6) _____ herders and two of which (maintain) (7) _____ themselves by farming. He (find) (8) _____ that in herding cultures, in which men (go) (9) _____ off by themselves for long periods of time, individuality (become) (10) _____ a highly valued trait, but in farming cultures, in which decisions (make) (11) _____ collectively, individuality (value) (12) _____ not so highly _____ . As both the herding and farming cultures (exist) (13) _____ in Africa for thousands of years, the two different personality types (have) (14) _____ a chance to become deeply ingrained in their respective cultures.

b. Few cultures in the world today (develop) (1) _____ as imaginative a cuisine as the Chinese. For thousands of years the Chinese (collect) (2) _____ and (experiment) (3) _____ with the vegetable and animal edibles available in the various parts of China. This fact does not mean that the Chinese of the past (resist) (4) _____ imported foods. On the contrary, the Chinese (adopt) (5) _____ foreign food-stuffs since the dawn of history. In prehistoric times, they (accept) (6) _____ wheat, goats, and sheep from central Asia. In later periods, peanuts and sweet potatoes (come) (7) _____ from coastal traders. More notable, however, (be) (8) _____ the introduction of Chinese foods to other parts of the world. Marco Polo, visiting China in the thirteenth century, (bring) (9) _____ back spaghetti, a form of Chinese noodles, to Europe. Some experts (trace) (10) _____ the origin of sauerkraut and catsup to China. Undoubtedly, as China once again (open) (11) _____ up to foreign visitors, its cuisine (influence) (12) _____ foreign food habits as it (do) (13) _____ in the past.

Small Group Assignment

Figurative Language

Figurative language, or **figures of speech,** are expressions that describe things more clearly by comparing them to something else. Figures of speech are not actually true, or literal, but they paint a word picture that helps us understand the object more clearly.

Since food is an essential area of human culture, many figurative expressions refer to food and cooking processes.

Similes

Similes are comparisons of one thing to another using the words *like* or *as*.

Beth eats *like a bird*. (Beth has a small appetite, similar to that of a bird.)

Metaphors

Metaphors are comparisons that *omit* like or as. The comparison is *implied* by the metaphoric use of a verb, noun, or adjective.

> Tony's shrill voice *grated* on my ears. (A verb metaphor that compares Tony's voice to the unpleasant screeching sound made when you grate, or scrape, something.)
>
> I haven't got the *dough* to buy new boots. (A noun metaphor that implicitly compares money, which one needs to buy things, to dough, the basis of bread, which one needs to live.)
>
> When my daughter wants a favor, she uses a *sugary* voice. (An adjective metaphor that compares a tone of voice to the sweet taste of sugar.)

Proverbs

Proverbs are old sayings in metaphoric form that teach a lesson or illuminate a common human situation.

> "Too many cooks spoil the broth." (A comparison is implied between a soup spoiled by too many cooks using their own ingredients and a job spoiled by too many people demanding that the work be done their own way.)

Form groups of three to complete the following exercises. After each assigned task, your instructor may have all groups discuss their answers.

1. Using Figures of Speech

Choose the figure of speech that best describes the given situation.

a. After knocking over the lamp, the little boy looked at his mother and said, "I'm very sorry." The mother's anger _____ .

buttered   *peeled*   *melted*

b. The children's constant fighting _____ on their mother's nerves.

sifted   *grated*   *boiled*

c. Angela looked at her boyfriend with soft, loving eyes. That look _____ him deeply.

chopped   *sliced*   *stirred*

d. Every day for the past month my neighbor's barking dog has woken me up at 5 A.M. I'm _____ .

fed up   *spilling the beans*   *burned out*

e. The band tried to _____ enthusiasm for the politician on the stand.

melt down   dampen   whip up

f. Mario loves to talk about profound, intellectual subjects. He's

_____ .

a rotten apple   an egghead   a carrot top

g. The committee voted to delay the project until next month. They

_____ .

put it on a high boil   put it on the back burner   burned it

h. On most television comedy shows, the laughter is faked and added to the sound track. This _____ laughter is intended to stimulate laughter in the home viewer.

frozen   garden-fresh   canned

i. Miguel's wallet with $40 in it was stolen. He was _____ .

boiling mad   sugary sweet   buttered up

j. The snow _____ over the city, _____ the rooftops.

chopped   grated   sifted

roasting   frosting   slicing

k. The difficulty with some parents is that they can _____ criticism, but they can't take it.

fold in   brew   dish out

l. As the day became warmer, Kim _____ his sweater and coat.

cut up   blended   peeled off

2. Understanding Proverbs

Read the following situations carefully. Then discuss and prepare a brief, but complete, explanation for each proverb that follows the situation.

a. John and Jane were dating steadily. But then John began to see other women, so Jane decided to see other men.
"What's sauce for the goose is sauce for the gander."

b. My sister loves the peace and tranquility of the countryside, and I love the constant activity of the city.
"One man's meat is another man's poison."

c. Ingrid enjoyed being president of the school board, but she became angry whenever someone criticized her decisions.
"If you can't take the heat, get out of the kitchen."

d. Ari had missed many classes, but he showed up for the midterm and told the instructor, "I'm not worried; I'm sure I'll pass." The instructor replied:
"The proof of the pudding is in the tasting."

e. I gave my daughter a dollar for her allowance. After she had spent it, she saw something else she wanted. But she had no money left.
"You can't have your cake and eat it too."

3. *Sharing Figurative Language*

Explain some proverbs or expressions that concern food or cooking in the language(s) represented in your group.

Some culture-specific patterns of dining among the Burmese are illustrated here: squatting around a low table, men and women eating together, children eating with adults, eating with the fingers of the right hand, consuming rice as a staple at every meal, all dishes on the table at one time.

Composition Development

Moving from General to Specific Statements: Funnel-Shaped Paragraphs

When developing compositions and paragraphs that support main ideas, the most frequently used pattern in academic writing is to begin writing from broad, general statements and move to increasingly specific, concrete statements. Since the general, abstract statements lead into narrower, more specific types of statements, this kind of development is rather like a funnel.

Examine the following graphic illustration of paragraph [1] of this chapter. Note that the sentences do not merely repeat each other; rather, they define, explain, or illustrate the preceding sentence in increasingly more specific terms. Also note that the repetition or restatement of key words such as *eat*/*edible*, *food*, and *taboo* keeps the sentences linked together.

> ***Introduction of essay's main idea:*** **All individuals must eat to survive—but what people eat, when they eat, and the manner in which they eat are all patterned by culture.**
>
> ***Introduction of paragraph's main idea:*** **No society regards everything in its environment that is edible and might provide nourishment as food.**
>
> ***Explanation*** **of paragraph's main idea and** ***introduction of specific concept of taboo:*** **Certain edibles are ignored, others are tabooed.**
>
> ***Explanation*** **of concept of taboo: These food taboos may be so strong that just the thought of eating forbidden foods can cause an individual to feel** *ill*.
>
> ***Example*** **of negative reaction: A Hindu vegetarian . . .**

Note in this example that the author has moved from the broadest, most general statement through a series of explanations and examples that become increasingly concrete and specific.

1. *Funnel-Shaped Paragraphs: The Reading Passage*

a. Number the sentences in paragraph [2] of the reading passage. Which sentence gives the paragraph's main idea? Which sentence(s) offer specific supporting details of the main idea?

   b. Number the sentences in paragraph [3]. The main idea is a definition. Which sentence states it? Which sentence gives an explanation of the definition? Which sentence offers an example of the main idea?

   c. Number the sentences in paragraph [5]. Which sentence introduces the general topic of the paragraph? Which sentence states the main idea? Which sentence gives an example of the main idea?

   d. Without looking back at paragraph [6], arrange the following summary sentences for the paragraph in correct order from broadest or most general to most specific.

   (1) The Hindu taboo of eating beef despite the need for food is an example. _____

   (2) Some culturally patterned food habits are difficult to understand. _____

   (3) If an Indian family ate its cows during a famine, it would not have bullocks for the next season's farming. _____

   (4) Certain food habits may seem irrational and detrimental to the survival of the group. _____

   (5) One anthropological explanation of the Hindu taboo on beef consumption views it as an adaptation to a specific environmental condition. _____

   e. Number the sentences in paragraph [7] of the reading passage. Then write the sentence number that belongs in the blank space.

   (1) An example of the assertion in the topic statement: _____

   (2) A conclusion referring back to the topic statement: _____

   (3) An explanation of the example: _____

   (4) A topic statement identifying the paragraph subject and making an assertion about it: _____

2. Sequencing Statements

In each set of statements, the sentences are out of logical order. Rewrite and rearrange them in funnel-shaped order from the broadest (most general) to the narrowest (most concrete or specific). Following each sentence, in parentheses, label it as an introduction, generalization for a topic statement, explanation, example, or detail of an example. Note: There may be more than one of each type of sentence in the paragraph.

a. (1) For thousands of years, the Chinese have collected and experimented with the edibles available in China.

(2) On the contrary, they have adopted foreign foods since the dawn of history.

(3) Few cultures in the world today have developed as imaginative a cuisine as the Chinese.

(4) This statement is not to say that they resisted imported foods.

(5) Even in prehistoric times, the Chinese accepted wheat, goats, and sheep from Central Asia.

b. (1) The Bushmen are an egalitarian and cooperative society.

(2) Participation in another culture forces a person to think about how to behave in a culturally approved manner.

(3) Richard Lee, a Western anthropologist, tells how he made a cultural error when he worked among the African Bushmen.

(4) Bushmen methods of hunting and gathering demand a high degree of sharing and an avoidance of competition.

(5) The Bushmen were offended, interpreting Lee's presentation of the ox as competitive and boasting.

(6) When Lee presented the Bushmen with an ox, he stressed its large size and the great amount of meat it would provide.

c. (1) Religion, economics, and family life all fit together to make up the cultural pattern of a society.

(2) Among the Kwakiutl, the potlatch is an important economic and social ceremony.

(3) Cultural elements cannot be viewed in isolation; they must be viewed in the totality of the culture.

(4) Canoes, food, and fish oil are distributed and even destroyed as the host tries to show how rich and generous he is.

(5) The potlatch is a feast at which many different kinds of wealth are given away by the host to impress his guests.

(6) In addition, the host may boast: "I am the great chief who vanquishes . . . I am the great chief who makes people ashamed."

3. *Forming Generalizations for Funnel-Shaped Paragraphs*

The topic statement for a well-developed funnel-shaped paragraph may consist of several sentences: an introduction to the topic, an explanation of the topic, and a sentence that narrows the topic down to a particular aspect or approach. The items that follow contain sets of related details. For each set, construct a topic statement of one to three sentences that proceeds in a funnel shape, from the broadest, or most general, to increasingly narrower statements.

a. (1) Thanksgiving turkeys are cooked, usually by roasting.

(2) Accompaniments such as vegetables, cranberry sauce, and cole slaw are bought and prepared.

(3) Several kinds of pie, both for the main meal and the dessert, are usually prepared.

(4) Some traditional Thanksgiving pies are mince and sweet potato, which are served with the turkey, and pumpkin and apple, which are served for dessert.

b. (1) Fast-food restaurants are located on almost every downtown corner.

(2) These restaurants serve working people who want a quick lunch and families and shoppers on a low budget.

(3) In a fast-food restaurant, you can sit over a cup of coffee or an inexpensive sandwich for several hours.

(4) Once in a fast-food restaurant I saw a man filling out his income tax statement over a cup of coffee.

c. (1) First, you have to put in the yeast and mix the ingredients for the bread dough by hand.

(2) Then you must allow the dough to rise for about one hour.

(3) When the dough has risen, you must punch it down and knead it for about fifteen minutes.

(4) The dough must be allowed to rise for a second time.

(5) Again, the risen dough must be punched down and kneaded.

(6) The dough must rise for a third time. Then it is baked for about fifty minutes to an hour.

4. *Paragraph Development: Funnel-Shaped Patterns*

Follow the directions for each item. After your first draft, revise your work into a well-developed, funnel-shaped paragraph.

a. (1) Make a generalization about human nutrition.

(2) Make an assertion about vegetables (or fruit) and human nutrition.

(3) Identify one of your favorite vegetables (or fruits) as an example of your assertion in (2).

(4) Provide several supporting details about your illustrative item in (3).

(5) State a conclusion about the subject related to the details you presented.

b. Brainstorm for three minutes all the details you can remember about your present kitchen. Group the details into related categories: appliances, storage space, utensils, and so on. Then compose a brief, funnel-shaped paragraph about a well-arranged kitchen.

(1) Make a generalization about the function of a kitchen.

(2) Assert an opinion about how kitchens should be arranged that includes two or three adjectives.

(3) Use the categories formed from your brainstormed details to name several important aspects of kitchens.

(4) Develop your paragraph about a well-arranged kitchen in funnel-shaped order from the most important, general items to the least important, more specifically detailed items.

c. Study the photograph of the Burmese family on page 48 at their meal. Write a funnel-shaped paragraph about the photograph.

(1) Introduce the topic of the photograph by making a generalization about eating patterns in different cultures.

(2) Make a statement of from one to three sentences about what a visitor to *your home* at mealtime would observe in terms of eating customs.

(3) Assume that the Burmese eating pattern in the photograph is typical of Burmese culture. Make a generalization about Burmese patterns of eating in comparison or contrast to the eating patterns described in (2). This statement will be your topic statement.

(4) Present several details from the photograph that support your topic statement about Burmese eating patterns.

(5) Draw a conclusion from the details in your paragraph about how you would feel if you were living in the Burmese culture and were constrained to follow Burmese eating customs.

d. Study the photograph of the Egyptian market at the beginning of the chapter. Write a funnel-shaped paragraph about the photograph.

(1) Introduce the topic of your paragraph by making a generalization about the activity of shopping for food.

(2) Add some assertions about shopping for food in your culture.

(3) Compare shopping for food as depicted in the photograph to shopping for food in your culture. This comparison will be your topic statement.

(4) Describe some aspects of the photograph that support your topic statement. You may use your imagination or your familiarity with similar market scenes to develop your details.

(5) Conclude with an opinion about the importance of food shopping in modern, urban cultures. Relate that opinion to your personal experiences of food shopping for your family.

Composition Topics

1. Compose a well-developed essay with funnel-shaped paragraphs on the following topic:

Fast-food restaurants are very popular in the United States. Many people believe they offer convenience, quality food, and reasonable prices. Do you agree or disagree? You may support your response by discussing the atmosphere, service, and other aspects of fast-food restaurants as well as the aspects mentioned above.

2. Compose an essay in which you relate the physical environment of your native or present residence to the food patterns of its people. First, identify the environment and give a general description of its features. Then, select one or two aspects of the environment as the focus of a funnel-shaped paragraph(s). Show how this aspect of the environment has influenced a specific food pattern in your culture. [Some aspects you might want to consider are climate (seasonal changes, rainfall, temperatures), types of land (mountainous, swampy, flat), availability of water (rivers, oceans, scarcity of water), and soil quality (fertile or infertile).]

Reproduction and the Family

The concept of "romantic love," in which a couple mate on the basis of physical attraction and common interests, is not a worldwide phenomenon. Here, a young American couple on a college campus display the physical demonstrativeness and self-involvement characteristic of romantic relationships. Other aspects of "romantic love" are informal or accidental introductions, assertion of individual preference over family or social dictates, and subordination of practical considerations to emotional needs. Would this scene be common in your native city? Explain.

Freewrite

Keep a journal for a week about interactions in your family. Then review your journal for a Freewrite focusing on the emotional experience of family living.

Vocabulary in Context

You will need to know the meanings of the following words to fully comprehend the reading passage. Use your dictionary as necessary.

Verbs	Nouns	Adjectives	Adverbs
abhor	perspective	erotic	
legitimize	indifference	heterosexual	
	intimacy	adolescent	
	preliminary	naive	
	puberty	(pre)marital	
	generation	celibate	
	flexibility		

Sentence Writing

Read each of the following items. Then compose a complete English sentence related to the item, using the given vocabulary words. The first one has been done.

1. Recent newspaper stories have highlighted the problems of runaways, those children from twelve to eighteen who leave their parents' home without permission and try to make a living on their own.

   indifference: *Children become unhappy if their parents show indifference to them.*

   adolescent (adj.): _____

   _____

   puberty: _____

   _____

   naive: _____

   _____

2. Life in an extended family of three generations has a number of economic and social advantages. However, it is also true that although three generations may share the same living space, they may not share the same social and moral values. Grandparents, parents, and children may see different solutions to a given problem.

perspective: _____

_____

flexibility: _____

_____

generation: _____

_____

3. Since the 1960s, the United States and Western Europe have undergone a so-called sexual revolution. Children have become familiar with sexual activity at an earlier age than before; advertising and the mass media have become more erotic; and legal marriage is no longer the only acceptable form of union between females and males.

intimacy: _____

_____

marital: _____

_____

preliminary: _____

_____

celibate: _____

_____

heterosexual: _____

_____

4. Magazines featuring erotic pictures and writing, that is, material intended to arouse sexual feelings, have become common sights on newsstands in the United States. Although many citizens support the right of any person to read or publish such materials, they nevertheless believe that such materials should not be openly displayed where children can easily view them.

erotic: _____

_____

abhor: _____

_____

legitimize: _____

_____

Reading: Reproduction and the Family

Key Concepts
- *Sexual reproduction*
- *Homosexual/heterosexual activity*
- *Sexual repression/sexual permissiveness*
- *Marriage: monogamy/polygamy*

[1]   Although the cultural components of food habits are relatively easy to study and understand, those of sexual habits are not. Of all the kinds of human behavior, sexual activity is the most likely to be viewed as "doing what comes naturally." Yet a cross-cultural **perspective** on sexual practices tells us that every aspect of human sexual activity is   5
patterned by culture and is influenced by learning.

[2]   Among humans, reproduction through sexual intercourse is, of course, biologically based. But every aspect of sexual activity among humans is culturally patterned. Contrary to being an expression of humanity's "animal" nature, sexual behavior in our species is uniquely   10
"human" in many ways. Human sexual behavior is not tied to reproduction, as is true for other animals, in which mating occurs only when the female is capable of conceiving a baby. Human females are biologically capable of sexual activity without a reproductive purpose. The human species has been freed from the rigidly patterned sexual behavior   15
of other animal species. The most notable aspects of human sexual habits are their variety and **flexibility.** And as is true of all human behavior, the cultural patterning of biological potential is the key to understanding our species.

[3]   Human culture teaches us how to respond to different parts   20
of the human body. What is considered **erotic** in some cultures evokes **indifference** or disgust in others. For example, kissing is not practiced in many societies. The Tahitians learned to kiss from the Europeans, but before this contact they began sexual **intimacy** by sniffing. The Trobriand Islanders, as described by anthropologist Bronislaw Mali-   25
nowski, "inspect each other's hair for lice and eat them . . . to the natives a natural and pleasant occupation between two who are fond of each other." Such activity may seem disgusting to us. But to the Trobrianders, the European habit of boys and girls going out on a picnic with a knapsack of food was equally disgusting, although it is perfectly acceptable for a   30
Trobriand boy and girl to gather wild foods together as a **preliminary** to sexual activity.

[4]   The idea of who is an appropriate sexual partner is also different around the world. The American negative reaction to homosexual activity is not shared by all cultures. In some societies, a period of   35
homosexual relationships is considered normal for an **adolescent** male, who is expected to, and apparently does, enter into a **heterosexual** marriage when adult. In still other cultures, such as in parts of Tahiti,

homosexual practices almost never occurred until they were introduced
by the Europeans. In these cultures, homosexual activity is not consid-   40
ered shameful or abnormal, as is largely true in some parts of the United
States; rather it is seen as an activity that does not make much sense if
members of the other sex are around. The ages at which sexual response
is believed to begin and end, the ways in which people make themselves
attractive, and the importance of sexual activity in human life are all   45
patterned and regulated by culture, and they affect sexual response and
behavior. A comparison of two cultures—the Irish of the island of Inis
Beag and the Polynesians of the island of Mangaia—helps demonstrate
the role of culture in this area of life.

[5]   The people of Inis Beag have been described as "one of the   50
most sexually **naive** of the world's societies." Sex is never discussed at
home when children are near, and practically no sexual instruction is
given by parents to children. Adults express the belief that "after marriage, nature takes its course." Women are not expected to enjoy sexual
relations; these are a "duty" to be endured, for to refuse to have sexual   55
relations within marriage is considered a mortal sin. Nudity is **abhorred**
by these islanders, and there is no tradition of sexual jokes. The main
style of dancing allows little bodily contact among the participants, but
even then some women refuse to dance because it means touching men.
The separation of the sexes begins early in Inis Beag and lasts into   60
adulthood. Other cultural patterns related to sexual repression* are the
absence of sexual foreplay, the belief that sexual activity weakens a
man, the absence of **premarital** sex, the high percentage of **celibate**
males, and the extraordinarily late age of marriage. As a female infor-
mant stated about sex, "Men can wait a long time before wanting 'it,'   65
but we women can wait a lot longer."

[6]   The people of the island of Mangaia in the South Pacific
present a strong contrast to those of Inis Beag. In this Polynesian culture,
sexual intercourse is one of the major interests of life. Although sex is
not discussed at home, sexual information is transmitted to boys and   70
girls at **puberty** by the elders of the group. For adolescent boys, a two-
week period of formal instruction about the techniques of intercourse is
followed by a culturally approved experience with a mature woman in
the village. After this experience, the boy is considered a man. (In Inis
Beag, a man is considered a "lad" until he is about forty.)   75

[7]   Sexual relations in Mangaia are carried out privately, but
there are continual public comments about sexual activity. Sexual jokes,
expressions, and comments are not only common but are expected as
part of the preliminaries to public meetings. This pattern of public verbal
references to sexual behavior contrasts with the public separation of the   80
sexes: Boys and girls should not be seen together in public, although

*The restraint or prevention of normal or natural desires.

practically every girl and boy has engaged in intercourse before marriage. The act of sexual intercourse itself is the focus of sexual activity. In Mangaia both men and women are expected to take pleasure in the sexual act. Female frigidity, male celibacy, and homosexuality are practically unknown. Thus different cultural attitudes about sex pattern the sexual feelings of males and females alike.

[8]   All cultures must include sexual instruction, either direct or indirect, for their members; for without sexuality leading to reproduction, a culture would survive only for one **generation.** Every society must solve the problems of regulating sexual unions between males and females, of providing economic support for the union and the children born to it, and of assigning responsibilities for the care of the children. The almost universal solution to these problems has been the relatively permanent union we call *marriage.* Its relative permanence provides a structure, the family, in which food and protection can be provided and children can receive the care needed for healthy development. Still another function of marriage is that it links different families and kinship groups. Thus marriage leads to cooperation among groups of people larger than the basic husband–wife pair—a great advantage for the survival of the human species.

[9]   Marriage refers to the customs, rules, and obligations that establish a special relationship between an adult male and female who have a sexual union, between the adult couple and any children they produce, and between the kinship groups of the husband and the wife. Both marriage and the family are cultural patterns. As such, they differ in form and functions among human societies. In the United States, the marriage tie is the most important in the formation of the family, but its importance is not true everywhere. In many societies, the most important family bond is between blood relations rather than between husband and wife. In some, the blood tie between generations (father and children or mother and children) is the most important.

[10]   *Monogamy,* the marital system that permits only one man to be married to one woman at any given time, is a law in the United States, but it is not in many of the world's cultures, which permit *polygamy,* or plural marriage. Most polygamous cultures practice *polygyny,* which is the marriage of one man to several women. A few permit *polyandry,* which is the marriage of one woman to several men. Anthropologists are coming to the conclusion that the most useful way to study sexuality, marriage, and the family is not to establish definitions that will apply to every known group; rather, they should look at the different ways in which the basic human needs of sexual regulation, infant care, division of labor, and establishment of rights and obligations within the family unit are **legitimized** in different societies.

Reading Comprehension

1. *True-False*

Indicate whether the following statements are true or false according to the information in the text. Be prepared to cite the sentence(s) that support your answer.

a. Reproductive ability among human beings is biologically based. _____

b. Human sexuality, like animal sexuality, is tied to the reproductive process. _____

c. Kissing is not a universal preliminary to sexual relations. _____

d. Homosexual relations among adolescent males will prevent them from forming adult heterosexual marriages. _____

e. The United States has a generally approving attitude toward homosexuality. _____

f. All styles of dancing are erotic and sexually related. _____

g. In the selection, Mangaian culture is used as an example of a sexually repressive society. _____

h. The age at which sexual activity begins is about the same all over the world. _____

i. Marriage based on romantic love is a universal institution. _____

j. The blood tie between a parent and a child may be stronger in some cultures than that between husband and wife. _____

k. Monogamous cultures do not permit divorce. _____

l. In a polyandrous culture, children of the same mother might have different fathers. _____

2. *Reading Review*

In oral discussion or in writing, answer the following questions based on the reading passage.

a. In what major way is human sexual behavior different from animal sexual behavior?

    b. Where did Tahitian society learn about kissing?

    c. What would be the Trobriand Islander reaction to heterosexual picnicking?

    d. What importance did homosexuality have in Tahiti before the coming of the Europeans?

    e. Why are the Inis Beag described as a sexually naive society?

    f. How is Mangaian society different from Inis Beag in its attitude toward sex?

    g. What is the essential purpose of marriage according to the passage?

    h. What ties in addition to marriage may be important in certain societies?

    i. What is the difference between monogamy and polygamy?

    j. What is the difference between polygyny and polyandry?

3. *Analyzing the Text*

What thought relationships are signaled by the following words or phrases? Use your chart of "Useful Signal Expressions" in Appendix B to guide you as necessary.

    a. Paragraph [1], sentence 1: *Although*

    b. Paragraph [1], sentence 2: *Yet*

    c. Paragraph [2], sentence 1: *of course*

    d. Paragraph [2], last sentence: *And*

    e. Paragraph [3], sentence 3: *For example*

    f. Paragraph [4], sentence 4: *until*

    g. Paragraph [5], sentence 4: *for*

    h. Paragraph [5], sentence 6: *because*

    i. Paragraph [6], next to last sentence: *After*

    j. Paragraph [7], last sentence: *Thus*

4. *Scanning*

Sometimes our purpose in reading is primarily to obtain specific facts or pieces of information about the subject of the selection. In this case we need not read every word; rather, we **scan,** or move our eyes quickly down the passage seeking only the details we want.

  ▪ **Scanning the Text.** To practice scanning, first locate the key words in the following questions that indicate the information wanted. (In the first six sentences, these key words are italicized.) Then scan the text to find the required information. In the blank spaces next to each item, write the relevant paragraph and sentence numbers from the text. The first one has been done.

a. Which sentence(s) identifies the main difference between *human and animal sexuality* with respect to *females* of the species? *Para [2] Sent. 4 and 5*

b. Which sentence(s) describes the *pre-European preliminary* to *sexual intimacy* among the Tahitians? _____

c. Which sentence(s) describes a *preliminary activity* to *sexual activity* among the *Trobriand Islanders?* _____

d. Which sentence(s) describes the *general attitude* toward *homosexuality* in the *United States?* _____

e. Which sentence(s) describes the way *Inis Beag women* are expected to *respond* to marital sexual relations? _____

f. Which sentence(s) describes the *Inis Beag attitude* toward *heterosexual dancing?* _____

g. Which sentence(s) describes the sexual training of adolescent boys in Mangaia? _____

h. Which sentence(s) describes the public attitude toward sexual activity in Mangaia? _____

i. Which sentence(s) describes the way Mangaian women are expected to respond to sexual relations? _____

j. Which sentence(s) describes the functions of marriage? _____
_____

k. Which sentence(s) defines marriage? _____

l. Which sentence(s) explains the difference between two basic systems of marriage? _____

m. Which sentence(s) defines the system of marriage in which one woman has several husbands? _____

▪ **Outline Completion by Scanning.** Scanning for details that support a main idea is a useful way to review material for an exam. Complete the following outlines with details scanned from the reading selection.

a. *Main Idea:* Different cultures have different concepts of sexually appropriate behavior.

Europeans - Kissing

_____

_____

_____

b. *Main Idea:* Inis Beag is a clear example of a sexually repressed culture.

_____

_____

_____

c. *Main Idea:* Marriage is the almost universal human solution to regulating the sexual union between a male and a female. However, the specific forms of marriage vary widely from culture to culture.

_____

_____

_____

_____

Vocabulary Study

1. Synonyms

Replace each italicized word or phrase in the following sentences with one word from the list.

abnormal
components
conceiving
kinship
obligations
reaction
regulating
verbal

a. Our *close relationship with family members* imposes certain economic and emotional *responsibilities*.

b. In the United States, *making rules about* education is a function of individual states, not the federal government.

c. Many different *elements* are necessary for democratic government, such as mass education and a free press.

d. The "wolf-children" and the "wild boy of Aveyron" had a *response* to dealing with other children that could be considered *very different from that of ordinary people.*

e. *Creating* great works of art is a uniquely human quality.

f. The instructor gave *oral* directions for the examination.

2. *Word Form Table*

Fill in the following table with the appropriate forms of the given words. Some words may have two forms.

	Verbs	Nouns	Adjectives	Adverbs
a.	abhor	_____	_____	_____
b.	xxx	indifference	_____	_____
c.	xxx	intimacy	_____	_____
d.	xxx	_____	celibate	_____
e.	xxx	_____	adolescent	_____

Use the correct form(s) from each lettered line to complete the same lettered sentence below.

a. Homosexual activity is considered normal in some cultures, is tolerated in others, and is considered an _____ act in still other cultures.

b. Nudity was viewed _____ , that is, without shame, in some South Seas cultures before the arrival of Christian missionaries.

c. American children often share their most _____ thoughts with their peers rather than their parents.

d. Priests in the Roman Catholic religion must remain _____ , but such _____ is not the rule in every religion.

e. Both physiologically and psychologically, _____ , or the period between thirteen and about sixteen years of age, can be very difficult.

3. *Word Formation*

Suffix *ly*: forms adverbs from adjectives. Adverbs describe a verb action or tell the kind or degree of adjectives. Underscore the adverbs in each phrase.

biologically based	extraordinarily late
uniquely human	culturally approved behavior
rigidly patterned	relatively permanent
particularly shameful	perfectly acceptable
sexually naive	completely abhorrent

Compose your own sentences that include these adverb phrases. You may use the content from the reading passage or make reference to your own native society or the society in which you are living now.

Writing Exercises

Sentence Types

There are three basic sentence types in English. They are all based on the thought unit of the main, or independent, clause.

Simple Sentence
This is a statement that contains one clause with one subject + main verb combination that expresses a complete thought.

> This *chapter discusses* sexuality, reproduction, and the
> (subject) + (main verb)
>
> **family in the human species.**

A simple sentence may have a compound subject of two or more items, a compound verb stating two or more actions, or both.

> *India and China* both idealize the extended family.
> (compound subject: note plural verb)
>
> **North Americans *idealize and emphasize* the needs of the**
> (compound main verbs)
>
> **individual above the group.**

1. *Sentence Combining*

Combine the given items to form a simple sentence with either a compound subject or a compound verb. The first one has been done.

a. Ruth Benedict was a famous anthropologist. Margaret Mead was a famous anthropologist.

Ruth Benedict and Margaret Mead were famous anthropologists.

b. The relationship between parents and children is a clue to the key values of a culture. The relationship between husbands and wives is a clue to the key values of a culture.

_____

_____

c. The Bushmen of south-central Africa hunt wild game for their food. The Bushmen of south-central Africa gather wild plants for their food.

_____

_____

d. In the past, almost all marriages in Asia were arranged. In the past, most marriages in Europe were arranged.

_____

_____

e. Physical survival is essential to the continuation of a culture. Reproduction is essential to the continuation of a culture.

_____

_____

Compound Sentence

A compound sentence consists of two or more independent clauses joined by a coordinating conjunction: *and* (addition), *but* or *yet* (reversal of thought), *for* (reason), *so* (result), *or* (choice).

Polyandry is a useful marriage system among the Todas,
(independent clause)

for they have fewer women than men.
(coord. conj.)   (independent clause)

A compound sentence may also be joined by a semicolon (;). It shows specific thought relationships between **independent clauses.** The following signal expressions may be used:

    time: then, next, later, now, afterwards

sequence:	first, second, . . . finally
addition:	in addition, furthermore, moreover, also
reversal:	however, nevertheless, in contrast, on the other hand
example:	for example, for instance
result:	thus, therefore, consequently, as a result

The Toda population has fewer women than
(independent clause)

men; therefore, polyandry is a useful marriage system for
(semicolon + signal)   (independent clause)

them.

---

1. *Sentence Combining*

Combine the given items to form either a simple sentence with a compound subject or a compound verb or a compound sentence that must include a coordinating conjunction or a semicolon. Use signal expressions as necessary. Label each completed sentence as simple or compound. The first one has been done.

a. The Iroquois followed the pattern of matrilocal residence.* Other Native American tribes also followed matrilocal residence. _____

The Iroquois and other native American tribes followed matrilocal residence. (simple)

b. Adult Iroquois women lived in a longhouse. Their children lived in a longhouse. _____

_____

_____

c. Each woman had a compartment in the longhouse. All her children had a compartment in the longhouse. _____

_____

_____

*A rule that states that a husband must live with his wife's family.

d.   A newly married Iroquois man moved to his wife's group. He spent most of his time with his mother's group. _____

_____

_____

e.   Married men hunted with men of the mother's group. Married men went on war parties with men of the mother's group. _____

_____

_____

f.   One girl in the mother's group cooked for the bridegroom. One girl in the mother's group prepared the bridegroom's clothes. _____

_____

_____

g.   This woman was called the bridegroom's "sister." The bridegroom was called her "brother." _____

_____

_____

h.   The bridegroom was obligated to help his "sister's" sons. It was not necessary for him to help his own sons. _____

_____

_____

i.   His own sons took their meals with their mother. They stayed with her most of the time. _____

_____

_____

j.   The father could be friendly with his own sons. The father could ignore his own sons. _____

_____

_____

k.   All the father's possessions were transmitted to his "sister's" sons. All the father's influence was transmitted to his "sister's" sons. _____

_____

_____

l.   Most cultures are patrilocal.* The matrilocal Iroquois family structure may seem strange to us. _____

_____

_____

Complex Sentence

A complex sentence contains at least one dependent and one independent clause. Each clause has its own subject + verb combination. However, the dependent clause is marked by one of the following subordinating adverbs or markers:

> time: when, while, before, after, since
> addition of description (adjective clause): who, which/that, where, whose
> reason: because, since, as
> reversal of thought: although, even though
> condition: if, whether, until, unless
> following verbs of telling or thinking: that, how, what, why, where, who, which, if, whether

---

Marriage has been defined as a union
(independent clause)

that unites a man and a woman to form a family.
(dependent clause—subordinate *that:* adds description)

Some form of marital union is practiced in every society
(independent clause)

although the details of the system may differ.
(dependent clause—subordinate *although:* reversal)

Because stability is important in raising children,
(dependent clause—subordinate *because:* gives a reason)

the institution of marriage always involves responsibility.
(independent clause)

---

*Residence and inheritance are through the father's side.

Note that in a complex sentence, when the dependent clause precedes the independent clause, it is followed by a comma.

1. *Sentence Completion*

Complete the following dependent clauses to make complex sentences. Punctuate correctly.

a. When our family has a problem _____

_____

b. _____

_____ because teenagers are rebellious.

c. Although weddings are happy occasions _____

_____

d. Since many parents are embarrassed to talk to their children about

sex _____

_____

e. _____

_____ before they get married.

f. If two generations live together _____

_____

g. _____

_____ who don't get along very well.

2. *Identifying Complete Thought Units*

Analyze each of the following items to determine if it is a complete independent clause with a subject and a main verb: If it is, mark it *IC* in the blank space and capitalize and punctuate it appropriately; if it is not and cannot stand alone as a sentence, mark it *Frag* (for *Fragment*) in the blank space and add as many words as necessary before and after the given item to make it a complete sentence with at least one independent clause. The first one has been done.

a. In a bookcase in the basement of my house, hidden away on a top shelf

Frag

there is a copy of Shakespeare's plays.

b. many people are worried about the influence of drugs on children
_____

_____

c. although there are many opportunities to participate in athletic contests
_____

_____

d. for example, becoming financially independent, getting an apartment away from home, obtaining a responsible job _____

_____

e. not many people have seen such things _____

_____

f. going away on a long vacation before work begins _____

_____

g. we'll help you to find the right payment plan _____

_____

h. who show affection for each other _____

_____

i. she knows that _____

_____

j. beginning in a relatively official tone, the politician gradually moved to a more intimate one as she warmed up to her audience _____

_____

k. that human beings are essentially peaceful and wish to live in harmony with their fellows _____

_____

l. she's apathetic _____

_____

m. where I first met you _____

_____

n. between fathers and sons or mothers and daughters living under the same roof _____

o. because you say so, that doesn't make it true ⎯⎯⎯⎯

p. excellent benefits such as an extensive medical plan, long, paid vacations, and a good pension system ⎯⎯⎯⎯

q. we never understood how she obtained such high grades without studying hard ⎯⎯⎯⎯

r. as a preliminary step to filing your application for college entrance ⎯⎯⎯⎯

3. *Paragraph Combining*

Rewrite the following paragraph using compound and complex sentence structures to combine the information given in each cluster into a single sentence. Some thought relationships are suggested for your guidance. The first one has been done.

(1) The extended family system has many benefits.
(2) The extended family system has been the most common family system in human history. (adding description)

The extended family, which has been the most common family system in human history, has many benefits.

(3) The extended family has several economic advantages.

(4) It can provide more workers than the nuclear family. (sequence)
(5) It contains older members. (addition)
(6) These older members can watch the small children. (adding description)

(7) The mother can work, too. (result)

(8) The extended family is useful for agricultural societies. (sequence)
(9) Farming families always need extra hands. (reason)

(10) Farm families have two choices in working their land.

(11) They may use their own family members.
(12) They may use hired laborers. (choice)

(13) The first choice is preferable.

(14) Then the family does not have to spend precious money to hire workers. (reason)

(15) In agricultural societies, land ownership is important.

(16) It is a source of power, pride, and prestige. (reason)

(17) The extended family system keeps the oldest son at home.

(18) The land goes to him at his father's death. (addition)

(19) The continuity of the family on the land is assured. (result)

(20) Purely agricultural societies are becoming fewer and fewer in our modern world.

(21) The extended family must adapt to a new, industrialized, urban world. (reason–result)

4. *Extended Paragraph with Sentence Variety*

Do you live in a nuclear or extended family situation? Describe some of the living arrangements, economic relationships, and emotional attachments that are basic to your family situation. Try to use the three different sentence types you have just studied.

Small Group Assignment

Interpreting Charts

Form groups. Read the introductions to each of the family kinship charts and answer and discuss the questions that follow.

In all societies, *kin,* or those we consider relatives, have special names. In every kinship system some relatives are classed together; that is, they are referred to by the same kinship term. For example, in the kinship language of English, the individual (called Ego) uses the term *aunt* to refer to both the mother's and father's sisters. In English the women who marry the brothers of either the father or mother are also called *aunt.* The English language puts these women together in the same category (aunt) because their relationship to Ego in terms of intimacy and authority is generally similar. In other cultures, however, where the father's sister and the mother's sister have different rights, obligations, and relationships to the individual (Ego), these female relatives are called by different kinship names.

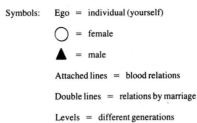

Symbols: Ego = individual (yourself)

○ = female

▲ = male

Attached lines = blood relations

Double lines = relations by marriage

Levels = different generations

English Language Kinship Terminology Chart

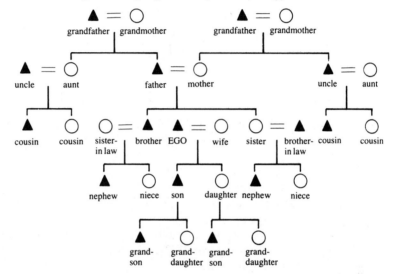

Questions

1. According to the chart, what does Ego call the father's brother and the mother's brother?
2. What is the term for the woman whom Ego marries?
3. What does Ego call the woman whom Ego's brother marries? What does this term mean?
4. What kinship term is the same for both males and females? Would you rather have different terms for males and females? Why or why not?
5. What does Ego call the male children of Ego's sister? What does Ego call the female children of Ego's sister?
6. Are the same kinship terms used for Ego's mother's side of the family as for Ego's father's side? If so, do you think using identical terms is a useful idea? Why or why not?

The Hawaiian system of kinship terms is found throughout Polynesia. It is relatively simple, using few kinship terms for different relatives. The

Hawaiian system emphasizes distinctions between generations, and it reflects the relative equality between the mother's and father's side of the family in regard to Ego. Within the Hawaiian kinship system, an individual may choose to live with either the mother's or the father's side of the family. By using the same terms for both biological parents and the brothers and sisters of these parents, Ego establishes intimacy with a wide group of people.

Hawaiian Language Kinship Terminology Chart

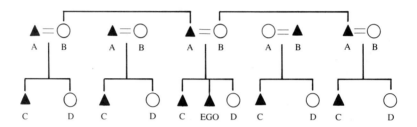

Questions

1. In Hawaiian terminology, is there any distinction between Ego's relatives on the father's side and on the mother's side? What does this lack of distinction mean?
2. Does the Hawaiian terminology distinguish between Ego's female cousins and Ego's male cousins? Do you think using identical terms is a good idea? Why or why not?
3. Why does Ego call female cousins by the same name that he or she uses for his or her sister?
4. The introduction asserts that the Hawaiian kinship system uses few names for categories of relatives. Support this statement by contrasting a category of kinship relations from the English kinship chart with one from the Hawaiian.

Describing Your Family Structure

Make a kinship chart of your family structure beginning with your parents' generation. Describe your family structure in a narrative composition, beginning with your parents' generation.

Composition Development

Subdividing a Topic

In writing an extended paragraph or a short essay, it is useful to begin by dividing the topic or given thesis sentence into three aspects or characteristics. Each of these will have its own general statement and supporting details or examples.

1. *Choosing Good Subtopics*

In the following exercises are a topic statement and a list of possible subtopics. First, write the key words for each aspect of the topic statement in the space provided. Then determine which three subtopics would be best for developing the composition. Think about why you eliminated the other possibilities: Were they too limited for development? Were they unrelated to the topic statement? Were they contradictory to the point of view? The first item is done for you.

a. **Topic Sentence:** Culture in its many forms raises humans above other mammals.

Key Topic Words: *Culture*

Key Point-of-View Words: *raises human beings*

Key Organizational Words: *many forms*

   (1) Humans' highly developed language systems

   (2) Humans' need for food, sleep, and reproduction— *omit: biological not cultural*

   (3) Humans' artistic creativity

   (4) Humans' economic systems

b. **Topic Sentence:** In modern society the word *family* has several different meanings.

Key Topic Words: _____

Key Point-of-View Words: _____

Key Organizational Words: _____

   (1) Communes* as families

   (2) Nuclear families (parents and dependent children)

   (3) Advantages of large families

   (4) Extended families (parents, children, other relatives)

   (5) Humanity as one family

c. **Topic Sentence:** There are many advantages to living in a large city.

Key Topic Words: _____

---

*A commune is a group of persons, many unrelated by blood or marriage, who share the same residence and financial responsibilities.

Key Point-of-View Words: _____

Key Organizational Words: _____

(1) Job opportunities

(2) Educational opportunities

(3) Pollution and crime

(4) Cultural opportunities

(5) Peacefulness and harmony of a small town

d. Topic Sentence: French schools may be strict, but they encourage politeness, respect for property, and good work habits.

Key Topic Words: _____

Key Point-of-View Words: _____

Key Organizational Words: _____

(1) American schools encourage individual expression.

(2) French schoolchildren wear uniforms.

(3) Careless or unsatisfactory work is not accepted in French schools.

(4) French schoolchildren learn to write in script at four years of age.

(5) Taking care of school equipment is required in French schools.

e. Topic Sentence: Children's play equips them for the physical, emotional, and mental demands of later life.

Key Topic Words: _____

Key Point-of-View Words: _____

Key Organizational Words: _____

(1) Doll play expresses feelings.

(2) Checkers was my favorite childhood game.

(3) Sports build body strength and coordination.

(4) Crossword puzzles are fun.

(5) Riddles and puzzles sharpen the mind.

2. *Generating Your Own Subtopics*

Carefully analyze the following statements for their topics and key word(s). Individually or as a class, list three meaningful subtopics of the main idea that could each be developed in its own paragraph.

a. Some art forms such as poetry and the novel cannot communicate fully across language barriers, but other art forms can.

(1) _____

(2) _____

(3) _____

b. The human body is a miraculous organism with all of its elements functioning together for its survival and development.

(1) _____

(2) _____

(3) _____

c. Language learning demands the mastery of several different skills.

(1) _____

(2) _____

(3) _____

d. Achieving a successful marriage requires effort in many different directions.

(1) _____

(2) _____

(3) _____

e. The schools have an important role to play in sex education.

(1) _____

(2) _____

(3) _____

f. If I were given the choice, I would never want to return in time to an earlier period of human development. The modern world is quite comfortable. There are too many modern inventions I couldn't live without.

(1) _____

(2) _____

(3) _____

3. *Practicing Subtopic Division*

Frequently in college writing assignments such as proficiency tests or essay examination questions, a generalization or topic statement for an essay is given to you, and you are expected to support it or provide your own similar generalization on the subject. For example, let us take the following generalization:

Introduction, including overall central idea: A family can be described in emotional, economic, and social terms.

Aspect 1: general statement about the emotional meaning of a family

Supporting details for the emotional meaning:

a. _____

b. _____

c. *(illustration)* _____

Aspect 2: general statement about the economic meaning of a family

Supporting details for the economic meaning:

a. _____

b. _____

c. *(illustration)* _____

Aspect 3: general statement about the social meaning of a family

Supporting details for the social meaning

a. _____

b. _____

c. *(illustration)* _____

Conclusion: restatement of central idea in the introduction

4. Completion of an Extended Paragraph with Three Aspects

Following is an incomplete paragraph that contains an introduction and a number of assertions that present related but different aspects of the main topic. In the space provided, add specific items that support the given aspects.

a. Weddings are by nature happy occasions in which both the bride's and groom's families participate with joy and enthusiasm. But a successful wedding, like any other successful affair, must be well and carefully planned in advance by both the bride's and groom's families. *(Aspect 1)* The bride's family has several major responsibilities. *(Write about two or three specifics.)*

_____

_____

_____

_____

(Aspect 2) The groom's family also has certain traditional obligations. *(Write about two or three specifics.)*

_____

_____

_____

_____

Composition Topics

1. In the United States today, some couples live together without being legally married. They say that love does not need a marriage certificate and that living together without a marriage license has many advantages. Do you agree or disagree? Using support from your readings, your own experience, or the experience of others, defend or contradict the given viewpoint. Use a three-subtopic organization for your essay.

2. There is currently a health crisis in the United States with problems such as AIDS, the spread of sexually transmitted diseases among young people, and an increasing rate of pregnancy among teenagers. Many people believe that if the schools taught courses in sex education, this would help prevent some of these problems. Do you agree or disagree? Support your opinion in a well-developed essay with some substantial, funnel-shaped paragraphs that explain your point of view. Review your essay to make sure that each paragraph treats only one subtopic.

Getting and Spending:
A Cross-Cultural View of Economics

With most of the modern world in transition from agricultural to technological economies, migrants to urban areas must find jobs that require little education and few specialized skills. Many immigrant women, such as these garment factory workers, supplement their families' incomes with wages from outside jobs. What other kinds of work do new urban immigrants typically perform? What role do labor unions play in this immigrant economy?

Freewrite

Freewrite about an early job experience. You may wish to describe how you obtained the job, the work you did, and the feelings you experienced in connection with it.

Vocabulary in Context

You will need to know the meanings of the following words to fully comprehend the reading passage. Use your dictionary as necessary.

Verbs	Nouns	Adjectives	Adverbs
distribute	consumption	material (goods)	rationally
expand	motivation		
	resources		
	prestige		
	aspect		
	priority		
	status		

Decide whether the italicized word in each sentence is appropriately used. If so, write C. If not, revise the sentence so that it illustrates the correct meaning of the italicized word.

1. The instructor *distributed* the examinations from the students after the test was over. _____

2. To *expand* our industrial base, we must find overseas markets for our products. _____

3. The American *consumption* of beef has put many cattle ranchers out of business. _____

4. If you have strong *motivation,* you will eventually obtain your college degree. _____

5. *Resources* such as nylon and plastic have many different uses. _____

6. In certain cultures, great *prestige* is achieved by owning an expensive car. _____

7. To be in a *status* of depression may interfere with the proper performance of your job. _____

8. The audience did not *aspect* the show to be as excellent as it was.

_____

9. Should elderly people get the highest *priority* in seating on public transportation?

_____

10. Rich vegetation, good soil, and plenty of rainfall are *material* goods desired by most people. _____

11. Often when we get angry, we do not think *rationally* and logically.

_____

Reading: Getting and Spending: A Cross-Cultural View of Economics

Key Concepts
- The economy: production, distribution, consumption
- Formal economics
- Material goods
- Social versus economic priorities
- Specialization of labor

[1]   Every society produces, **distributes,** and uses goods and services. Therefore, every society has an economy, a system that manages the process of production, distribution, **consumption,** or use. The people of every culture learn specific economic behavior. They have certain **motivations** and make certain economic choices that their society has taught them.   5

[2]   *Formal economics* states that people make **rational** economic choices that result in their well-being and profit. It studies the production and consumption of goods in an industrialized market economy. It assumes that the economy runs on rational choices such as those a businessperson makes: Should the firm cut down or **expand** its production in a certain situation? Should it purchase a new machine or hire more laborers? Where should it locate its plant? Will it manufacture shoes or gloves? How much will be spent on advertising its product? All these decisions are assumed to be rational, that is, based on the desire to make the greatest possible profit from limited **resources.**   10   15

[3]   Formal economics also assumes that individuals as well as businesses act rationally in making decisions about how to spend their incomes. Individuals may have many desires, but they usually have only limited income to fulfill those desires. Therefore, decisions about how   20

to spend that income—whether to buy a car, give the children a private school education, place a down payment on a house, or take a vacation—must be weighed rationally before they are made. Decisions about how to spend time are similarly weighed. Should one spend one's leisure time with one's family, in a second job, or back in school studying for an advanced degree to improve one's future economic chances?

[4]   Formal economics focuses on the Western industrial market economy. However, its key assumptions about rational decision making, limited resources, and the importance of profit do not apply to all societies. For example, in some traditional societies economic choices are made as the result of a different value system from that common in the United States. For instance, in hunting and gathering societies such as that of the !Kung of south-central Africa, people have not been trained to desire many **material** goods. Therefore, they do not have to work all day, every day to fulfill their needs; they can get enough food and other essentials and still have plenty of leisure time left over. From our point of view, people who do not use their leisure time to further their work and profit are "lazy." But not everyone feels the need for more possessions and services—more "stuff"—than they already have.

[5]   In our society, high social **status** or respect is closely tied to the possession or consumption of certain "brand name" goods and services. For example, all cars serve the same basic function of transportation; however, certain cars known to be expensive have more **prestige** than do other cars that may be just as useful. In addition, we are willing to pay extra for those services that our cars automatically perform for us: automatic windows, automatic trunk openers, automatic gear shifts. In other societies, such prestige may not be associated with the display of goods but rather with generosity in giving goods away to others. People who own and display much more than others may be thought stingy and may lose rather than gain prestige.

[6]   In the United States, we generally place economic priorities above social ones. In some societies, however, social relations have a higher **priority** than economic ones. For example, in many Asian countries, a businessperson will leave his or her work to show hospitality to a guest even if it means the loss of a day's income. The more traditional a society is, the more it is expected that friends, relatives, and neighbors will help each other financially in time of need without a formal contract for paying back the loan. Furthermore, in many non-Western cultures, even those whose standard of living is quite low, people will go into debt for social or religious ceremonies such as a feast or a funeral.

[7]   In nonindustrial societies few aspects of behavior are purely economic. Most activity has a mixed social, ceremonial, or moral **aspect** to it, as well as having an economic one. For example, the Ponape people of the South Pacific often hold huge feasts at which the host serves the pig and beer and the guests bring such prestigious foods as yams and

breadfruit. These feasts have an important economic purpose. They provide a way for extra food to be distributed around the village without shaming those farmers whose crops are inferior. They also permit food to be eaten that would otherwise be wasted, since the Ponape do not have refrigeration or other means for preserving food. But, these feasts 70 also serve important social purposes. They bring people together and allow them to gain prestige by acting modestly about their contributions; at these Ponape feasts, one gains prestige not only by bringing extra food but by praising the contributions of others as better than one's own. The social aspects of the Ponape feasts may be hidden from outsiders, 75 but they are understood and respected by the members of the Ponape culture.

[8]   Other aspects of the economy that may differ greatly from one culture to another are the basic unit of production, the sexual division of labor, and the degree of specialization of labor. In agricultural soci- 80 eties, the *unit of production* is most frequently the extended family that consists of several generations of relatives. The *specialization of labor* is usually by sex and age only. The men perform all tasks related to farming, whereas the women perform all the work related to house-keeping, gardening, and child care. Social and economic activities are 85 usually integrated in such societies, and often decisions that appear to be economically "irrational" have a hidden meaning in terms of the culture's beliefs or values.

[9]   On the other hand, in industrial societies, the unit of produc-tion is usually a business firm outside the family structure that is mo- 90 tivated almost entirely by economic interests. Typically there is a high degree of specialization of labor: Workers may belong to different unions depending on the different type of job they perform within an industry, or a company may have a dozen vice-presidents, each with a narrow area of responsibility. 95

Reading Comprehension

1. Identifying Key Terms

Next to each item below taken from the business section of an American newspaper, put a *P* if it is primarily a form of *production*, a *D* if it is primarily a form of *distribution*, and a *C* if it is primarily a form of *consumption*. Be prepared to explain your responses.

a. Businesses kept a tight hold on labor costs this quarter. _____

b. Traders worry that conflict in the Persian Gulf may disrupt supplies of

oil to the United States. _____

c. Housing construction spending fell 1.1 percent in June, probably because of overbuilding and the new tax law. _____

d. The advertising firm of Chiat/Day won the Nissan (Japanese auto firm) $150 million advertising account. _____

e. Cellular phone companies are regaining popularity as investments because of advances in the technology. _____

f. The Russians have been trying to increase their exports to the United States to make the trade balance more equal. _____

g. Nonfarm business productivity rose at an annual rate of 1.4 percent from April to June. _____

h. The Tandy Corporation aggressively attacked other computer makers with their new personal computers such as the 1000TX, which is three times faster than the IBM PC and sells for under $2000. _____

i. The Federal Trade Commission will seek to prevent a Texas grocery store chain from buying sixty Safeway food stores, as that might unfairly reduce competition. _____

j. Prices paid by Third World consumers are rising again, with inflation up in Argentina, Brazil, and Yugoslavia. _____

2. *Reading Review*

In oral discussion or in writing, answer the following questions based on information in the reading passage.

a. What does the discipline of formal economics study?

b. What does the word *rational* mean as it is applied in economics?

c. Why do most families have to make decisions about whether to spend their money on a new car, a child's education, or a vacation?

d. Give some examples of material goods that are important in your society.

e. What does *brand name* mean?

f. What is a *contract?* What are some occasions when people make contracts with each other?

g. What is the importance of refrigeration in food consumption?

h. What similar purpose is served by a Ponape feast and a party in your culture?

i. What is the sexual division of labor that is typical of agricultural societies?

j. Would labor unions be useful in a small family business? Why or why not?

3. *Analyzing the Text*

Circle the letter of the correct response or follow other directions as given.

a. In paragraph [1], the thought relationship between the first and second sentences signaled by the word *therefore* is
(1) contrast **(2)** result **(3)** reason **(4)** addition

b. In paragraph [2], the expression *that is* in the last sentence indicates that the writer is
 (1) adding more information about the word *rational*.
 (2) giving a reason for the word *rational*.
 (3) giving a condition for the word *rational*.
 (4) restating the meaning of the word *rational*.

c. In paragraph [3], the word *also* in the first sentence and the word *similarly* in the fourth sentence both suggest that the writer is
 (1) contrasting one idea with another.
 (2) adding pieces of information that are alike.
 (3) presenting a time order of events.
 (4) putting ideas in a reason–result context.

d. In paragraph [4], which signal words indicate a contrast between ideas?

 _____ and _____

e. In paragraph [4], which signal expressions introduce examples?

 _____ and _____

f. In paragraph [5], what contrast about cars is presented? Which word is the signal that introduces the contrast? _____

g. In paragraph [6], what is the purpose of the signal *furthermore?*

 _____

h. In paragraph [7], what thought relationship is signaled by the word *since* in the sixth sentence?
 (1) reason–result **(3)** emphasis
 (2) time order **(4)** reversal of a statement

i. In paragraph [7], the Ponape people are introduced as an example. In your own words, what are they an example of, according to the text?

j. In paragraph [8], what is the relationship between the third and fourth sentences? *(The specialization . . . child care.)*
 (1) Sentence 4 is a result of sentence 3.
 (2) Sentence 4 is an explanation of sentence 3.
 (3) Sentence 4 sets a condition of sentence 3.
 (4) Sentence 4 is a contradiction of sentence 3.

k. In paragraph [9], the adjective clause *that is motivated almost entirely by economic interests* specifically describes
(**1**) industrial societies   (**3**) a business firm
(**2**) a unit of production   (**4**) a family structure

4. *Summary Outlines*

Complete the following paragraph outlines with information or examples from the text. Use complete sentences of your own words.

Paragraph [1]:   The economy is a system for managing the process of _____ , _____ _____ , and _____

Paragraphs [2] and [3]:   Formal economics is based on the idea that people make thoughtful economic choices.

Example **a:**   A businessman _____

Example **b:**   An individual _____

Paragraphs [4] and [5]:   Western industrial societies and some traditional societies have _____ economic values.

a.   Western people work _____

b.   In Western society, respect is _____

c.   Traditional people may/may not desire/ display _____

Paragraphs [6] and [7]:   A central idea of these paragraphs is that ____ _____

Example **a:**   Some people will go in debt for a marriage or a funeral.

Example **b:**   _____

Example **c:**   _____

In most traditional societies, economic activities _____

Paragraphs [8] and [9]:   Traditional and industrial economies differ from each other in several ways.

Traditional **a:** _____

b: There is little specialization of work.

c: _____

Industrial: **a.** Production is mostly through business firms whose main interest is profits.

b. _____

Vocabulary Study

1. Responding to Questions with Vocabulary Words

Respond to the following questions using the word(s) in italics in a sentence of your own composition.

a. In general, do you *assume* that a husband or a wife earns the larger income in the family?
b. How can you *fulfill* your dreams of becoming a college graduate?
c. Do you live in an ethnically *integrated* neighborhood? If so, which ethnic groups are integrated there?
d. Do your car trunk and hood open *automatically* or manually?
e. Describe the way a person would be *modestly* dressed for entering a house of worship.
f. What kinds of food might a *stingy* person offer his or her guests?
g. What kinds of business does the *hospitality* industry include?
h. What do you think attracts people to a window *display?*
i. Give some examples of desirable *moral* qualities.

2. Word Form Table

Fill in the following table with the appropriate forms of the given words. Some nouns or adjectives may have two forms.

	Verbs	*Nouns*	*Adjectives*	*Adverbs*
a.	xxx	generosity	_____	_____
b.	rationalize	_____	_____	_____
c.	_____	decision	_____	_____
d.	_____	_____	_____	financially
e.	_____	_____	economic	_____

Use the correct form(s) from each lettered line to complete the same lettered sentence below.

a. Are your holiday gifts to your children so _____ that you go into debt?

b. Is your budget based on a _____ analysis of your income? When you buy something you don't really need, do you _____ your decision by telling yourself that you deserve some luxuries for working so hard?

c. Who _____ how to spend the money in your family? Some people act _____ about making important purchases such as a car or a piece of furniture.

d. My _____ are always in a mess because I don't keep track of my bank statements.

e. In a recession, a nation undergoes _____ hardship as people lose their jobs and families try to _____ by cutting back their purchases.

3. *Word Formation*

Prefixes *un, ir, im, in:* syllables attached to the front of an adjective, meaning "not."

uncertain	irrational
unconscious	irresponsible
undeveloped	
unessential	immodest
ungenerous	impermissible
unlimited	impossible
unmotivated	
unproductive	inexpensive
unspecialized	informal

Write one brief paragraph with a topic sentence and use supporting details in related sentences that include at least five adjectives with a prefix meaning "not." You may use words from the preceding list and/or add your own.

Writing Exercises

Structures for Relating Past Events

Past Perfect and Past Perfect Continuous Tenses

The past perfect tense is most commonly used when *two* related actions from the past are discussed together and one of the past actions happened *earlier* than the other. The use of the past perfect tense emphasizes the *earlier* occurrence, the fact that it happened *previous* to the other past action, which is reported in the simple past tense.

> **Mary thought about her present job. She *had* never *held***
> (past perfect)
>
> **such an important position before in her entire life.**
>
> **Although Mary *had* never *held* such an important**
> (past perfect)
>
> **position, she felt certain that she could handle her new responsibilities.**

The past perfect continuous tense emphasizes the ongoing or continuous nature of the earlier past action.

> **Because Mary *had been working* as a bank teller for many**
> (past perfect continuous)
>
> **years, she was familiar with the bank's financial system.**

Connective adverbs such as *before, after, when, until, because, since,* and *although* are commonly used to join clauses of sentences involving the past perfect.

1. *Sentence Combining*

Each of the following items contains two sentence kernels that are dated or that suggest a specific time period. Combine the two items into one complete, correct English sentence by putting the item that happened *first in real time* into the past perfect/past perfect continuous tense and the event that happened later into the simple past/past continuous. Use the appropriate signals of time, reason, or contrast as given. Make whatever changes are necessary for sentence correctness. The first one has been done for you.

a. **(1)** I applied to college. (Until)
   (2) I never realized that financial aid was available for part-time students.

   Until I applied to College, I had never realized that financial aid was available for part-time students.

b. **(1)** I enrolled in college. (By the time)
   (2) I saved money from earlier jobs.

   _____

   _____

   _____

c. **(1)** I went to school for several semesters as a part-time student.
   (2) I became a full-time student. (before)

   _____

   _____

   _____

d. **(1)** I decided to take the TOEFL test in 1976. (When)
   (2) I was already studying English for many years. (1970–1975)

   _____

   _____

   _____

e. **(1)** I arrived in the United States. (Until)
   (2) I did not read English newspapers on a regular basis.

   _____

   _____

   _____

f. **(1)** I lived in a large city in my native country. (Because)
   (2) I was not frightened by living in Chicago.

   _____

   _____

   _____

g. **(1)** I did not have much experience making friends with foreigners.
   (Although)

(2) I was looking forward to making new friends in the United States.

_____

_____

_____

2. Sentence Completion

Read the following paragraph. Using the information given in it, complete each item in the exercise with a clause in the past perfect tense. Use whatever guide words are given in parentheses.

My parents have always been proud of their children's ability to earn their own spending money. My brother got a job delivering newspapers before his twelfth birthday. He was conscientious about his work and wouldn't go to school until all his papers were delivered. Because my brother's paper route grew in size, his employer promoted him to a truck loader, which increased my brother's earnings quite a bit. My sister was also a hard worker. For several summers she worked as a companion to an elderly woman in our neighborhood, and she kept this work part-time while she went to high school. When she graduated, she had over $1,000 in the bank. With this money, she took a trip to New York City. She saw snow and subways for the first time. Many aspects of New York City impressed her favorably. When she returned, she decided she would go to nursing school in New York City.

(a) By the time my brother was twelve, _he had already gotten a job delivering newspapers._

(b) My brother wouldn't go to school until he _____

_____

(c) His employer promoted him because _____

_____

(d) Before she entered high school, my sister _____

_____

(e) When she graduated from high school, she (save) _____

_____

(f) My sister's trip to New York was the first time that _____

_____

(g) By the time she returned home, _____

_____

3. *Paragraph Composing with Past Perfect Tenses*

The past perfect tenses are useful for telling about situations that turned out differently from what we expected or hoped. In one paragraph, narrate a situation or event in which the results were different from what you had expected or hoped for. Use the past perfect or past perfect continuous tense to emphasize those actions in the earlier past. Then review your paragraph for the appropriate use of the past perfect tenses. Here are some topic suggestions:

> the unexpected difficulties or benefits of a specific job
> a surprising result from a job interview
> the unanticipated difficulties of going to college
> a vacation that was unexpectedly pleasant or unpleasant
> a reversal of feelings about a person you met
> an unexpected liking or dislike of a newly tasted food
> the unexpected pleasures or inconveniences of acquiring a pet

Direct and Indirect Speech

Direct or Quoted Speech

Direct or quoted speech records the exact words spoken by someone. Only the quoted words and their punctuation go inside the quotation marks. In dialogues, interviews, or media accounts of important talks, you will find speech in its direct, or quoted, form. When the quoted speaker is talking about himself or herself, direct speech uses the first person pronouns, *I, my, me, mine, we, our, us, ours.*

Direct speech is usually introduced or completed by the narrative part of the sentence, which has a subject and a verb of telling or thinking. The narrative part of the sentence is *outside* the quotation marks.

Advertising executive Michael Keenan stated, "We have a
(narrative)   (exact words)

surprising number of men looking for secretarial work today."

---

1. *Rewriting for Direct Speech*

Use the following statement as the topic sentence for a paragraph about a job interview or a conference with an instructor or counselor that you remember well.

I remember (identify job interview in a phrase) *because it went especially well/badly/turned out unexpectedly for me.*

Write one paragraph about this interview or conference in which you put some of the information in the form of direct quotations. Begin each new quotation (your direct speech and the direct speech of the other person) on a new line.

Indirect or Reported Speech

Indirect or reported speech is a report of what another person has said or written. Reported speech is especially useful in academic work for the purpose of paraphrasing, summarizing, and using brief narratives to support generalizations.

In reporting the thoughts and words of others, we may use a wide variety of narrative verbs or verbs of telling or thinking.

admit	doubt	inform (+ obj.)	prove	suggest
announce	estimate	imply	realize	tell
answer	explain	know	reply	think
ask	feel	mention	say	understand
believe	guess	notice	see	wonder
claim	hope	observe	show (+ obj.)	
discover	indicate	point out	state	

These verbs are followed by clause markers of reported speech: *that* (for reported statements); *what, why, who, where, how* (+ quantity word); *who, which* (for reported information questions); *if* (for reported conditional questions); *whether* (for reported choice questions). The clauses that follow these markers are called noun clauses, because they function like noun objects of the narrative verb.

Reported speech *never* includes quotation marks. The pronouns used are usually in the third person: *he/she, his/her, him/her, his/hers, they, their, them, theirs.*

Changes from Direct to Reported Speech

Study the following changes that occur when direct speech becomes indirect speech.

Direct Speech		**Indirect Speech**
will	becomes	would
can	becomes	could
is *(simple present)*	becomes	was *(simple past)*
felt *(simple past)*	remains	felt *(simple past)*
	becomes	had felt *(past perfect)*
have been transformed *(present perfect)*	becomes	had been transformed *(past perfect)*

had remembered	remains	had remembered
(past perfect)		*(past perfect)*
this, these	become	that, those

Rewriting for Indirect or Reported Speech
Study the examples.

Direct Speech: The new employee said, "I'm satisfied with my salary."

Indirect Speech: The new employee said that he was satisfied with his salary.

Direct Speech: "Why has consumption of this new product gone down?" asked the marketing manager.

Indirect Speech: The marketing manager asked why the consumption of the new product had gone down.

Direct Speech: "I don't know whether we should expand our production now or wait until the end of the year," the firm's accountant wondered.

Indirect Speech: The firm's accountant wondered whether they should expand their production then or wait until the end of the year.

1. Rewriting for Indirect Speech

The following excerpts are from interviews with a supervisor who is searching for a secretary and a secretary who is seeking employment. Their remarks are in direct speech. Choose one of the interviews to write up as one paragraph of reported speech. Select at least five direct speech statements to report in your paragraph, using appropriate narrative verbs and noun clause markers. You may frame your reported interview with an appropriate introductory and concluding statement.

Advertising Executive:
"I need a secretary with excellent typing skills."
"Our office has a relatively formal dress code because our image is important for our business."
"Why don't more men go into the secretarial field?"
"Age is not a factor with our firm. We will hire a mature person with the right skills."
"If I can't find a good secretary soon, I'll have to hire a temporary person."
"What has happened to all the young people who want to start from the ground up?"
"I hope I can find someone who will stay at least two years."

Secretary:

"What type of positions do you have open in the secretarial area?"

"I can type sixty words per minute, and I am learning to use a word processor."

"I'm extremely reliable. I wasn't absent for a single day on my last job."

"I don't want to work in an office where formal attire is required, because I don't have the extra money to spend for new clothing."

"My children are grown, so I don't expect to have problems with personal emergency leave."

"I have an even temper and can handle a busy office without becoming nervous."

"Why did your last secretary leave?"

"What is the salary difference between a typist and a secretary?"

Small Group Assignment

Active Listening

Form groups of three. Designate each group member as A, B, or C. A is the speaker, B the note-taker, and C the attentive listener.

Now study the following list of topics. You will have five minutes to think about what you want to say on *one* of the topics. You may take notes for your talk. Speaker A will talk for three minutes. Note-taker B will listen and take notes. Attentive listener C will listen carefully *without* taking notes. No one may interrupt the speaker while he or she is talking.

When three minutes are up, A will stop talking. C will report as accurately as he or she can what was said by A. C will find expressions of indirect speech useful. For example: *"He said that. . . ." "He added that. . . ."* After C has reported on A's talk, A and B will discuss the report. Was it accurate? Were all the major points and significant details included? Did C report some of his or her own ideas rather than the speaker's?

Participants will then exchange roles until all have had a chance in each. When everyone has had a chance at each role, the class as a whole will discuss reactions to the different demands of the roles.

Topics (choose one side of one topic about which to speak)

Labor unions are harmful/beneficial to workers.

The government should/should not own the natural resources of a country (for example, mines, oil supplies, forests).

Public employees (police, fire officers, teachers, sanitation) should/should not be allowed to strike.

The credit card system is beneficial/injurious to most people.

Time/Money/Learning experience is the most important benefit a job can offer.

Government should/should not play a major role in solving the unemployment situation.

Writing a Persuasive Paragraph

Now use your notes to write a paragraph supporting your point of view.

Composition Development

Unity and Coherence

In developing an essay, it is important that you follow the principles of unity and coherence. **Unity** means that your material is unified, that is, all of what you have included is relevant to your topic statement or some aspect of your topic. If you wander from your subject or contradict your central idea (without deliberately introducing a reversal of thought), your writing will lack unity.

Coherence refers to the logical sequence of your statements and the connections you make between them so that readers can follow your ideas. The sequence of ideas by time—from earliest to most recent—or by funnel-shaped development—from most general to most specifically detailed—are examples of coherent sequences.

The use of signal expressions for your various thought expressions and the repetition of key words from paragraph to paragraph are also important in making your essays coherent. Use the page "Useful Signal Expressions for Coherence" in Appendix B as a reference.

Unity and coherence begin with your introduction, for it is here that you give your reader a clear idea of your topic, your point of view, and the aspects of the topic that organize your composition.

1. *Analyzing a Paragraph*

Read the following paragraph that focuses on the economic aspect of marriage in traditional societies. Then answer the questions that follow.

(1) Marriage may be defined as a union in which persons of the other sex join to form a new family. (2) Families in all societies place certain constraints on the choice of suitable mates for marriage. (3) For example, even in the most modern, industrialized societies, brothers and sisters, or even first cousins, are not permitted to marry each other. (4) Until recent times, in both industrialized and traditional societies, the selection of mates was arranged, or at least supervised closely, by the parents, who were primarily directed by practical considerations rather than emotional

factors. (5) For instance, economic, social, and political situations were important factors to consider in planning a marriage. (6) Even today, parents in a traditional family will look for suitability of the couple in such areas as social and financial position and educational level. (7) For example, although most societies permit a *man* of high social, economic, or educational level to marry a woman of a lower level, they disapprove of a woman doing the same. (8) Today, however, as societies urbanize and industrialize, the arranged-marriage system is becoming less strict. (9) For instance, in some traditional cultures, parents arrange only the preliminary introduction—from then on, the young man and young woman are free to continue or end the relationship. (10) Yet it still remains true that in the majority of the world's cultures, the practical considerations of the parents and the advice of the matchmaker are more influential in marriage than the emotions of the young people. (11) So long as marriage affects the whole family economically and socially and not just the two people who wed, this realistic outlook is bound to continue over much of the world.

Questions
Respond with appropriate answers for items **a** through **i.**

a. Which sentence states the main idea of the paragraph?
b. What key word in sentence 2 is repeated in 3? What word(s) in sentence 3 explain that key word?
c. In sentences 2 and 3 the expressions "all societies" and "most societies" are used. What phrase in sentence 4 corresponds to those expressions?
d. Sentence 5 is an explanation of which phrase from sentence 4?
  (1) industrialized and traditional societies
  (2) practical considerations
  (3) emotional factors
e. What is the function of sentence 7?
  (1) It repeats a key term of sentence 3.
  (2) It reverses the information in sentence 4.
  (3) It illustrates the suitability of sentence 6.
f. What is the function of sentence 8?
  (1) It changes the direction of the paragraph to some extent.
  (2) It provides a specific example of the paragraph's main idea.
  (3) It enlarges the definition of the word *marriage*.
g. Sentence 9 is
  (1) an example of sentence 8.
  (2) a reversal of sentence 8.
  (3) a cause of sentence 8.
h. Sentence 10
  (1) states the effect of sentence 9.
  (2) introduces a new aspect of sentence 9.
  (3) reverses the thought of sentence 9.

    i. The expression "so long as" in the last sentence suggests that the writer
       (1) is placing the subject in the framework of time.
       (2) is telling a personal anecdote about the subject.
       (3) is offering a new definition of the subject.

2. *Sequencing a Paragraph*

Read the introduction to this scrambled paragraph on arranged marriage. Arrange sentences **a–j** in a coherent sequence. Eliminate any sentences that are not relevant to the topic. Be prepared to discuss your sequence choices.

Introduction and main idea

In some societies marriage is considered more than just a relationship between the two individuals involved. Such societies view marriage as affecting the family and the social group as well. In such cultures, parents usually follow the traditional system of arranged marriages for their children.

a. In arranging a marriage, the parents often use a go-between or marriage broker.

b. In addition, the marriage broker will explain the background of each candidate to the parents.

c. This system of arranged marriages is many thousands of years older than the modern American system of marriages based on individual choice.

d. My sister had a beautiful wedding paid for by my parents.

e. The parents, sometimes in consultation with the marriageable child, may select two or three of the best candidates.

f. The marriage broker will show photographs of possible mates to the parents.

g. It seems unfair that the girl's family has to pay for most of the wedding arrangements.

h. If the two young people like each other, discussions about financial arrangements, wedding preparations, and such will take place.

i. The parents will take into consideration such background factors as religion, economic status, level of education, and social class.

j. Then a meeting of the parents and the young couple will be arranged.

3. *Breaking Essays into Paragraphs*

Divide each of the following essays into five paragraphs: an introduction with the topic statement, three paragraphs for the body, and a conclusion. Underscore the main idea or topic statement of each of the three body paragraphs. Then answer the questions that follow.

A. Some years ago, two American psychologists named Robert Rosenthal and Lenore Jacobson conducted studies to find out why success comes more easily to some people than to others, even when their basic abilities are about the same. Initially they conducted laboratory experiments with rats to find the answer to their question. The first hypothesis they formed was that the expectations of the experimenters in the laboratory would influence the behavior of their subjects, the rats. The concept behind this hypothesis was that of "the self-fulfilling prophecy." That is, if we are led to hold certain expectations about ourselves, we will, in fact, fulfill those expectations. What people think of us and expect of us is communicated to us by their words, their attitudes, and their behavior to us. The procedure for the experiment was not complicated. First, a number of Rosenthal and Jacobson's students were given a group of rats and a maze* for the rats to run through. Some of the students were told that their rats were "bright" and were descended from a group of rats that had done well in running the maze previously. Other students were told that their rats were "duller" than the first group. Later, both groups of students filled out questionnaires asking for their opinions of their rats' personalities and intelligence. The results of the experiment were interesting, and they confirmed the idea of the self-fulfilling prophecy. The rats labeled bright did well, whereas the rats labeled dull did poorly. Students who handled the "bright" rats seemed to expect more from them and accordingly handled them in such a fashion: They spoke gently to them and handled them frequently. On the other hand, the students who worked with the "dull" rats handled them roughly and spoke loudly to them. Apparently the students did have certain expectations about their rats because of what they had been told, and they communicated these expectations to the rats; indeed, the rats fulfilled those expectations. Rosenthal and Jacobson finally drew the conclusion that expectations can powerfully influence the behavior of subjects. They later went on to apply this conclusion to other groups of subjects including teachers and students.

B. Benjamin L. Whorf was one of the first American linguists to recognize the intimate connections among language, culture, and psychology. He understood that it is not only the actual physical aspects of something that make people act a certain way but also their *perception* of the situation. And, that perception is often shaped by language. Whorf provided several interesting examples of how, unconsciously, language helped cause some accidental fires. In one plant for wood distillation, the metal distilling containers were insulated with a

*A confusing, intricate, complicated network of passages, many of which end in blank walls.

material prepared from limestone. This material was called "spun limestone." No attempt was made to protect this insulating material from excessive heat or contact with open flames, probably because its name, which ended in *stone,* implies resistance to fire. But after a long period of use, the spun limestone did catch on fire, and to everyone's surprise, it burned vigorously. In another case, an electric glow heater on a wall was seldom used, so one of the workers used it as a coat hanger. One night, he entered the room and snapped on the switch, which he thought turned on the light. When no light appeared immediately, he figured that the bulb had burned out. He then hung his coat over the switch and thus could not see the glow as the heater began to work. The heat ignited the coat, which then set fire to the building. In a third instance, a coal-fired melting pot was used to reclaim lead in a factory. Next to this red-hot melting pot was a dump pile the workers called "scrap lead"—a misleading label, for the pile contained old radio condensers, which still had paraffin paper between them. Gradually, the warmth of the melting pot heated up the "scrap lead" pile. Soon the paraffin blazed up and set fire to the roof. Such examples, which could be greatly multiplied, show us how certain behavior is affected by the linguistic formulas in which the situation is spoken of and by which it is analyzed. Whorf emphasized that our world is "to a large extent unconsciously built up on the language habits of the group." He concluded, "we always assume that the linguistic analysis made by our group reflects reality better than it does."

C. After psychologists Rosenthal and Jacobson performed their initial experiments testing the validity of the self-fulfilling prophecy with laboratory rats, they found that expectation really did influence the ability of the rats to run their mazes. The two psychologists hypothesized that the self-fulfilling prophecy would operate in the classroom as well as in the laboratory. They believed that teachers' expectations about their students would affect the students' achievement. For instance, it was their hypothesis that if teachers were told that certain children were "bright," the teachers would form higher expectations about them. These higher expectations would be communicated to the students in various ways, and the students would, in fact, do better work. To validate the hypothesis, it was essential that the teachers' expectations be formed solely by what they were told about the students. The psychologists devised an experiment to test their prediction about the impact of self-fulfilling prophecy. The experiment began in 1964 in a California elementary school. First, a number of selected children were given a test by the experimenters. The experimenters then told the teachers that certain children had tested well and could be expected to make good academic progress. In fact, these "bright" children had done no better than other children on their tests. Thus the higher expectations of these children existed only in the teachers' minds. Later in the year, the teachers were asked to describe the personalities and potential for success of their students. They described the children who had been labeled "bright" in positive ways and rated their chances for success high. All the children were tested four different times during the next two years. The children who had been labeled bright and rated highly by their teachers did, in fact, show greater intellectual gains than the others. Younger children made the highest gains, perhaps because they were more easily influenced by their teachers' attitudes than older children. For all teachers, however, the experiment seemed to show that teachers' expectations are influential in how children learn. Thus, teachers' attitudes play an important part in students' intellectual achievement. Teachers should be made aware of this influence, and then be sensitive to how they communicate their expectations.

a. Discuss the paragraph divisions and topic statements you selected for each essay with your class. Number the paragraphs in each essay for reference.

b. In essay A the paragraph about the procedure of the experiment contains several signals of sequence. Underscore them.

c. What thought relationship is indicated by the expression "on the other hand"?

d. Why is the word *bright* in quotation marks?

e. One of the last sentences in the essay on expectations includes the signal word *indeed*. Does this word signal contradiction, result, or emphasis of the previous assertion?

f. The three body paragraphs of essay B contain concrete examples of the main idea. Underscore the signal expressions that introduce each example. What order do the paragraphs follow: from most important to least important? simple listing? from least important to most important? chronological?

g. Several of the paragraphs are organized by chronological sequence. Underscore the time signals in each paragraph.

h. In essay C, the following signal expressions are used: *For instance* (sentence 4); *if* (sentence 4); *in fact* (sentences 5, 11, 16); *thus* (sentence 12); *however* (sentence 18). What thought relationship is indicated by each of these signals?

i. In the experimental procedures paragraph of essay C, several signals of sequence are used. Underscore these.

4. Sentence Combining

The following sentences are from student essays introducing the topic of immigrants who became economically successful in their new cultures. Combine these sentences in whatever ways seem best to you, making all necessary changes for sentence fluency. Add your own signal expressions for coherence to each paragraph as appropriate.

a. (1) The event described happened a while ago.
(2) I was taken by my family on a visit.
(3) The visit was to friends of the family.
(4) The drive took a long time.
(5) My family stopped at a house.
(6) The house was beautiful.
(7) The house was suburban.
(8) The house had a big yard.
(9) There were plants in the yard.
(10) There were vegetables in the yard.
(11) There were lots of different kinds of vegetables.
(12) I had the feeling of peace.
(13) I had the feeling of quiet.
(14) The surroundings gave me these feelings.

b. (1) I take pride in telling about an uncle.
(2) The uncle is named Mr. L. A. F.
(3) The uncle came to the United States.
(4) The time was after World War I had ended.
(5) The uncle was a sailor.
(6) The uncle was sometimes a fisherman.
(7) The uncle was sixteen on his arrival in the United States.
(8) The uncle came from China.
(9) The uncle came to the United States by ship.
(10) The uncle had only a small sum of money.
(11) The uncle worked as an apprentice.
(12) This was in the beginning.
(13) This was in a laundry shop.
(14) His salary was only fifty dollars a month.

c. (1) The person I am going to tell about had a dream.
(2) The dream was to find success.
(3) The dream was about America.
(4) This person is called C.
(5) C came from an island.
(6) The island is Cyprus.
(7) The time was ten years ago.
(8) C is a cousin.
(9) C is thirty years old.
(10) C was a waiter.
(11) C worked in a restaurant.
(12) The restaurant was in a hotel.
(13) The hotel was big.

(**14**) The hotel was luxurious.
(**15**) C is successful now.
(**16**) He has a lot of money.
(**17**) He has a lot of property.

d. (**1**) My family always talked about an aunt.
(**2**) The aunt is my mother's sister.
(**3**) The aunt earned her own living.
(**4**) She took care of her children.
(**5**) The aunt's husband had died.
(**6**) The aunt had no help from others.
(**7**) The aunt did not show sadness.
(**8**) The aunt made herself strong.
(**9**) The aunt opened a factory.
(**10**) The factory was for sewing.
(**11**) The aunt ran it well.
(**12**) I like to listen to my aunt's story.
(**13**) I think it is a model.
(**14**) The model is good for others.
(**15**) The aunt's story teaches others to believe something.
(**16**) The belief is that women can rise to an equal position.
(**17**) The position is equal to that of men.
(**18**) Men earn a living.
(**19**) Men solve problems.
(**20**) Men gain success.

5. Composing a Unified Paragraph

In a free enterprise economy, where you have many choices of the same product, you are voting for or against a company every time you select one item over another. You can get an even stronger vote when you write a letter to a company telling them why you do or don't like their product, why you buy it or won't buy it.

Think about a product you favor (one cereal or type of bread, for example) or a product you won't buy (maybe war toys, or baby food with sugar in it). Write a letter to the company stating your feelings.

Composition Topics

1. Intelligent consumerism means that you are careful about where and how you spend your money. An aware consumer can do many things to get the most for his or her dollar: look for sales ads; read labels on food for the ingredients; use credit methods to advantage, not disadvantage. Discuss why you think it is important to be an active consumer

This Caribbean commercial area mixes traditional market stalls run by local women with more modern stores. Each type of business contributes to the local economy. What are some characteristics of the commercial areas of your neighborhood? Are most of the businesses small, family-run enterprises, or are they more impersonal chain stores with hired help? What part does advertising play in the commerce of your country's economy?

and describe some of the ways in which you handle your money wisely. Aim for unity in each paragraph of your essay and coherence through the use of signal expressions.

2. It is very difficult these days to find a secure, interesting job that offers a good salary. Colleges should function primarily to prepare students for these jobs by offering them career programs in technical fields and business. Students should not be required to take liberal arts courses, such as history or art appreciation, that will not help them to make a living after they graduate.

   Do you agree or disagree with the above statement? Support your opinion with references to your reading, your own experience, or the experience of others you know.

The Cultural Patterning of Time

In every culture, various events are viewed as time markers for the human life span. In American culture, high school graduation, marriage, and a sixtieth birthday, as pictured here, are celebrations that mark important periods of life.

Freewrite

Freewrite about a ceremony in your family, religion, or culture that marks a significant point in a person's life. What changes are expected at this point of life?

Vocabulary in Context

You will need to know the meanings of the following words to fully comprehend the reading passage. Use your dictionary as necessary.

Verbs	**Nouns**	**Adjectives**	**Adverbs**
calculate	perseverance	conscious	skeptically
evoke	dimension	obsessive	
instill	disdain	cumulative	
merge	sociability		
	intuition		

Word Scramble
Skim the entire paragraph below for meaning. Then unscramble the letters in parentheses to form the correct form of the vocabulary word for the blank space.

The sense of time is a cultural (1) (sieodnmin) _____ that is (2) (linlstide) _____ so early that we are not even aware we have learned it. Americans think that other cultures (3) (auaccellt) _____ time in the same way they do. In the time-obsessed American culture, Americans regulate the days with calendars, schedules, and clocks that tick off the seconds as well as the hours. Americans see time, like money, as having a (4) (mlvuatuice) _____ value: It can be "banked," or saved up for later use, as in vacation days or sick days from work. Sometimes the American compulsion about time (5) (eokves) _____ the amusement or the (6) (dndsiia) _____ of others whose cultures do not measure time so strictly. The American concept of time as a commodity is rational and makes perfect sense to Americans, who believe that it is a universal human (7) (tniouitni) _____. But other concepts of time are just as reasonable in the context of other cultures.

Sentence Writing

Look up the meaning of any word in the lists that does not appear in the scrambled word paragraph and write an original sentence for each.

Reading: The Cultural Patterning of Time

Key Concepts
- *Dimensions of culture "out of awareness"*
- *Time as a commodity*
- *Newtonian law of motion*
- *Time value of repetition and persistence*

[1]   In his book *The Silent Language,* anthropologist Edward Hall theorizes that perceptions of time and space are different in different cultures and that these perceptions are culturally patterned. Hall called these **dimensions** of culture "out of awareness," because people are not **conscious** of having learned them. It may well be true that most   5
important aspects of culture, such as our perceptions of our physical environment or our food tastes, are learned "out of awareness." And certainly our perceptions of time and space are among the most deeply instilled of our cultural values. For example, members of modern, industrialized Western societies are conditioned to view time, space, and   10
matter in Newtonian terms. Sir Isaac Newton, the seventeenth-century English scientist, transformed mathematics and science to such an extent that even though we may not be able to list or explain his discoveries, we are influenced by them. Newton formulated several laws of motion that are basic to the Westerner's understanding of the universe. His first   15
law of motion states that every body in the universe continues at rest or in uniform motion in a straight line unless it is compelled to change that state by other forces acting upon it. This notion also underlies the concept of time in Western culture, and to Westerners it appears that it should be an intuitive concept of time shared by all people everywhere.   20
But as anthropologists have demonstrated through their studies of other cultures, these Newtonian "laws" are not universal. They are **instilled** by a specific culture, thought system, and language.
[2]   "Time is human; nature knows only change." In fact, "telling time" is a strictly human invention. All cultures have some system of   25
measuring duration, or keeping time, but in Western industrial societies we keep track of time in what seems to other peoples almost an **obsessive** fashion. We view time as motion on a space, a kind of linear progression measured by the clock and the calendar. Our sense of time leads us to imagine it as a ribbon or a scroll marked off into equal blank   30
spaces, suggesting that each of these spaces can be filled with an entry. This perception contributes to our sense of history and the keeping of

records, which are typical aspects of Western cultures. In Western industrialized societies, records, annals, diaries, and accounting ledgers
play an important role. We are fascinated by sequencing, dating, chart-   35
ing, and measuring pieces of time. We **calculate** not only the seasons
but also the years, months, weeks, days, hours, minutes, seconds, and
even thousandths of seconds. We find it useful to divide the past into
named periods such as "the Renaissance" or "the classical age." And our
linguistic treatment of time has guided many other aspects of our lives.   40
For example, literature is taught in schools by being divided into periods—or framed time slots—rather than by being treated in a thematic
fashion that cuts across time boundaries.

[3]   Although our perceptions of time seem natural to us, we must
not assume that other cultures operate on the same time system. For   45
instance, why should we assume that a Hopi raised in the Hopi culture
would have the same **intuitions** about time that we have? In Hopi
history, if records had been written, we would find a different set of
cultural and environmental influences working together. The Hopi people are a peaceful agricultural society isolated by geographic features   50
and nomad enemies in a land of little rainfall. Their agriculture is successful only by the greatest **perseverance.** Extensive preparations are
needed to ensure crop growth. Thus the Hopi value persistence and
repetition in activity. They have a sense of the **cumulative** value of
numerous, small, repeated movements, for to them such movements are   55
not wasted but are stored up to make changes in later events. The Hopi
have no intuition of time as motion, as a smooth flowing line on which
everything in the universe proceeds at an equal rate away from a past,
through a present, into a foreseeable future. Long and careful study of
the Hopi language has revealed that it contains no words, grammatical   60
forms, constructions, or expressions that refer to what we call time—
the past, present, or future—or to the duration or lasting aspect of time.
To the Hopi, "time" is a "getting later" of everything that has been
done, so that past and present **merge** together. The Hopi do not speak,
as we do in English, of a "new day" or "another day" coming every   65
twenty-four hours; among the Hopi, the return of the day is like the
return of a person, a little older but with all the characteristics of yes-
terday. This Hopi conception, with its emphasis on the repetitive aspect
of time rather than its onward flow, may be clearly seen in their ritual
dances for rain and good crops, in which the basic step is a short, quick   70
stamping of the foot repeated thousands of times, hour after hour.

[4]   Of course, the American conception of time is significantly
different from that of the Hopi. Americans' understanding of time is
typical of Western cultures in general and industrialized societies in
particular. Americans view time as a commodity, as a "thing" that can   75
be saved, spent, or wasted. We budget our time as we budget our money.
We even say, "Time is money." We are concerned in America with

being "on time"; we don't like to "waste" time by waiting for someone who is late or by repeating information; and we like to "spend" time wisely by keeping busy. These statements all sound natural to a North American. In fact, we think, how could it be otherwise? It is difficult for us not to be irritated by the apparent carelessness about time in other cultures. For example, individuals in other countries frequently turn up an hour or more late for an appointment—although "being late" is at least within our cultural framework. For instance, how can we begin to enter the cultural world of the Sioux, in which there is no word for "late" or "waiting." Of course, the fact is that we have not had to enter the Sioux culture; the Sioux have had to enter ours. It is only when we participate in other cultures on their terms that we can begin to see the cultural patterning of time.

[5]   Americans have a sense of time that is oriented toward the future, not an infinitely extending future, but the foreseeable future. We look back at the past only to measure how far we have come in the present, and we look at the present as a stepping stone to foreseeable future accomplishments. We project ourselves into the future by producing calendars, programs, schedules, and budgets for upcoming periods of time. Other cultures do not share such a future orientation. Navajos, for instance, look **skeptically** at the promise of benefits in even the foreseeable future; whereas the future among Hindus is conceived of in terms of more than a lifetime, as extending infinitely through many rebirths and lifetimes.

[6]   Just as other cultures' concepts of time may irritate Americans when we come up against them in our activities, so our concept of time may **evoke** amusement or even **disdain** from people in other cultures. For example, many foreigners must have been puzzled by an article in the *New York Times* business section that described a man who defined himself as a "time consultant." This expert suggested that one way to use time more efficiently was to program the subconscious* to consider a plan of action for the following day while falling asleep. In this way, he said, one's sleeping time would be well spent, not wasted. Such a notion is considered perfectly rational in the American business community. But in an agricultural community, where one cannot control the elements governing crop growth, or in a nonindustrialized nation, where the speed of a walking animal or a human hand controls production, such a perception of time would be valueless. With these different, culturally patterned views of time that exist all over the world, it is no wonder that some American businesspeople come into conflict with businesspeople from other cultures, where **sociability** is more important than using every minute of one's time for business.

---

*That level of the mind in which mental operations occur without our being aware of them.

Reading Comprehension

1. *True–False*

After each statement write *T* for true, *F* for false, or *NI* for no information, according to the information given in the reading passage.

a. Perceptions of time and space are said to be learned "out of awareness" because not everyone has them. _____

b. Newton's law of motion is fundamental to Western views about time and space. _____

c. Westerners are likely to measure, divide, and mark time periods with great exactness. _____

d. The Hopi people view time as a flowing line, as Western people do. _____

e. Industrialization is a factor that leads Americans to view "time as money." _____

f. Americans consider it acceptable to arrive at an appointment an hour late. _____

g. People in the Iroquois culture are always late for work. _____

h. The American sense of time is directed most strongly toward the ancient past. _____

i. In Hindu culture, birth, life, death, and rebirth are viewed as part of an ongoing life cycle. _____

j. Time consultants could play a valuable role in agricultural societies. _____

2. *Reading Review*

In oral discussion or in writing, answer the following questions based on information in the reading passage.

a. Why does paragraph [1] present the theories of Sir Isaac Newton?
b. Explain the proverb "Time is human; nature knows only change" in your own words.
c. What is the central idea of paragraph [2]?

d. According to paragraph [3], what aspect of time do the Hopi people value most?

e. How is the Hopi view of time shown in their ceremonial dances?

f. Explain the saying "Time is money" in your own words.

g. What is the American view of punctuality? How is it similar to or different from the view of time in your own culture?

h. What is the main idea of paragraph [5]?

i. What is a time consultant?

j. How can different views of time cause conflicts among businesspeople from different cultures?

3. *Analyzing the Text*

Circle the number of the statement that best completes the given sentence according to the text.

a. Certain aspects of our behavior are labeled "out of awareness" because
   (1) we don't do them frequently.
   (2) we aren't conscious that we have learned them.
   (3) no one else knows that we do them.
   (4) they aren't important to our lives.

b. An example of culturally ingrained behavior would be
   (1) an individual talent such as that for drawing.
   (2) our feelings of how we should treat our parents.
   (3) the color of our hair, eyes, and skin.
   (4) none of the above.

c. Newtonian concepts of time, space, and matter are
   (1) common to every culture.
   (2) particular to educated people only.
   (3) related to Western culture and thought patterns.
   (4) unique only to Newton and his scientific associates.

d. The Hopi and Sioux concepts of time
   (1) are shared by the majority of people in the United States.
   (2) are a minority cultural view in the United States.
   (3) do not exist.
   (4) are based on the first Newtonian law of motion.

e. The concept of *time as a commodity* means that
   (1) people who work long hours make good wages.
   (2) time is equated with money.
   (3) it is easy for Westerners and non-Westerners to do business together.
   (4) Americans have irrational cultural patterns.

f. Westerners view time as wisely spent
   (1) when it is filled with small, repeated actions.

    (2) when waiting for someone.

    (3) when one is being sociable.

    (4) when it is put to use in earning income.

g. The purpose of this chapter's reading passage is

    (1) to illustrate different cultural patterns of time.

    (2) to explain Newtonian laws of motion.

    (3) to analyze Hopi culture and customs.

    (4) to criticize Americans for their profit motives.

h. The Arab proverb "Past and present are as alike as two drops of water"

    (1) is similar to the Western industrialized concept of time.

    (2) is similar to the Hopi concept of time.

    (3) suggests a society that emphasizes the scientific method.

    (4) implies that the society is oriented toward the foreseeable future.

4. *Drawing Inferences*

One way we can test our understanding of written material is by drawing **inferences,** or conclusions, that seem likely to be true based on the information given. Circle the number of the statement that appears to be the correct inference based on the information given in the reading selection.

a. A Western businessperson would be *most* likely to

    (1) be an hour late for a business appointment.

    (2) drop in on his or her boss for a social conversation.

    (3) use her or his lunch hour for making a business deal.

    (4) have his or her children visit at the office.

b. If you were planning to visit a Sioux festival, it would probably be *most* important that

    (1) you call in advance if you were going to be late.

    (2) you arrange for transportation well in advance.

    (3) you have an exact schedule of the time various events are going to take place.

    (4) you be prepared to stay beyond the time scheduled for the events.

c. Which of the following methods of invitation would be *most* likely to come from a typical American mother?

    (1) We're having a birthday party for our daughter on May 15. Come early, stay late.

    (2) We're having a birthday party for our daughter on May 15, 2:30 to 4:30. Please let us know if you can come.

    (3) We're celebrating our daughter's birthday at home on May 15. Drop in.

d. Which of the following points of view seems most *opposite* the Western perception of time?

    (1) A journey of 1,000 miles begins with a single step.

    (2) Busy hands are happy hands.

(3) Time is money: Don't waste it.
(4) He who hesitates is lost.

Vocabulary Study

1. *Distinguishing Meanings from Context*

Words may have different meanings depending on their **context,** or usage, in a sentence. Circle the number of the sentence in which the italicized word is closest in meaning to the italicized word in the given sentence.

a. Every body in the universe continues in *uniform* motion in a straight line unless it is compelled to change.
   (1) American soldiers wear khaki-colored *uniforms* in summer and winter.
   (2) The institution's executives presented a *uniform* appearance of neatness and conservatism.
   (3) The dancers' legs kicked to the music in *uniform* rhythm.

b. Newton's first law is the *notion* that underlies the Western concept of time.
   (1) The inattentive student didn't have a *notion* of what the instructor would ask on the exam.
   (2) My *notions* about recent political events are based on a careful reading of several daily newspapers.
   (3) My uncle's store sells fabric, ribbons, trimming, and other sewing *notions*.

c. Western industrialized societies keep track of time in an almost obsessive *fashion*.
   (1) The *fashion* for baking homemade bread has long disappeared from the American household.
   (2) Many men enjoy looking at such *fashion* magazines as *Gentleman's Quarterly*.
   (3) My mother always listened to her children's problems in a sincerely interested *fashion*.

d. Among the Hopi, extensive preparations are needed to *ensure* good crop growth.
   (1) The policeman *ensured* that there was no one in the store before he entered.
   (2) You can *ensure* good grades by attending class, studying, and periodically reviewing your notes.

e. Westerners are *conditioned* to view time in a linear manner.
   (1) The beautician *conditioned* her client's hair with a special lotion.
   (2) Some parents *condition* their children to be respectful of authority.
   (3) Air-*conditioned* restaurants are sometimes too cold for comfort.

f. Americans have an *orientation* to the foreseeable future.
  (1) The kitchen's *orientation* was toward the east to catch the rising sun.
  (2) Freshman students benefit from an *orientation* program that introduces them to the college.
  (3) The early Puritan colonists of America had a strong *orientation* toward work and religion.

g. The Sioux *conception* of time is quite different from that of the Hindu culture.
  (1) The *conception* and birth of Mrs. Smith's child took place in Paris.
  (2) A child's *conception* of love begins very early in life.

2. *Word Form Table*

Fill in the following table with the appropriate forms of the given words. Some nouns or adjectives may have two forms.

	Verbs	Nouns	Adjectives	Adverbs
a.	_____	_____	extensive_____	_____
b.	compel_____	_____	_____	_____
c.	_____	intuition_____	_____	_____
d.	conceive_____	_____	_____	_____
e.	_____	_____	_____	significantly___

Use the correct form(s) from each lettered line to complete the same lettered sentence below.

a. Italian scientist Enrico Fermi worked _____ in the area of nuclear physics.

b. My instructor is _____ about starting class exactly on time.

c. A sense of time and space is not _____; it is taught by culture.

d. Can you _____ of an original way to celebrate your birthday?

e. Anthropologists have shown that there is cultural _____ to most human activity.

3. Word Formation

Prefix *in/im:* syllable attached to the front of a word, frequently meaning "in" or "inside." Prefix *ex:* syllable attached to the front of a word meaning "out" or "outside."

inhale	exhale
implicit	explicit
impose	expose
inject	eject
intensive	extensive
interior	exterior
internal	external
introvert	extrovert

Write a second sentence that is related to the first one given, using the appropriate word in parentheses. You may include the additional words in parentheses in your sentence if you wish. The first has been done.

a. There is a lot of factory smoke and gasoline fumes from traffic in my neighborhood.

(inhale/exhale: air) *Inhaling this bad air makes me sick.*

b. We just painted our apartment, hung wallpaper, and built new book-shelves.

(interior/exterior: attractive) _____

c. My cousin loves to socialize and meet new people.

(introvert/extrovert: personality) _____

d. Certain newspapers and magazines cater to people's interest in the lives of movie and television stars.

(impose/expose: private lives) _____

e. Fortunately, the person hit by the car was not seriously hurt.

(*internal/external: no bleeding*) _____

_____

_____

f. I studied Russian in a nine-week program in which we were in class for eight hours a day.

(*intensive/extensive: course*) _____

_____

_____

g. There was a drunk man at the movies who was causing a disturbance.

(*inject/eject: manager*) _____

_____

_____

h. The directions for putting together the bicycle are clear and detailed.

(*implicit/explicit: easy to assemble*) _____

_____

_____

Writing Exercises

Structures for Sentence Efficiency

In Chapter One, adjective clauses were introduced as a means of adding description to a noun within a single sentence.

Review: Adjective Clauses

The following items contain two or more thoughts that review some details from previous chapters.

1. Sentence Combining with Adjective Clauses

Combine each group of sentences into one complete sentence, using one or more of the given items as the information for the adjective clause. Make whatever other changes are necessary. Punctuate your revised sentences according to whether their adjective clauses are essential or nonessential. The first one has been done.

a. **(1)** Celebrations of birth are part of all cultures.
   (2) Celebrations of birth vary from group to group.

Celebration of birth, which vary from group to group, are part of all cultures.

b. **(1)** Culture is the source of our humanity.
   (2) Culture both constrains and frees us.

_____

_____

c. **(1)** Music is noise with rhythm and pattern.
   (2) Music is common to all cultures.

_____

_____

d. **(1)** Victor couldn't focus his eyes.
   (2) Victor's eyes were unsteady and expressionless.

_____

_____

e. **(1)** The crowd gathered around Victor.
   (2) The crowd expected to see a noble savage.

_____

_____

f. **(1)** The psychologist educated Victor, the "wild boy."
   (2) The psychologist was perceptive and sympathetic.

_____

_____

g. **(1)** Kamala and Amala were brought to an Indian orphanage.
   (2) The director kept a diary about them.

_____

_____

h. **(1)** Kamala had many nonhuman characteristics.
   (2) These were the result of her early isolation.

_____

_____

i. **(1)** Cannibalism is rare.
    (2) Cannibalism occurs in nonritual contexts.

_____

_____

j. **(1)** The people of Inis Beag have cultural patterns.
    (2) These patterns repress sexuality.

_____

_____

2. *Paragraph Composing with Adjective Clauses*

a. Study one of the photographs in this text. Compose statements containing adjective clauses about the subject of the photograph. Remember that adjective clause statements will have one main, independent statement about the subject and one dependent piece of information beginning with an adjective clause marker.

(Opening photograph, Chapter One)

This little girl, who is wearing a party hat, is celebrating her seventh birthday.

b. Explain the job of a time consultant using adjective clause statements as appropriate. Begin with a definition of a time consultant as a person *who* performs certain functions. Continue your paragraph with a brief statement of why a time consultant could or could not be useful to you.

Adjectives

The descriptive information given in an adjective clause may sometimes be reduced without losing any of its meaning by changing the structure of the sentence.

> **All cultures have medicines *that are effective and traditional*.**
>
> **All cultures have *effective traditional medicines*.**
>
> ***Structural change:* The relative clause *that are effective and traditional* has been changed to a *modifying phrase* composed of the adjectives *effective* and *traditional* to describe the noun *medicines*. These modifiers *precede* the noun they describe.**

1. *Sentence Reduction Using Adjectives*

Reduce the following sentences by changing the information in the italicized relative clauses into noun modifiers. Make whatever changes are necessary in revising and rewriting the sentences. The first one has been done.

a. All societies divide labor into some tasks *that are only for males and some that are only for females*.

All societies divide labor into male and female tasks.

b. There are important differences in culture between women *who live in cities* and women *who live in farming areas*.

_____

_____

c. Anthropologist Edward Hall discovered that different cultures have perceptions about time *that are different*.

_____

_____

d. Newton formulated laws of motion *that are basic and significant*.

_____

_____

e. The division of labor *that is by sex* has been studied among the people *who live in Israel*.

_____

_____

f. The people *who farm in Abkhasia* are famous for their life span, *which is long and productive.*

_____

_____

g. Societies *that are industrialized* seem to calculate time in a fashion *that is almost obsessive.*

_____

_____

h. The Hopi value activities *that have persistence and repetition.*

_____

_____

Descriptive Phrases Following Nouns

> **Important studies on Samoan culture were carried out by Margaret Mead, *who was a well-known anthropologist.***
>
> **Important studies on Samoan culture were carried out by Margaret Mead, *a well-known anthropologist.***
>
> *Structural change:* **The adjective clause *who was a well-known anthropologist* has been reduced to an *appositive,* or *descriptive phrase*, that *follows* the noun it is describing. Appositives are set off with commas.**

> **People *who want to be well informed* about other cultures will enjoy anthropology.**
>
> **People *wanting to be well informed* about other cultures will enjoy anthropology.**
>
> *Structural change:* **The adjective clause *who want to be well informed* has been reduced to a *present participial phrase*, that is, a group of words beginning with the present participle (*-ing* form) of a verb, *wanting* (to want). Present participial phrases may either be essential (no comma) or nonessential (comma).**

The following information, *which was written by an anthropologist,* explains child-rearing patterns among the Rajputs of India.

The following information, *written by an anthropologist,* explains child-rearing patterns among the Rajputs of India.

Structural change: The adjective clause *which was written by an anthropologist* has been reduced to a *past participial phrase,* that is, a group of words beginning with the past participle of a verb, *written* (to write). Past participial phrases may be either essential (no comma) or nonessential (comma).

Retirement is a time of life when older Americans still enjoy close friendships, numerous social activities, and an energetic lifestyle. Americans designate these later years as "the golden years" and the older population as "senior citizens" to emphasize the active role people still enjoy at this stage of their lives. What roles do older people play in your culture?

1. *Sentence Reduction Using Adjectives and Appositives*

Replace the italicized material in each sentence with either adjectives that precede the noun or appositive phrases that follow the noun. The first one has been done.

a. Otilia Arosemena, *who is a Panamanian politician,* considers herself a woman *who is quite liberated* for her culture.

Otilia Arosemena, a Panamanian politician, considers herself quite liberated for her culture.

b. This Panamanian leader, *who has been a hard worker* since her school days, played a role *that was major* in getting the vote for women *who are from Panama.*

_____

_____

_____

c. Her husband, *who is the vice-minister of agriculture,* leaves her alone to pursue her interests, *which are social and political.*

_____

_____

_____

d. She has one daughter *who is a ballet dancer* and one son *who is a physician.*

_____

_____

_____

e. Arosemena, *who is a natural born fighter,* favors independence *of culture and economics* for the people *who live in Panama.*

_____

_____

_____

f. Is feminism, *which is widespread,* a feature of your culture?

_____

_____

_____

Write one brief paragraph about a well-known political leader in your culture or country. Try to use descriptive structures such as adjective clauses, adjective-noun combinations, and appositives.

2. *Sentence Reduction Using Present Participial Phrases*

Reduce the following sentences by changing the italicized information in the relative clauses into present participial phrases. Follow the punctuation given for the clauses. The first one is done for you.

a. The Rajputs are a people *who live* in the western part of India.

   The Rajputs are a people living in the western part of India.

b. They are a group *that claims* descent from ancient warrior kings.

   _____

   _____

c. Today, however, the Rajputs are villagers *who farm* the soil.

   _____

   _____

d. Rajput houses are built with separate quarters for males and females, *which follows* spatial patterns typical of the rest of India.

   _____

   _____

e. Rajput women practice *purdah,* so *they wear* a veil in front of all male strangers.

   _____

   _____

f. Rajput women restrict their movement to their own homes, *where they confine* themselves to their own sections and courtyards.

   _____

   _____

3. *Sentence Reduction Using Past Participial Phrases*

Reduce the following sentences by changing the italicized information in the relative clauses into past participial phrases. Combine all of the items into one sentence. Make whatever changes are necessary. The first one is done for you.

a. Rajput women of India, *who are accustomed* to a life *that is restricted* to domestic work and child rearing, have certain values about bringing up their children.

Rajput women of India, accustomed to a life restricted to domestic work and child rearing, have certain values about bringing up their children.

b. Rajput infants *will be picked up* only if hungry. Rajput infants *will be attended to* only if hungry. Rajput infants otherwise spend most of their time in their cots.

_____

_____

_____

c. Blankets *that are wrapped* around them protect them from insects and the evil eye.

_____

_____

_____

d. But *when they are wrapped* in blankets and *when they are protected* in this manner, the infants are not very mobile. (*Note:* Here dependent time clauses, not adjective clauses, are to be reduced.)

_____

_____

_____

e. Praise and attention, *which are not given* freely, are thought to spoil a child.

_____

_____

_____

f. Rajput children, *who are discouraged* from being self-reliant, thus gradually learn the values and customs *that are required* of them.

_____

_____

_____

4. *Using Descriptive Phrases in a Paragraph*

Write a paragraph about the way a homemaker, a working person, or a student in your culture or your present society might divide his or her day. Begin your paragraph with a topic statement that introduces your subject. Use descriptive phrases and adjective clauses where appropriate.

Series of Parallel Items

A series is a group of three or more expressions that are related in meaning and parallel in form because they all belong to the same category of items in a sentence. All the items in a series must take the form of the first item, which governs the series pattern. Commas separate all the items in a series; the last item is preceded by *and* or *or*.

Everything that human beings *know, feel, and think* is determined by their participation in a human culture.
(A series of plural present tense verbs that give examples of *everything*)

The Bushman's hunting methods, the American's senior prom, the ancient Greek's appreciation of tragic drama, and the Navajo's healing ceremonies are all examples of culture.
(A series of adjective + noun expressions as subjects of the main verb *are*)

---

1. *Sentence Combining*

Combine each group of sentences into one sentence that contains a series of parallel items. Make whatever changes are necessary for sentence correctness. The first one has been done.

a. (1) The psychologist who cared for Victor, the "wild boy," was young.
   (2) The psychologist who cared for Victor, the "wild boy," was perceptive.
   (3) The psychologist who cared for Victor, the "wild boy," had sympathy.

   The psychologist who cared for Victor, the "wild boy," was young, perceptive, and sympathetic.

---

b. (1) Celebrations of birth are part of most cultural systems.
   (2) Celebrations of marriage are part of most cultural systems.

(3) Celebrations of victory in warfare are part of most cultural systems.
(4) Celebrations of successful harvests are part of most cultural systems.

_____

_____

_____

c. (1) Victor couldn't focus his eyes.
(2) Victor couldn't distinguish between sweet and fetid smells.
(3) Victor wasn't able to speak in any human language.

_____

_____

_____

d. (1) Victor was captured in a French forest.
(2) Victor was brought to Paris.
(3) Victor was shown to huge crowds.

_____

_____

_____

e. (1) Practically everything humans perceive is learned through participation in their culture.
(2) Practically everything humans know is learned through participation in their culture.
(3) Practically everything humans think is learned through participation in their culture.
(4) Practically everything humans value is learned through participation in their culture.

_____

_____

_____

f. (1) Ethnocentrism is when we think that our culture is the best.
(2) Ethnocentrism is when we think that our language is the best.
(3) Ethnocentrism is when we think that our values are the best.
(4) Ethnocentrism is when we think that our ways of doing things are the best.

_____

_____

_____

2. *Sentence Composition*

Use a series of parallel items to compose an original sentence on a separate piece of paper in which you

a. describe your family.
b. describe some activities you do at school.
c. describe some weekend activities.

3. *Proofreading*

Proofreading means looking over written work to catch and correct mistakes. Some of the following sentences contain errors in the punctuation and form of a series of parallel items. On a separate sheet of paper, revise the incorrect sentences. If a sentence is correct, write *C* after the sentence.

a. A liberated women will have independence, education and self-respect no matter what culture she lives in.
b. In modern societies, an educated wife can stop a man from doing wrong by talking to him, make him see his mistakes, and correct them with him.
c. Some of the obstacles to romantic love are differences in culture, education, religion, financial, and race.
d. As children grow up, they imitate what their parents do, say and think.
e. In modern marriages, both spouses should help each other by doing their housework together, sharing the care of their children, and plan activities for the whole family.
f. Love is wonderful. When it happens, the couple doesn't see anybody else, don't care about anything and don't think about anything but their love.
g. If we make our lives so busy with work or studies, we don't have time to see our family or we couldn't enjoy outings with our friends. And we won't have time for participation in sports.
h. Engineering is one of the most popular fields for young Americans. You can earn a good salary as an engineer, and there may be the chance to travel. You will gain respect for being in a useful profession.

Small Group Assignment

Paragraph Reconstruction

Form groups. You will have five minutes to read the following paragraph as many times as you can. *Do not take notes.* Your instructor will then read the paragraph aloud twice. With your books closed, have your group try to reconstruct the paragraph as closely as possible to the original. The first sentence and the following terms will be put on the board to aid your reconstruction: *issei, nisei, kibei, sansei, yonsei,* and *gosei.*

The Perspective of Time Among Japanese-Americans

Most immigrant groups in America only distinguish between native and foreign born persons. But the Japanese in America have a different name for each generation. They call immigrants from Japan *issei,* which means "first generation." They call the children of at least one *issei* parent *nisei,* which means "second generation." They call those children born and raised in the United States but educated in Japan by the name *kibei.* They call the children of *nisei* and *kibei, sansei,* which means "third generation." They call the children of *sansei, yonsei,* and they call the children of *yonsei, gosei.*

Discussion

What are some of the formal or slang words in your language that refer to immigrants of different generations? Why do some terms for new immigrants, like the American term "greenhorn," have negative associations?

Composition Development

Summarizing

The ability to summarize is an important academic skill that can be applied to a variety of purposes: reviewing lecture and text material for examinations, condensing key texts to include in term papers or class presentations, briefly retelling a narrative as part of a critical evaluation, or digesting technical material for decision making in a field situation.

To summarize a book, a textbook chapter, an article, or any other long piece of writing requires that you **condense** the content to its essentials:

Its *identification*—title, author, date (where relevant), purpose, audience, and writing level where this is related to purpose.
Its *overall main idea* and the *most important subtopics* or supporting ideas.
The most *significant supporting details,* examples, or methods of development.
The author's *main conclusion(s)* based on the material presented in the text.

The length of a summary in relation to the original material varies. For short articles, one rough determination is to have approximately the same number of summary sentences as there are paragraphs in the original. Another is to have the summary be about 15-25 percent of the length of the original piece.

Characterization of a Summary

A summary generally has the following characteristics of organization and style:

It is written in ordinary paragraph-essay form, although it may contain various kinds of lists for the purpose of brevity.

It begins with the identification of the material to be summarized.

It clearly states the overall main idea of the original work.

It discusses the author's main points and their supporting details in the order followed in the original.

It is written in the reader's *own words,* which filter and condense the author's thoughts.

It *does not* include large pieces of direct quotations from the original.

It *does not* contain the reader's reaction to or opinions about the piece.

Writing a Summary

The prerequisite to writing a good summary is a thorough, careful reading of the original the first time. While reading the text, you should underscore, take notes in the margin, or in some other way annotate the main ideas and significant details. Then you can use these notations for your summary.

1. Mapping the Selection

Prior to summarizing, skim the selection so you can group together those paragraphs that deal with the same major topic or idea. Use a separate sheet of paper to "map" the selection, that is, to list the paragraphs that go together, to state the topic of the grouped paragraphs, and to express the main idea, viewpoint, or topic development of the grouped unit. Study the following example of a map of the reading selection from Chapter Two, "Culture and Food Habits."

Para. No.	Topic	Key Point(s)
[1]	Intro.—some diff. food taboos	Diff. cultures have diff. food patterns related to religion, physical environment
[2],[3],[4]	3 diff. methods of getting food	Hunting & gathering—oldest Pastoralism—herding plus trading Agriculture—producing food from ground; opened way for civilization

[5]	Relation of food-getting methods to physical environment	Groups sharing an environment exploit it in diff. ways
[6],[7]	Some reasons for cross-cultural food patterns	Biological—Asian aversion to dairy products Long-term benefits to society—Hindus against killing cows

Now map Chapter 5 following the same guidelines.

2. Summary Introduction

Begin the summary with a statement that identifies the original piece. Indicate the author's overall main idea and purpose.

> **In *The Silent Language*, anthropologist Edward Hall *theorizes* that certain aspects of perception such as those of time and space are learned "out of awareness," without our knowing we have learned them. Hall's book is intended for nonspecialists. Its purpose is to reduce cross-cultural misunderstanding in daily life. It is written in a highly readable style with many interesting, specific examples.**

Note the italicized expression *theorizes*. This verb is important to a summary since it is a key part of the main idea statement. The following list contains other useful verb combinations:

analyzes a situation or structure (divides it into its different components)
explains a situation (makes something intelligible to the reader)
compares or contrasts two or three items (shows how they are similar to or different from each other in related and significant areas)
discusses a situation or problem (investigates or debates a question by presenting its various sides in objective language)
describes a structure, environment, or series of events (presents a mental picture by using concrete words; presents the characteristics of someone or something)
evaluates a work or a result (examines with the purpose of placing a value on something)

3. Composing the Summary Body

After mapping the original text and writing the summary introduction, you are ready to compose the summary using your mapped material as a basis.

As you proceed, check the original piece for specific points or developmental patterns to include. But, do *not* use whole sentences or pieces of the text for your summary. Do *not* use the writer's figures of speech. If you find yourself copying more than a few words from the original, stop and ask yourself, what is the main idea of this piece of text? Say the answer aloud without looking at the text, and then write down what you said. This technique will help you summarize properly *in your own words*.

4. *Revising for Efficiency*

The following items were written by various students as part of their summaries of an article on engineering and the recent changes that have taken place in both the field and the type of person who enters that field. The items are not necessarily incorrect, but they are too wordy for a summary and could benefit from revision. Utilize adjective clauses, descriptive phrases, and parallel items in your revisions. Follow the directions for each item and rewrite it on a separate sheet of paper.

a. (1) Times are changing in engineering. (2) This is the factor that has changed, that engineers used to be males who came from workingclass families, but now many engineering students come from families that are more middle and even upper class.
(Use adjectives to reduce relative clauses; reduce the number of clauses in (2).)

b. (1) In the last two decades, not only the social background of engineers has changed. (2) The racial and sexual composition has changed, too. (3) And also, the national background of engineers has changed, as there are now many foreign students in engineering. (4) This is in addition to all the women and minority Americans who are becoming engineers.
(Combine the information in (2) and (3) into a series; combine the related information of (3) and (4) into a series sentence.)

c. (1) Engineering does not guarantee a job. (2) It depends on the economic situation. (3) It also depends on the supply of engineers. (4) An average of 53,000 engineering jobs was open yearly until 1985. (5) Most of these jobs were in private industry. (6) The average engineer will begin with $28,000, whereas the liberal arts graduate may only earn around $24,000 in his or her first working years.
(Combine sentences so that there are no more than four; eliminate some detailed information that is too specific for a summary.)

d. (1) The kinds of engineering jobs that are employing new engineers who are recent engineering school graduates are electrical engineering, civil engineering, and mechanical engineering. (2) These are the different kinds of engineering jobs open nowadays.
(Reduce to one sentence with as little repetition as possible.)

e. (1) The article mentions Elena N. as a typical new engineer. (2) Elena is a woman, and she is from Nicaragua, from a wealthy family there.

(3) She graduated from M.I.T. in industrial engineering. (4) She immediately got an excellent position with a high salary. (5) She began earning $36,000. (6) Like many foreign engineering graduates, Elena says, "I want to go back and help the institutions in my country do a more efficient and effective job for the people. (7) After a few years training on the job here in the United States, I will return to my country and apply what I have learned there."
(Combine (2) and (3) using an appositive and adjectives; condense quoted material and report it in your own words.)

    f. (1) In this article the author says that engineering is the only field in which women start with higher salaries than men do. (2) I think the author is wrong here, because men and women studying the same field and getting the same position are supposed to get the same salary. (3) Also, women have little difficulty finding a job in engineering.
(Eliminate one sentence as an opinion.)

5. *Pair Summary Revision*

The following is a summary of an article that discusses the different food patterns of wives who have jobs outside the home and those who don't. The summary is not as efficiently written as it might be. Some statements are too detailed for a summary. There are adjective clauses that could be reduced to appositives or simple adjectives. Some sentences might be combined with others without losing any important information. Rewrite the summary with a partner, deciding together how you would change the expression of the given information. Treat this version as a first draft. Then write a final version.

Food and the Working Wife

The woman who works and who lives in an urban area is adding to the budget of her family, but she is also doing much that upsets their patterns of eating. Let's start with some facts that are a surprise: The working woman, whether she is an office worker or a professional, entertains more than her counterpart who does not work. She also uses fewer canned or frozen foods than the nonemployed wife. And her husband almost never helps with the food shopping or preparation. Susan Sieverman was the research director for this report. This report was published in *The Ladies Home Journal* magazine. The report was based on a questionnaire that was sent to 500 urban households. The survey showed that women who are employed are likely to skip breakfast. Or they may eat breakfast out. Or they will quickly eat a cold breakfast that doesn't require any cooking. But at dinner they will cook regular meals, just like the wife who is not employed outside the home. Working women cook beef more than do women who don't work. And working women are more likely to serve wine rather than beer or soda at dinner. The report's director, who was Susan Sieverman, said she was surprised that working wives used fewer convenience (canned, frozen, packaged) foods than nonworking wives. But she concluded that this case was true partly because working wives tend to have smaller families than nonworking wives. It makes sense that a woman with only one or two children would have more time to cook a nice meal from scratch than a mother with three or more children, especially as children are so fussy about what they will and won't eat.

6. *Three-Minute News Summarizing*

Select an issue of daily interest from the newspaper for a topic. Read several articles (over a period of days if necessary) on the topic and summarize each one in a few statements. Then compose a "news summary" in the form of a three-minute oral presentation that states a main idea about your chosen topic and uses the summarized articles as supporting evidence.

7. *Expressing Ideas Efficiently*

Compose a twenty-word telegram to a local or national politician urging his or her action on an important social, economic, or political issue.

Composition Topics

1. Attitudes and perceptions about time are one of the most important dimensions of our lives. The following question is from a university writing test. It asks you to consider the dimension of time in your life.

   Some people work too hard and too much. In their effort to succeed in school or work, they often do not have time to build good relationships with their friends and families. This effort to succeed is just not worth it.

   Do you agree or disagree? Support your viewpoint with references to your experience, the experience of others you know, or your reading. (You may wish to refer to the reading passage of this chapter.)

2. It has been said that punctuality is the virtue of kings. Reflect on and discuss the quality of punctuality and the importance it plays in various aspects of your life. Develop the body of your essay with at least one concrete example of a situation in which punctuality or the lack of it affected you in a significant manner.

6

The Cultural Patterning of Space

Compare and contrast the New York City skyline pictured here with the skyline of your own native town or city. What are the most prominent buildings in your native skyline? Is your skyline uniform or broken up in the heights and shapes of buildings? Downtown New York City mixes commercial, residential, industrial, and educational space. Is this mixed use of space characteristic of your native city or town?

Freewrite

Think of a location you know well. Write about it for five minutes. Then choose one word from your Freewrite and write about it for another three minutes. Again, choose one word from your Freewrite and write about it in further detail for one additional minute.

Vocabulary in Context

You will need to know the meanings of the following words to fully comprehend the reading passage. Use your dictionary as necessary.

Verbs	**Nouns**	**Adjectives**	**Adverbs**
radiate	centralization	urban	densely
designate	intrusion	characteristic	
segregate	barriers	secular	
infringe		sacred	
precede		abstract	
		objective	
		subjective	

Antonyms

An antonym is a word or phrase that means the *opposite* of a given word. Each of the following sentences has a set of antonyms in parentheses. Choose the appropriate item to fill in the blank space in each sentence.

1. (segregate/integrate) Since 1954, American school systems have not been permitted to _____ black and white children in different schools.

2. (urban/rural) Long distances between neighbors, lack of or infrequent public transportation, and distant cultural, educational, shopping, and recreational centers are some disadvantages of _____ areas.

3. (characteristic/uncharacteristic) The ideal of each child having his or her own room is _____ of American culture because of its emphasis on individualism and independence.

4. (densely/sparsely) Because the Sahara Desert has so little water and vegetation, it is _____ populated.

5. (secular/sacred) In the Middle Ages, criminals could not be taken from a church. This fact illustrates one function of _____ space.

6. (centralization/decentralization) The educational system in the United States, in which each of the fifty states controls its own programs and funds, is an example of _____ .

7. (segregated/integrated) In many American colleges today, dormitories are _____ , that is, men and women share the same living space.

8. (precede/follow) American custom provides that politeness be shown to women by men and to older persons by younger ones; therefore, in entering a room, women will _____ their male escorts, and older people will _____ younger ones.

9. (objective/subjective) It is more difficult for instructors to grade a _____ exam such as an individual essay than a multiple-choice test.

10. (abstract/concrete) It is easier to learn mathematical concepts if we begin with _____ examples such as counting stones, sticks, or money.

Reading: The Cultural Patterning of Space

Key Concepts
- *Cross-cultural spatial perceptions*
- *Centralization*
- *Concepts of superiority and inferiority*
- *Personal space*
- *Adaptation to a spatial environment*

[1] Like time, *space* is perceived differently in different cultures. Spatial consciousness in many Western cultures is based on a perception of *objects in space,* rather than of space itself. Westerners perceive shapes and dimensions, in which space is a realm of light, color, sight, and touch. Benjamin L. Whorf, in his classic work *Language, Thought and Reality,* offers the following explanation as one reason why West-   5

erners perceive space in this manner. Western thought and language mainly developed from the Roman, Latin-speaking, culture, which was a practical, experience-based system. Western culture has generally followed Roman thought patterns in viewing **objective** "reality" as the foundation for **subjective** or "inner" experience. It was only when the intellectually crude Roman culture became influenced by the **abstract** thinking of the Greek culture that the Latin language developed a significant vocabulary of abstract, nonspatial terms. But the early Roman-Latin element of spatial consciousness, of concreteness, has been maintained in Western thought and language patterns, even though the Greek capacity for abstract thinking and expression was also inherited.

[2]   However, some cultural-linguistic systems developed in the opposite direction, that is, from an abstract and subjective vocabulary to a more concrete one. For example, Whorf tells us that in the Hopi language the word *heart,* a concrete term, can be shown to be a late formation from the abstract terms *think* or *remember.* Similarly, although it seems to Westerners, and especially to Americans, that objective, tangible "reality" must **precede** any subjective or inner experience, in fact, many Asian and other non-European cultures view inner experience as the basis for one's perceptions of physical reality. Thus although Americans are taught to perceive and react to the arrangement of objects in space and to think of space as being "wasted" unless it is filled with objects, the Japanese are trained to give meaning to space itself and to value "empty" space. For example, in many of their arts such as painting, garden design, and floral arrangements, the chief quality of composition is that essence of beauty the Japanese call *shibumi.* A painting that shows everything instead of leaving something unsaid is without *shibumi.* The Japanese artist will often represent the entire sky with one brush stroke or a distant mountain with one simple contour line—this is *shibumi.* To the Western eye, however, the large areas of "empty" space in such paintings make them look incomplete.

[3]   It is not only the East and the West that are different in their patterning of space. We can also see cross-cultural varieties in spatial perception when we look at arrangements of **urban** space in different Western cultures. For instance, in the United States, cities are usually laid out along a grid, with the axes generally north/south and east/west. Streets and buildings are numbered sequentially. This arrangement, of course, makes perfect sense to Americans. When Americans walk in a city like Paris, which is laid out with the main streets **radiating** from centers, they often get lost. Furthermore, streets in Paris are named, not numbered, and the names often change after a few blocks. It is amazing to Americans how anyone gets around, yet Parisians seem to do well. Edward Hall, in *The Silent Language,* suggests that the layout of space **characteristic** of French cities is only one aspect of the theme of **centralization** that characterizes French culture. Thus Paris is the center of France, French govenment and educational systems are highly

centralized, and in French offices the most important person has his or her desk in the middle of the office.

[4] Another aspect of the cultural patterning of space concerns the functions of spaces. In middle-class America, specific spaces are **designated** for specific activities. Any **intrusion** of one activity into a space that it was not designed for is immediately felt as inappropriate. In contrast, in Japan, this case is not true: Walls are movable, and rooms are used for one purpose during the day and another purpose in the evening and at night. In India there is yet another culturally patterned use of space. The function of space in India, both in public and in private places, is connected with concepts of superiority and inferiority. In Indian cities, villages, and even within the home, certain spaces are designated as polluted, or inferior, because of the activities that take place there and the kinds of people who use such spaces. Spaces in India are **segregated** so that high caste* and low caste, males and females, **secular** and **sacred** activities are kept apart. This pattern has been used for thousands of years, as demonstrated by the archaeological evidence** uncovered in ancient Indian cities. It is a remarkably persistent pattern, even in modern India, where public transportation reserves a separate space for women. For example, Chandigarh is a modern Indian city designed by a French architect. The apartments were built according to European concepts, but the Indians living there found certain aspects inconsistent with their previous use of living space. Ruth Freed, an anthropologist who worked in India, found that Indian families living in Chandigarh modified their apartments by using curtains to separate the men's and women's spaces. The families also continued to eat in the kitchen, a traditional pattern, and the living room–dining room was only used when Western guests were present. Traditional Indian village living takes place in an area surrounded by a wall. The courtyard gives privacy to each residence group. Chandigarh apartments, however, were built with large windows, reflecting the European value of light and sun, so many Chandigarh families pasted paper over the windows to recreate the privacy of the traditional courtyard. Freed suggests that these traditional Indian patterns may represent an adaptation to a **densely** populated environment.

[5] Anthropologists studying various cultures as a whole have seen a connection in the way they view both time and space. For example, as we have seen, Americans look on time without activity as "wasted" and space without objects as "wasted." Once again, the Hopi present an interesting contrast. In the English language, any noun for a location or a space may be used on its own and given its own char-

55

60

65

70

75

80

85

90

*A caste is a division of society, a hereditary class into which one is born, with rigid rules about occupations and social associations.

**The material remains of past civilizations, such as fossils, monuments, pottery, and so on.

acteristics without any reference being made to another location or space. For example, we can say in English: "The room is big" or "The north of the United States has cold winters." We do not need to indicate that "room" or "north" has a relationship to any other word of space or location. But in Hopi, locations or regions of space cannot function by themselves in a sentence. The Hopi cannot say "north" by itself; they must say *"in* the north," *"from* the north," or in some other way use a directional suffix with the word *north.* In the same way, the Hopi language does not have a single word that can be translated as room. The Hopi word for room is a *stem,* a portion of a word, that means "house," "room," or "enclosed chamber," but the stem cannot be used alone. It must be joined to a suffix that will make the word mean *"in* a house" or *"from* a chamber." Hollow spaces like room, chamber, or hall in Hopi are concepts that are meaningful only in relation to other spaces. This pattern of spatial perception among the Hopi seems to be similar to their pattern of time perception, in which periods of time are not seen as *separate* pieces of duration, as they are in the Western cultures, but are integrated as pieces of a connected pattern.

[6]   Anthropologists do not know why one culture develops one type of time-space perception and another culture develops another type. Spatial perceptions may be adaptations to specific environments: the degree of population density, the amount of arable land, the absence or existence of natural **barriers** such as the sea or mountains, or the amount of distinguishing landmarks in the region. For instance, among some Eskimo peoples, whose environment is a vast snow plain with few landmarks visible for most of the year, spatial perception is highly developed. The Eskimos must learn to make careful distinctions among different spatial elements, as their lives may literally depend on these distinctions when they are hunting far from home.

[7]   In some cultures a significant aspect of spatial perception is shown by the amount of "personal space" people need between themselves and others to feel comfortable and not crowded. North Americans, for instance, seem to require about four feet of space between themselves and people near them to feel comfortable. On the other hand, people from Arab countries and Latin America feel comfortable when they are close to each other. People from different cultures, therefore, may unconsciously **infringe** on each other's sense of space. Thus just as different perceptions of time may create cultural conflicts, so too may different perceptions of space.

Reading Comprehension

1. True–False

After each statement write *T* for true, *F* for false, or *NI* for no information, according to the information given in the reading passage.

a. Ancient Roman culture was based on practical and concrete thinking. _____

b. Ancient Greek culture emphasized abstract thinking. _____

c. European cultures generally value inner personal experience more than non-European cultures do. _____

d. The Japanese concept of *shibumi* means beauty in flower arranging. _____

e. The Peoples' Republic of China is an example of a highly centralized society. _____

f. Japan and the United States are similar in that both cultures use the same space for a variety of different purposes. _____

g. In India, public and private space is separated for males and females. _____

h. The Hopi language locates places only in connection with other spaces or directions. _____

i. The density of population is rarely a factor in the development of a culture's spatial perception. _____

j. Arab, Latin American, and North American cultures all have similar perceptions of personal space. _____

2. *Reading Review*

In oral discussion or in writing, answer the following questions based on information in the reading passage.

a. Briefly explain the difference between the thinking patterns of the ancient Greek and Roman cultures.

b. What does the *shibumi* concept in Japanese design refer to? How is this concept different from the Western concept of space?

c. What similarities are there in the way Americans perceive both time and space?

d. Give an example of how the theme of centralization is demonstrated in French society.

e. Give your own example of the concept that Americans generally designate specific spaces for specific purposes.

f. Give an example of how the Indian culture separates space by religious or sex-based criteria.

g. Why did the Indians of Chandigarh paste paper over their windows?

h. In your own words, briefly explain how the Hopi language refers to a room or location.

i. Explain the term *personal space* and illustrate it with a reference to your own behavior.

3. *Analyzing the Text*

Use a separate sheet of paper to respond to the following questions.

a. Underscore the topic sentence of paragraph [1]. Does the paragraph develop by example, explanation, or chronological reporting?

b. In paragraph [2], a number of different signal words are used to relate one thought to another. Indicate the thought relationships signaled by the following expressions:

however	(sentence 1)	Thus	(sentence 4)
for example	(sentence 2)	for example	(sentence 5)
similarly	(sentence 3)	such as	(sentence 5)
in fact	(sentence 3)	however	(sentence 8)

c. What two arrangements of space are being compared and contrasted in paragraph [4]?

d. In paragraph [4], what does the pronoun *it* refer to in the sentence "It is a remarkably persistent pattern, even in modern India."

e. In paragraph [5], the author states that "the Hopi present an interesting contrast." Explain the contrast that is the topic of that paragraph.

4. *Applying Key Concepts*

(1) Review the key concepts listed at the beginning of the chapter. Then next to each of the following items, write the key concept that it illustrates.

a. The chair of the judge presiding over a courtroom is raised above the seats of the other participants.

_____

b. Americans entering a crowded restaurant will wait in line for their own table rather than share a table with strangers. This case is not true of people in many parts of Europe and Asia.

_____

c. Southern Italian villages near the sea, attacked and invaded throughout history, have mostly been built with the houses clustered together.

_____

d. Elementary school children all over France follow the same curriculum and do the same lessons at any given point in time.

_____

e. China has never had much wood for fuel. Most commonly, Chinese food is cut into small pieces and cooked for a short period of time.

_____

f. Eskimos living in the northernmost regions of North America, where the land is covered with snow most of the year, can distinguish between flat and slightly hilly land under the snow that a non-Eskimo wouldn't notice.

_____

g. Studies done in American college libraries have shown that if there were many empty seats, students already seated would become uncomfortable and annoyed if a newcomer sat down in the chair next to them.

_____

h. English has dozens of words for different types of architectural structures based on their function, whereas Hopi has only one basic word for a building regardless of its use.

_____

(2) Consider the following question about "personal space" in class discussion or in writing.

a. When you enter a train or bus with a friend, how do you arrange the space between you for conversation?

b. When a train or bus is uncrowded, where do you generally choose your seat? Why?

c. When the train or bus is crowded, how do the sitting passengers establish spatial barriers? How do the standing passengers establish spatial barriers?

d. How do people on a crowded train or bus react if someone bumps into them accidentally? How do you react?

e. Do people on trains and buses in your native country behave differently than people do in the United States? Explain.

Vocabulary Study

1. Vocabulary Items

Complete each blank item with one word from the given list of words. Use your dictionary as necessary.

> barriers
> designate
> inappropriate
> infringe
> intrusion
> modify
> radiate
> sequentially

a. In many European cities, streets _____ out from a circle, plaza, or square.

b. During a parade, the police set up _____ to prevent traffic from moving in the streets.

c. The secretary's _____ into the meeting was necessary because the chairperson had an important telephone call.

d. In a democratic society, the government should not _____ on the rights of citizens to express their political views.

e. My professor will _____ two outstanding students to represent the college in the debate.

f. American buildings are numbered _____ , with odd and even numbers on opposite sides of the street.

g. Reading a newspaper in a college classroom is _____ behavior.

h. The dance instructor tried to _____ the steps of the routine for her beginning students.

2. *Word Form Table*

Fill in the following table with the appropriate forms of the given words. Some nouns or adjectives may have two forms.

	Verbs	*Nouns*	*Adjectives*	*Adverbs*
a.	modify	_____	_____	xxx
b.	_____	function	_____	_____
c.	_____	intrusion	_____	_____

d. _____   _____   characteristic   _____

e. _____   _____   persistent_____   _____

Use the correct form(s) from each lettered line to complete the same lettered sentence below.

a. The engineer had to make a major _____ in the original plans for the bridge.

b. The bridge had to _____ as both a railway trestle and an automobile road.

c. Teenagers sometimes think their parents are _____ in asking questions about their activities.

d. One major _____ of French culture is centralization.

e. Most immigrants work _____ to better the lives of their children.

2. *Word Formation*

Prefix *super:* meaning "above," "over," "beyond the usual."

superficial	superintendent	supersede
superhuman	(a) superior	supersonic
superimpose	superlative	superstructure
		supervise

In an unabridged dictionary, look up the meanings of each of the words in the preceding list. Note particularly the derivation of the word and the meaning of its stem. On a separate sheet of paper, write the primary definition of each word, and under the definition write a sentence using the word.

The prefix *sub* is the opposite of *super;* it means "under" or "lower." Explain the meaning of the following words and provide examples of their use.

subcutaneous	substructure
sublease	subterranean
submarine	suburban
submission	subway
subordinate	

Writing Exercises

Passive Voice Review

A verb tense may be in the active or passive voice.

Active: **Different cultures perceive the use of space differently.**

Passive: **The use of space is perceived differently by different cultures.**

The active verb indicates that the subject of the sentence is the *doer* or performer of the verb action. In the passive voice, the subject position is not taken by the doer of the action, but by the *receiver* of the action. In passive voice, the doer or performer of the action either is not mentioned at all or becomes the agent. The agent is introduced by the preposition *by*.

Active: **The Japanese see the same space as having many different functions.**

Passive: **The same space is seen as having many different functions by the Japanese.**
_(agent)

The agent or performer of the action is omitted in a passive voice sentence if the agent is unknown, if the agent is common knowledge, or if the agent is unimportant.

The New York skyline is known for its tall buildings.
(agent is common knowledge, "by everybody")

Chandigarh was designed according to European perceptions of light and space. *(agent unimportant)*

The passive voice uses some form of the verb *to be* as an auxiliary plus the past participle of the main verb.

> Males and females *are segregated* in public space in India. *(simple present tense)*
>
> A great deal of work *is being done* in space perception research. *(present continuous tense)*
>
> Chandigarh *was designed* by a French architect. *(simple past tense)*
>
> Research on population density *was being conducted* in New York last year. *(past continuous tense)*
>
> The results of this study *haven't been published* yet. *(present perfect tense)*
>
> Many surveys *had been sent* out before the study got under way. *(past perfect tense)*
>
> Such studies *can be used* to improve the quality of human life. *(future/modal)*

Note that passive verb forms must be singular or plural depending on the item in the *subject position*.

Passive Verb Forms

1. Distinguishing Between Active and Passive Verbs

Mark each of the main verbs in the following paragraph either *A* for active or *P* for passive. Mark whether the verb and its subject/receiver is singular or plural.

Baffin Island Eskimos, who hunt for their food supply, have excellent visual skills. The explanation for this lies in their physical environment. The Eskimos' land consists of endless snowfields without any distinctive landmarks. The Eskimos are required to travel widely over this unmarked landscape to find enough food to survive. Thus visual skills are developed as a kind of survival tool. Eskimo youngsters are trained in space perception at an early age, for when they grow up, they too will roam in search of food over the vast snowfields where every distinctive landmark is buried for most of the year.

2. Formation of Passive Simple Present Tense Verbs

Fill in the blank spaces with the correct passive form of the verb in parentheses.

The Eskimo pattern of child rearing (to condition (1) _____ primarily by their physical environment and their food-getting patterns. Children (to give) (2) _____ lots of freedom to roam the land, and punishment that would constrain them (to avoid) (3) _____ . Individualism, self-reliance, and curiosity (to encourage) (4) _____ . The Eskimos teach their children to develop personal skills that (can utilize) (5) _____ for food getting and survival in their difficult environment. Children (to teach) (6) _____ to hunt and fish when they are quite young. Eskimo children (to educate) (7) _____ early to be participating members of their culture.

3. Verb Choice: Active or Passive Forms, All Tenses

Choose the active or passive form of the verb in parentheses as appropriate to complete each sentence.

a. The main duties of the Indian housewife (have always been seen/have always seen) (1) _____ as tending the children, caring for the home, and serving hot, tasty meals throughout the day and evening. It is an ideal of the Indian middle class that women (should not move/should not be moved) (2) _____ around freely outside the home. Women generally (have not encouraged/have not been encouraged) (3) _____ to attend meetings of a purely social nature, because such social activities (have viewed/have been viewed) (4) _____ as a waste of time that (should spend/should be spent) (5) _____ in the care of the home. Religious activities, however, (have always considered/have always been considered) (6) _____ appropriate for women. Therefore, many Indian women (have formed/have been formed) (7) _____ clubs whose stated purpose is religious but whose activities (offer/are offered) (8) _____ sociability as well. Since Indian wives (have freely permitted/have been freely permitted) (9) _____ to attend such club meetings, both their needs and the ideals of their society (serve/are served) (10) _____ by such activities.

In Japanese homes, the same space serves many functions. Here a Japanese family gathers for dining, reading, and relaxation around the stove, which serves for both cooking and heating. Notice the absence of fixed walls and heavy, hard-to-move furniture.

b. In Eastern Europe, Jewish women (had limited/had been limited) (1) _____ to a secondary, domestic role in the household. Primary importance (had given/had been given) (2) _____ to the man in his role as biblical student. Frequently, the wife (took/was taken) (3) _____ the role of family provider, whereas her husband and son (allowed/were allowed) (4) _____ to spend their lives in study. However, when Eastern European Jews (moved/were moved) (5) _____ to Israel, some of them (decided/were decided) (6) _____ to create a new social pattern: the *kibbutz,* a collective agricultural settlement. The earliest *kibbutzim* (organized/were organized) (7) _____ on principles of strict social equality and nonsexist roles. The communal approach to child rearing (had freed/had been freed) (8) _____ women for nondomestic production. Recently, however, some *kibbutzim* (have returned/have been returned) (9) _____ to more traditional sex-role patterns, and women once more (are limiting/are being limited) (10) _____ to domestic and mundane tasks.

4. *Sentence Completion*

Fill in the correct form of the verb, active or passive, to complete the blanks in the following paragraph. Verb tenses and singular or plural forms will be suggested by sentence content.

Agricultural societies of the past usually (to characterize) (1) _____ by the pattern of extended families. Sons (to remain) (2) _____ with their parents even after they (to marry) (3) _____ and several generations of one family (to inhabit) (4) _____ the same piece of property. Even today, in largely agricultural countries such as China or India, the extended family pattern (to find) (5) _____ in many villages, towns, and cities. In the extended family pattern, the family (to continue) (6) _____ through time as a permanent social unit. As older members (to lose) (7) _____ through death, newer members (to gain) (8) _____ through birth, adoption, or marriage. In ancient cultures, relationships between the generations, such as father and son, (to give) (9) _____ more importance than the relationships between people in the same generation, such as husbands and wives. The changing patterns of family membership (to study) (10) _____ by anthropologists and sociologists over the past half century in order to improve our understanding of this essential social unit.

5. *Composing*

a. Descriptions of places often include passive forms, since the writer wishes to emphasize the objects that are being described rather than the person or agent connected to them. Choose a private or public space that is familiar and significant to you, and describe the arrangement of its furniture, its decoration, or its equipment so that the reader understands why it is comfortable, interesting, or important to you.

> *My favorite place for studying is the college library, which is located in the atrium of our main building.*

b. The formation, structure, function, and other aspects of a particular social group may be described using passive voice sentences to emphasize the characteristics of the group rather than the people involved in it. Write an extended paragraph in which you discuss such a group in which you have participated (for example, a school club, a religious organization, an athletic team).

> *My soccer team was formed in Brooklyn in 1989.*

c. Rituals, celebrations, and other special events are often described with passive voice sentences that emphasize the activities and items of the event rather than the people performing the action. Compose a description of such an event, using passive voice sentences as appropriate.

> *My sister's wedding was held in the most beautiful church in our native city.*

Small Group Assignment

Analyzing a Poem

Listen to your instructor read the following poem aloud. Then study it silently for five minutes, with the aim of reconstructing it as well as you can from memory, with your book closed.

The New Post*
by Chi Hsueh

He has left the boundless plain
Taken leave of his well-loved village
Exchanged the waving wheat for the ocean waves
Laid down his hoe and taken up a gun.

This new recruit come to the island,
Will he miss home?

The sea's tossing waves remind him
Of wheat rippling in the breeze;
The fishing boats under full sail
Of heavily laden carts at harvest time.

The new recruit come to the island
Feels at home.

Have someone write on the board the class's recall of the words, phrases, and lines and their approximate position in the poem. When no one can remember any more of the poem, open your books and compare the class reconstruction with the original.

1. *Discussing the Poem*

Form small groups to discuss the following questions about the poem. Have one person record your group's responses. When the group work is finished, re-form as a class to discuss your answers.

   a. The subject of this poem is not explicitly identified. Which words or phrases in the title and the poem suggest that it is about a soldier?
   b. What feeling or emotion does the poem explore in the first two stanzas, or sections of the poem?
   c. What kind of environment did the soldier come from? What occupation did he formerly have? Which lines explain your answer? How is his new place different from the one he left? Which lines explain your answer?
   d. The poet makes two comparisons in the third stanza. What are they? Which of them has been referred to earlier in the poem?
   e. What is the soldier's feeling in his new post? How do the comparisons in the third stanza explain his feeling?
   f. The rhythm of the first stanza is carried by a series of parallel structures,

*From *Chinese Literature*. Reprinted by permission of China Books and Periodicals, Inc.

beginning with "He has left . . . " Which words in the next three lines continue the parallel structure?

g. In line 9 the poet has condensed the comparison by leaving out some words at the end of the line. What are the words left out?

2. *Composing*

With the entire class, compare your feelings on arrival in a new place to that of the soldier's in the poem. Did you find any similarities between the new place and the one you had left? What kinds of experiences may help a person feel at home in a new place? Do you feel that you will become "at home" in the United States? Why or why not? Write about your ideas in an extended paragraph.

Composition Development

Paragraph Development by Examples and Illustrations

A great deal of academic and professional career work involves communicating general ideas or principles. But texts written entirely in generalized or abstract terms are difficult for readers to absorb. Therefore, a good writer uses a variety of developmental methods to support his or her generalized assertions and make them clear and concrete. In previous chapters you learned to support your ideas with explanatory and descriptive details and chronologically ordered events. In this section you will learn about supporting assertions by using examples and illustrations.

Examples are statements about specific types, forms, or variations of subjects, assertions, or general statements. Brief specific examples support assertions by demonstrating to the reader that types or forms of the subject do exist. Examples or illustrations within a paragraph do not have to be long. Even a short series of specific types of items or a one- to two-sentence example can be useful in enriching a paragraph and making general or abstract statements concrete.

Reread paragraph [2] of the reading selection of this chapter. What is the overall main idea of that paragraph? What example is used to support the main idea in concrete terms? What is a secondary generalization or assertion in the paragraph? What example is provided to make that assertion clearer? In this paragraph the word *shibumi* is translated into an abstract idea: the essence of beauty. What two examples are given to make this abstract idea concrete?

Skim paragraph [3]. What is the overall main idea? What example is given to help the reader visualize the main idea? What expression is used to introduce the example? What concrete example is given in this paragraph to support the assertion that the theme of centralization is important in French culture?

In paragraph [4], what example is used to support the assertion that the segregation of space is a characteristic pattern of India that has persisted for thousands of years? Is there an introductory expression for that example? If so, what is it?

State the overall main idea of paragraph [5] in your own words. What example is given to explain it? What introductory expression is the link between the idea and the example given?

In paragraph [6], what examples are given to support the assertion that different peoples have different ideas of personal space? What expression is used to introduce the example?

Signal Expressions for Incorporating Examples

for example, for instance, + an independent clause
one example, another example, a third example . . . is
an illustration, an example of this + verb
such as + a series of parallel items
the example of, the case of . . . + verb (usually for an extended example)
also, in addition are useful signals for adding examples

1. Filling in Signal Phrases for Examples

Fill in the blank spaces with an appropriate signal phrase for examples. Include proper punctuation.

a. (1) Among the Cheyenne, the play of both boys and girls is an imitation of and preparation for adult roles. (2) Boys _____ have learned to ride bareback, use the lasso, and shoot with bow and arrow by the time they are six or eight. (3) Girls _____ learn to ride early, and even as toddlers they take on domestic responsibilities _____ helping their mothers carry wood and water and taking care of younger children.

b. (1) The women's liberation movement of the past decade has accounted for many changes in language as well as behavior. (2) The term *Ms.* _____ has been widely introduced as a nonsexist title for both married and unmarried women. (3) _____ of this linguistic development is the increasing use of nonsexist designations

_____ *chairperson* or *businessperson* for *chairman* or *businessman.* (4) Married women are increasingly retaining their maiden names or hyphenating them with their husband's name, a practice that already occurs in Latin American countries _____ Puerto Rico and Mexico. (5) And some women who were born with surnames having male suffixes _____ *man* or *son,* are changing them. (6) _____ of a Long Island woman, El-len Cooperman, who recently petitioned for a name change to Coop-erperson, shows the changing times.

c. (1) Although Asian countries are generally more conservative in social customs than Western cultures, there have been several notable ex-amples of women leaders, both past and present, in both China and India. (2) In China _____ there have been several powerful empresses _____ the Empress Wu in the sev-enth century and the Empress Dowager Tzu Hsi in the early twentieth century. (3) In India, _____ a modern political leader was Indira Gandhi, the daughter of the late Prime Minister Nehru.

d. (1) Different cultures have different perceptions of time. (2) North Americans _____ place a high value on punctuality. (3) Latin Americans, however, have a relaxed attitude about being on time for appointments. (4) _____ of a culture with a relaxed feeling about time is the Sioux, which does not even have a word for "lateness." (5) The future orientation of the American culture _____ contrasts with the attitudes about the future in other cultures. (6) Navajos _____ are skeptical about predicting or planning for the future, even the foreseeable future.

2. *Choosing Relevant Examples*

To serve their purpose of clarifying general statements or assertions, ex-amples must be *apt,* that is, they must be specific instances of the subject stated in the general statement or assertion.

List A contains a number of general statements or assertions. List B contains examples. Write the number of the example from list B that is most appropriate in the blank space provided in list A. When you have finished the exercise, your instructor will call on class members to read the general statements and examples that comprise the paragraph. Note how the examples give concreteness to the passage.

List A

a. The basic division of labor among the Dani of New Guinea is by sex, with the men doing the heavy work. _____

b. The women do the light work. _____

c. The Dani are relatively self-sufficient in their basic economy.

_____

d. In contrast to the Dani, there are many other agricultural cultures that cannot maintain themselves on the fruits of their farming labor.

_____

e. Tepoxtlán men, like many farmers elsewhere, cannot support their families on the meager produce of their small, infertile landholdings. They must seek other sources of income. _____

f. Women and children, too, must help with part-time, income-producing activities to prevent hunger. _____

List B

(1) For instance, many Tepoxtlán men work as temporary agricultural workers in the United States.

(2) such as fighting, building houses, and clearing fields and gardens.

(3) An illustration is the S. family, in which the wife raises turkeys and pigs, the children sell flowers, and the entire family produces charcoal.

(4) For example, a Dani woman's tasks may include planting, weeding, cooking, and making salt.

(5) One example of such a group is the peasantry of Tepoxtlán, a small village sixty miles outside of Mexico City.

(6) For instance, Dani villagers provide their own food, clothes, and shelter from the materials found or grown in the area.

Illustrations, which are actually extended descriptions of people, places, and reports of events, are also useful to support generalizations and abstract ideas—they *show* the reader something instead of merely asserting something. Illustrations bring meanings alive when they are specific and concrete in detail. They are effective when they are appropriate, that is, when they are closely related to the assertions or generalizations. Study the following boxes about paragraphs [2] and [3] of the reading passage in Chapter One, which show how the author used illustrations to support the topic statements.

Paragraph [2] Topic Statement: *Culture is necessary for the survival and existence of human beings as human beings.*

Extended description of the wild boy with many specific details about his animal-like behavior and his lack of human traits.

Restatement of Main Idea: *[Jean-Marc-Gaspard Itard] believed that Victor appeared subnormal because he had not participated in normal human society.*

Paragraph [3] Topic Statement: *Its [the case of the wolf-children] meaning is the same, however: Participation in human culture is necessary for the development of human characteristics.*

Extended description of the wolf-children with many specific details about their wolflike behavior and their inability to get along in a human environment.

Restatement of Main Idea: *Apparently, without early human contact, human beings will not develop a "human nature" that allows them to feel comfortable with others of their species.*

3. *Analyzing Illustrative Materials*

In class discussion, comment on the following student paragraphs in regard to how well they use illustrative details to support their main ideas. Ask yourself the following questions about each item: (1) Is a main idea clearly expressed before the illustration is presented? (2) Does the illustration clearly support the main idea, or is it vague, or even contradictory to it? (3) Is the illustration itself well written with vivid, concrete details? (4) Does the illustration include details that are not relevant to the main ideas? (5) Is there a solid concluding statement that reinforces the topic statement?

A. The hardest part of making a new life in a new culture is finding a job. Most immigrants who want to get a good job have language problems that make it very difficult for them. This is like the story of my friend. He was a doctor when he was in his native country. Because he does not know English very well, he cannot be a doctor in America. So he finally found a job as a cook in a restaurant. The restaurant is a very famous one. It attracts tourists from all over the world, and sometimes he finds someone who speaks his native language with him. Every morning before work, my friend goes to language school. Now, after a few years, he is completing his studies to be a doctor in America.

B. Immigrants get used to the American life, and they don't want to leave their jobs, which offer them money, and go back to their native countries. For example, I have a relative who lives in Connecticut and now has a gas station of his own that returns a big profit for him. A couple of years ago he was a partner with others, but now it's his own individual property. Last summer he did go back to Greece and bought land and an apartment, because nobody knows what will happen in the future. He wants to live in Greece because his old friends are there.

C. Most immigrants come to America to settle down. Most of them have their families, jobs, businesses, and houses in America. They don't want to leave all those things in America. Most people are busy working and living. They hardly think about their native country. One of my father's friends came to America more than twenty years ago. He has two restaurants. Every day he and his wife go to their restaurants. They work until one o'clock in the morning. They have to work the whole year long. They have no time to think of anything else. Working and living is the only thing they can think of.

4. *Composing Examples to Support General Statements*

Each of the following general statements or assertions would communicate better if it were supported by some concrete examples. Compose one or two such examples for each item, using a variety of the signal expressions for introducing examples.

Assertion: **New York City mixes commercial, residential, and educational space in the same area.**

Example: **For instance, in Greenwich Village, many business firms, clothing stores, a major university, and numerous apartment buildings share the same streets.**

---

a. Food does more than fill our stomachs. In every culture, certain foods are associated with specific celebrations.

b. A recent survey found that most working people and students do not eat an adequate breakfast.

c. The word *family* in its narrowest sense means a mother, father, and their biological children. However, the family unit in a broader sense may consist of many other persons.

d. Time perceptions differ from culture to culture.

e. Every major city has its own special character, feeling, or rhythm.

f. Many older people have skills and knowledge that today's younger people lack.

g. Today's young people are familiar with complicated technology that their parents and grandparents find difficult or impossible to master.

h. In my native language (name it), verb (nouns, prepositions, articles, adjectives, adverbs) are formed and used differently than in English.

i. Proverbs provide a clear and easily memorized way of communicating the wisdom of a particular society.

Composition Topics

1. Imagine that you are a member of a community group in your neighborhood. A donation of money has been made to your group to improve neighborhood facilities of various types (for example, the branch public library, the local hospital, the neighborhood school, drug rehabilitation centers, health clinics, day care centers, athletic facilities, the local park, street cleaning, and beautification).

Compose an essay in which you present your ideas on the best way to spend this donation to improve your neighborhood. Divide your main idea into three subtopics. Develop each subtopic in a separate paragraph. Use concrete details and examples to support your ideas for neighborhood improvement.

2. There is an English saying, "A man's home is his castle." Write an essay that presents your interpretation of this proverb. Develop your essay with two or three paragraphs that explain *how* a man's home is his castle. You may wish to conclude with a proverb from your own culture that conveys the same idea.

The Arts in a Cultural Context

In many societies, artistic and religious elements are combined to give pleasure and communicate spiritual values. Here, the value of peaceful meditation associated with Buddhism is represented in this splendid statue from a Chinese temple. Describe the physical appearance of some statue, painting, object, building, or decorated garment that is connected with the religious system of your culture. Explain what emotional and artistic message this item conveys.

Freewrite

Freewrite about a piece of art (music, literature, film, painting, or the like) that you have enjoyed. What emotions does it bring out in you? Can you explain why?

Vocabulary in Context

Verbs	**Nouns**	**Adjectives**	**Adverbs**
appreciate	symbol	imaginative	merely
inspire	insight	universal	
	innovation	conservative	

Synonyms

Read the following paragraphs that summarize some of the main ideas of this reading selection. Substitute an appropriate word from the vocabulary list for each of the italicized expressions. Put your chosen words in the same form as that given. Rewrite the paragraph on separate paper.

All societies have art, that is, forms of *creative* expression that represent ideas or emotions through *signs*. To *enjoy and admire* the art of a society, it is helpful to know something about its cultural patterns. Although some people from other cultures may be *stimulated* by the art of a different society, many people dislike art that is not familiar to them.

The role of the artist in society is not *everywhere the same.* In Western cultures, the artist is typically seen as being in opposition to society, as one who has deeper *perceptions* about life than others. Artists usually work on *new ideas;* they do not *simply* repeat the artistic forms of the past. Artists in non-Western societies are usually more *traditional* in their artistic representations.

Reading: The Arts in a Cultural Context

Key Concepts

- *Symbolic communication*
- *Graphic arts/plastic arts/performance arts*
- *Cross-cultural artistic preferences and values*

[1]   Plato, the ancient Greek philosopher who devoted much of his writing to the subject of education, stated that "the well educated are those who are able to sing and dance." In every culture, singing, dancing, and other arts such as painting, sculpture, the writing of prose and poetry, and the playing of musical instruments have an important role. Every society offers a way for its people to gain pleasure from

5

creative and **imaginative** activity. The application of beauty, skill, and style beyond the **merely** practical is as much a **universal** human need as the need for food, sleep, and protection from the weather.

[2]   Art refers to any human object or activity that tries to meet   10
the standards of beauty in a specific society. For example, in Japan, tea drinking is an art, because it is associated with a special ritual of beautiful service; whereas in the United States, tea drinking is not an art but merely an ordinary activity. The great variety of artistic forms and styles in each culture makes the study of art rewarding. In addition, art ex-   15
presses some of the basic themes and values of a culture, so it provides **insights** into different cultural patterns and the different ways in which people view the world around them.

[3]   Art is a form of symbolic communication. For example, some dance movements may symbolize, or represent, the movements of an-   20
imals. Religious paintings or statues may be **symbols** of gods, saints, or certain spiritual values. Sometimes such paintings or sculptures are believed to actually *be* the thing they show. For instance, ceremonial masks are sometimes believed to take on the supernatural power of the spirits or beings that they represent.   25

[4]   Art may also symbolize a specific emotion or communicate a specific meaning. This kind of artistic symbolism varies from culture to culture, and we must know the specific cultural traditions to understand it. For instance, in Western music, the use of the minor scale traditionally **inspires** the emotion of sadness. In India, certain *ragas,* musical pieces,   30
are traditionally associated with different times of the day or evening. In Chinese opera, a blue cloth waved across the stage is immediately recognized as representing a river by a Chinese audience. These traditional artistic elements are like a code that people in those cultures have been taught to understand.   35

[5]   A third way in which art is symbolic is that it may reflect certain kinds of social behavior or social values. For example, a study of Navajo music reveals that the Navajo believe there is only one right way to sing each kind of song; this strict regulation is consistent with the generally **conservative** nature of Navajo social life. American jazz,   40
however, places a high value on **innovation,** freedom to experiment, and an individual's interpretation of a piece; this value is typical of American society in general. We may say that art helps make cultural values concrete and visible.

[6]   Two basically different notions of art exist in modern times.   45
One is the idea of "art for art's sake." This idea, which is typical of modern Western societies, means that the artist, using his or her imagination, creates only for the purpose of giving pleasure. However, in past societies and in many traditional societies today, art is not a special, separate activity removed from everyday life. Rather, art is a part of   50
all aspects of culture. For example, among the Inuit Eskimo people,

there is no separate word for *art*. All "artificial" objects are named together as "that which has been made." Inuit artistic skill is applied in making objects used in everyday life such as tools, weapons, or religious charms. Among the Inuit, as among many other nonindustrialized peoples, such skills as dancing, weaving, making pottery, singing, or playing a musical instrument are not performed as separate "artistic" behaviors but are integrated into everyday life.

[7]   Because art is so deeply rooted in cultural traditions, it is difficult to talk about standards of beauty in any universal manner. What is beautiful in one culture may not be beautiful in another. Each culture has developed its own traditions of what is acceptable in artistic content and style. It is sometimes difficult to appreciate art whose content and style are different from our own. However, we can learn something about the cultural values behind a specific work of art to help us appreciate its value. For example, although many Western artists such as Pablo Picasso were inspired by African masks without knowing anything about African cultures, most of us can **appreciate** African art more if we study something about the society that produced a specific work.

[8]   Cultures differ not only in their ideas of beauty but in the various types of art they prefer. In some cultures, masks and painting are the most important ways of expressing artistic values and technical skill. In other cultures, verbal skills are more important, producing a wealth of myths, folktales, and word games, but relatively little painting, sculpture, or pottery. Although every culture has dramatic performances as part of its religion, some cultures have developed this skill more than others. We do not know of any culture, no matter how harsh its environment or how simple its technology, that does not have some form of art. In fact, it is sometimes exactly those societies with a harsh environment and a relatively simple social structure, such as that of the Inuit Eskimo, that place a high value on artistic skill.

[9]   Some types of art may be more easily appreciated outside their cultural settings than other types. The graphic and plastic arts such as painting, sculpture, carving, work in precious metals or other valued materials (for example, bone, horn, or ivory), clay and pottery making, basketry, weaving, embroidery or other skills related to the making or decoration of garments, and architecture are perhaps most able to be enjoyed or admired across cultural contexts. Examples of graphic and plastic arts can be removed from their cultural settings and exhibited in museums or used or worn by people from other cultures. Their color, shape, and texture photograph well and can give pleasure to outsiders through illustrated books. On the other hand, verbal arts such as poems, word games, myths, dramas, or prose works do not easily cross cultural boundaries. Not only is there the language barrier, but verbal arts are usually so deeply rooted in the mind and the history of a culture that

even if we understand the vocabulary word by word, we may still miss the essence of the artistic work.

[**10**]   Music and dance are performance arts that appear in every culture. Music is often said to represent the "soul" of a people in a highly emotional form. Music, dance, and song frequently involve other dec-   100
orative arts such as masks, body paint, or costume; all of these aspects have symbolic value. Both music and dance in human societies are used to communicate a wide range of ideas and emotions. Although these thoughts and notions may not always be clear to us as outsiders, we nevertheless can take pleasure in the rhythm, movement, and emotion   105
of a dance or musical performance without completely understanding the social values behind them.

Reading Comprehension

1. *True—False*

After each statement write *T* for true, *F* for false, or *NI* for no information, according to the information given in the reading passage.

a. Singing, dancing, and painting are more important to human society than eating, sleeping, and providing shelter. _____

b. The art of tea drinking is practiced only in Japan. _____

c. A mask, statue, or painting may be a religious symbol. _____

d. Italian opera uses symbolic colors to represent aspects of nature. _____

e. Navajo music and American jazz are noted for their freedom and flexibility. _____

f. "Art for art's sake" means that artistry should be integrated into the objects of everyday living. _____

g. European artists were influenced by African masks because they had a deep understanding of African culture. _____

h. Societies living in harsh environments never develop complex artistic traditions. _____

i. Nonverbal art such as sculpture is most easily appreciated by people from other cultures. _____

j. Music, dance, and textile design are called performance arts.

———————

2. *Reading Review*

In oral discussion or in writing, answer the following questions based on information in the reading passage.

a. What are some basic human needs?

b. According to the text, why is tea drinking an art form in Japan but not in the United States?

c. Why is the study of art worthwhile?

d. Why do many religions use paintings, masks, or sculptures to communicate their beliefs?

e. How are jazz musicians and Navajo musicians different in their view of music?

f. Summarize the two basically different ideas about the artist's place in society held by Western societies and more traditional societies.

g. Why is it difficult to judge works of art from different cultures as beautiful or ugly?

This sign, and the realistic sculpture of the worker painting it, is a piece of public art in Paris, France. The words say, "There is no art without liberty." Discuss this statement.

   h. According to the text, which types of art are the most difficult to appreciate by outsiders? Why is this so?

   i. What is meant by "graphic" and "plastic" arts? To what extent can these
be appreciated outside their specific culture?

   j. Why do you think music is sometimes called the "soul" of a people?
Why is the art of dance enjoyable even if we don't know its cultural
meanings?

3. *Analyzing the Text*

Respond to the following questions as directed.

   a. In paragraph [5], music, painting, and writing poetry are considered as
     (1) examples of imaginative activity.
     (2) more important than food and sleep.
     (3) ways for cultures to communicate.
     (4) aspects of life meaningful only in Western culture.

   b. In paragraph [2], sentence 2, the word *whereas* signals
     (1) a reason and its result.
     (2) an example.
     (3) an addition of description.
     (4) a contrast.

   c. In paragraph [3], which two expressions signal an illustration of a general
idea?

   d. In paragraph [4], the statement that art symbolizes emotion is an addition
to the previous paragraph's idea that art is symbolic communication.
Which word or expression in paragraph [4] signals that addition?

   e. In paragraph [5], a sequence of statements is signaled by
     (1) *For example* . . .
     (2) *however,*
     (3) *A third way* . . .
     (4) the semicolon.

   f. In paragraph [6], to what item does the description "typical of modern
Western societies" apply? What word serves as the adjective clause
marker for this information?

   g. In paragraph [6], what expression introduces the example of objects of
everyday life?

   h. What is the thought relationship of the first sentence of paragraph [7]?

   i. What contrast of ideas is signaled by the word *However* in paragraph
[7]?

   j. In your own words, what is the main idea of paragraph [8]?

   k. Which expression in paragraph [9] signals a contrast between different
kinds of artistic production?

   l. The last sentence of paragraph [10] contains two expressions of contrast.
What are these?

4. *Paraphrasing*

Circle the number of the sentence that is closest in meaning to the given statement from the reading selection.

a. The application of beauty, skill, and style beyond the practical is as much a human need as the need for food, sleep, and protection from the weather.

(1) Filling out applications is a practical skill for human beings.

(2) Human beings need to eat, sleep, and shelter themselves from the weather.

(3) Human beings' food and shelter does not need to be beautiful or practical.

(4) Human beings need decoration and art as much as food, rest, and shelter.

b. The great variety of artistic forms and styles makes the study of art rewarding.

(1) Great artists receive great rewards.

(2) There are many different ways to reward artists for their years of work.

(3) Studying the arts is worthwhile because of the many different types of artistic expression.

(4) Artists who study many different styles of expression are superior.

c. Many religions put their beliefs in material form so that people can see or touch them as they worship.

(1) Material objects such as paintings or statues are often used by religious groups to communicate spiritual ideas.

(2) Different religions use different materials in their ceremonies of worship.

(3) People who worship material goods do not truly have religious beliefs.

(4) Religious beliefs take many different forms such as seeing, touching, or worshipping certain spirits.

d. Because art is so deeply rooted in cultural traditions, it is difficult to talk about standards of beauty in any universal manner.

(1) Some art is more difficult to understand than other art.

(2) There are so many traditions of art and culture in the universe, it is difficult to learn them all.

(3) Ideas of what is beautiful and artistic are almost the same in every culture.

(4) Ideas of style and beauty depend on each culture's traditions and values.

e. Modern Western cultures emphasize an artist's originality and innovation.

(1) In Europe and the United States, artists are judged by how new and different they are.

(2) In Europe and the United States, an artist must use modern Western themes.

(3) In Europe and the United States, the role of the artist receives little emphasis.

(4) Modern Western nations think that art and culture are important.

Vocabulary Study

1. Vocabulary Clusters

Different areas of knowledge have their own vocabulary of items that relate to each other in a general sense, but have distinctive meanings. Use a dictionary or encyclopedia as necessary to obtain the meaning of the items in one or more of the following clusters. Then write a brief paragraph about one or more of the cluster topics, using some of the vocabulary items.

Music: concert, recital, chamber music, percussion instruments, symphony, orchestra, conductor, overture, jazz, blues, opera, aria
Painting, drawing: pastels, fresco, canvas, chiaroscuro, icon, Impressionism, abstract art, engraving, lithography, calligraphy
Stone, metal and woodwork: sculpture, chisel, marble, marquetry, mosaic, cast, mold, bronze, terra-cotta, enamel, filigree, relief, pedestal
Textiles: spinning, weaving, fiber, loom, weft, warp, brocade, linen, embroidery, block print, crochet, batik

2. Word Form Table

Fill in the table with the appropriate forms of the given words. Some nouns or adjectives may have two forms.

	Verbs	Nouns	Adjectives	Adverbs
a.	_____	imagination	_____	_____
b.	inspire	_____	_____	_____
c.	_____	innovation	_____	_____
d.	_____	symbol	_____	_____
e.	_____	_____	conservative	_____

Use the correct form(s) from each lettered line to complete the same lettered sentence below.

a. Children often play _____ with ordinary household objects such as clothespins or kitchen utensils.

b. Ministers in African–American churches are noted for being dramatic and _____ speakers.

c. The French Impressionist painters are admired for their _____ in the use of light and color.

d. The colors of a nation's flag are usually _____ of the country's values.

e. The _____ of a culture's artistic heritage should be strongly supported by the government.

3. *Word Formation*

Suffix *ion:* an ending that forms nouns from verbs; signifies "action," "state," "instance of," or "result."

application	education	integration
appreciation	expression	opposition
association	imagination	production
communication	imitation	protection
conversation	innovation	reflection
creation	inspiration	representation

Choose ten words from the preceding list and note down the verb form of each. Use your dictionary as necessary. On a separate sheet of paper, write a meaningful sentence or a pair of sentences that uses both the verb and noun form of the word.

Protect → Protection

The best way for museums to protect their paintings is to hire security guards for protection.

Writing Exercises

Sentence-Level Patterns of Reason and Result

In developing a topic by reasons, you must be able to express the thought relationship of *reason leads to result* clearly and efficiently.

1. *Recognizing Reason and Result Clauses*

Study the following sentences. Label as *reason* the clause that tells *why* something happened. Label as *result* the part of the sentence that tells the *outcome or effect* that took place.

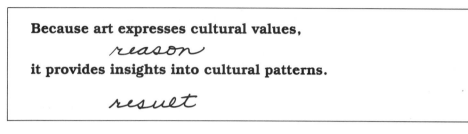

> **Because art expresses cultural values,**
>
> *reason*
>
> **it provides insights into cultural patterns.**
>
> *result*

a. Art is a universal aspect of human experience; therefore, it is worthy of study by anyone who wishes to understand our species more completely.
b. Because art is deeply rooted in cultural traditions, it is difficult to talk about universal standards of beauty.
c. People find it easier to communicate spiritually with visible objects; consequently, many religions embody their spiritual values in paintings or sculptures.

In Western artistic tradition, the artist's self-portrait, like that of Fred Baar, pictured here, is a frequent subject. The self-portrait reflects the focus on individualism that is central to Western values. Self-portraits are not commonly found in the art of traditional societies, where the well-being of the group is the highest value.

d. Since Navajos are conservative in their social values, they believe that foreign music is dangerous and inappropriate for them.

e. Modern Western societies value individualism and innovation; the Western artist, therefore, is judged by his or her unique and original expression.

f. As a result of their harsh physical environments, some groups such as the Inuit Eskimos place an especially high value on artistic expression.

Sentence Patterns for Expressing Reason-Result Relationships

Reason-result (cause-effect) relationships may be expressed in several structurally different manners.

[1] Separate Sentence Units. These employ the signal expressions *therefore, consequently, thus, for that reason, as a result* in the effect, or result, clause.

Masks play an important part in many African religious rituals. Therefore, a great deal of creative imagination and energy goes into the making of an African mask.

---

[2] Compound Sentences. Here two independent clauses are joined by a semicolon or the conjunction *so*. In using the semicolon construction, the signal expressions follow the same pattern as in [1].

Masks play an important part in many African religious rituals, so a great deal of creative imagination and energy goes into the making of an African mask.

---

[3] Complex Sentences. The dependent reason clause begins with *because, since,* or *as*. The dependent clauses beginning with these adverbial terms must be attached to an independent, or main, clause.

Because masks play an important part in many African
(dep. clause)

religious rituals, **a great deal of creative imagination and energy goes into the making of an African mask.**

---

1. *Expressing Reason-Result Relationships*

On a separate sheet of paper, rewrite the following pairs of sentences so that they express a reason-result relationship. You may combine the sentences or leave them separate, but try to use all the reason-result sentence patterns and signal expressions at least once.

a. **(1)** Tea drinking is considered an art form in Japan.
   (2) Tea drinking in Japan is a ceremony performed according to standards of beauty and skill.

   Because tea drinking in Japan is a ceremony performed according to standards of beauty and skill, it is considered an art form in Japan.

b. **(1)** Stories, jokes, and drama do not cross cultural boundaries easily.
   (2) The audience must understand the language to appreciate them.

c. **(1)** The Inuit believe that everyday objects should be beautiful.
   (2) They use artistry and technical skill in making weapons and tools.

d. **(1)** Capitalist societies have a high degree of specialization in labor.
   (2) There may be many vice-presidents in a single company.

e. **(1)** American advertisers spend a lot of money on ads in teenage magazines.
   (2) American teenagers consume enormous amounts of junk food and soft drinks.

f. **(1)** Americans and Sioux have different concepts of time.
   (2) A Sioux might have some difficulty adjusting to work in a large American firm.

g. **(1)** In India men and women are segregated in many public places.
   (2) An Indian woman visiting the United States might feel shy at first.

h. **(1)** The Japanese are trained to make good use of all available space.
   (2) Even a small Japanese house is usually comfortable.

2. *Sentence Expansion*

Each item given is a reason (cause) that could lead to a specific result (effect). On a separate sheet of paper, add your own sentence or clause to the given one to produce a reason-result statement. Use appropriate signal expressions.

> **Dorothy Lee is a Western-trained anthropologist.** *(reason)*
>
> **Because Dorothy Lee is a Western-trained anthropologist,** *(reason)*
>
> **she looks at the world in a scientific way.** *(result)*

a. Victor, the "wild boy," grew up alone in a forest.
b. An American might feel ill at the thought of eating snakes.
c. In Ponape society, people do not boast about their contributions to feasts.
d. North Americans and Latin Americans have different concepts of time.
e. American cities are usually laid out in a grid, with sequentially numbered streets and buildings.
f. The theme of centralization is important in French culture.
g. The Indian families living in Chandigarh did not like the large glass windows in their homes.
h. Sioux Indians were able to keep their jobs in American firms.
i. Music is called the "soul" of a people.

3. *Paragraph Combining*

Combine the individual sentences of the tale of "The Intelligent Crow and the Water Pitcher" into longer, fluent sentences, making whatever structural changes are necessary. You will have to add signal expressions of *time order, reversal of thought,* and *reason-result* at various points in your narrative. When you have finished, answer the questions that follow in complete sentences expressing reason–result.

a. Once there was a crow.
b. He was thirsty.
c. He had not drunk anything in days.
d. The weather had been very hot.
e. All the pools of water had dried up.
f. The crow came upon a pitcher.
g. The pitcher was nearly empty.
h. The pitcher had only a little water at the bottom.
i. The crow put his beak into the pitcher.
j. The crow's beak could not reach the bottom.
k. The crow could not drink the water.
l. The crow tried to break the pitcher.
m. The crow tried to get at the water.

n.   The crow could not break it.
o.   The crow tried to overturn the pitcher.
p.   The crow was not strong enough to overturn the pitcher.
q.   The crow had no more ideas.
r.   The crow was about to fly away in despair.
s.   The crow got a new idea.
t.   The crow picked up a pebble.
u.   The crow dropped the pebble into the pitcher.
v.   The crow dropped more pebbles into the pitcher.
w.   There were many pebbles in the pitcher.
x.   The water level kept rising.
y.   The water level rose to the brim.
z.   The crow was able to drink.
   (1) Why was the crow thirsty?
   (2) Why was the pitcher nearly empty?
   (3) Why couldn't the crow reach the water in the pitcher?
   (4) Why did the crow try to break the pitcher?
   (5) Why did the water level in the pitcher rise?
   (6) The moral of this tale is "Necessity is the mother of invention." Explain that proverb and add some reasons why you believe it is or is not a valid expression.

Small Group Assignment

Folktales are a form of artistic activity popular in many traditional cultures. They communicate important societal values in a form that everyone can understand. Read the following Indian folk tale. What value do you think it teaches?

Once there were six blind men who wished to discover what an elephant was like. The first man reached up and felt the elephant's ear and said that the elephant was like a fan. The second felt the elephant's tail and said that the elephant was like a rope. The third, feeling the elephant's leg, said that the elephant was like a tree. The fourth man felt the elephant's trunk and said that the elephant was like a snake. The fifth man seized the elephant's tusk and said that the elephant was like a stick. The last man, touching the elephant's side, said that the elephant was like a wall. And all of them were right.

Pair/Group Composing

Close your texts and listen carefully as your instructor reads the story of the blind men and the elephant. The key elements will be placed on the blackboard.

first man—elephant's ear—fan
second man—elephant's tail—rope
third man—elephant's leg—tree
fourth man—elephant's trunk—snake
fifth man—elephant's tusk—stick
sixth man—elephant's side—wall

Without turning to your text, recreate the story in one complete paragraph with whatever artistic additions you wish to add. Use either direct speech (quotations) or indirect speech to communicate the comments of the blind men about the elephant.

Story Telling

Write out a folktale from your culture. What cultural value does it communicate?

Composition Development

Topic Development by Reasons

A good writer supports topic statements with various kinds of specifics: illustrations, descriptive and chronological details, examples, and explanations. An additional method of support is by reasons. **Reasons** are explanatory statements that answer the question *why*.

1. Analyzing Paragraphs Developed by Reasons

Study the following paragraphs. On a separate sheet of paper, restate the main idea of the paragraph in your own words. Below your restatement, list in brief note form the reasons that support the main idea.

a. College students involved in career and professional degree programs sometimes dislike having to take liberal arts courses such as those in social science. They ask themselves: "What can such courses do for me?" The answer: "A lot." Anthropology is a good example. First, anthropology contributes to an understanding of the genetic and cultural differences among human groups. It helps remove the blinders of ethnocentrism, that is, looking at the world only through the narrow lens of one's own culture or class. Anthropology also teaches that major differences among human groups are cultural not biological. Furthermore, because anthropology studies people within their own cultural context, it prohibits judgments of inferiority or superiority; it accepts only *differences*. And finally, anthropology helps one understand one's own culture and its impact.

b. Anglo (Western) doctors in California have complained that the Mexican–American community is not using the medical services provided for them. There are a number of reasons why Mexican–Americans are hesitant to use the Anglo health-care system besides its high cost. One main reason is that Mexican–Americans hold beliefs about the causes and cures of illness that are not recognized as valid by Anglo doctors. A second factor of some importance is the Mexican–American belief that if one gives in to sickness, one is morally weak. Furthermore, Mexican–Americans cannot make the quick decisions about treatment customary in Anglo health care, because for them such decisions involve family members and close friends.

c. There are several reasons why physical anthropologists study nonhuman primates, especially monkeys and apes. Studying these animals can provide some clues to help us understand human chemistry and physiology. More important, research on nonhuman primates has helped us better understand the human physical structure and its unique aspects. Of major importance is the contribution primate research has made to our understanding of human behavior patterns.

d. Some anthropologists want to drop the word *race* as a classification for human groups. Their first reason is the obvious fact that human history has always involved migration and mobility, which results in interbreeding between different human groups. Therefore, there are no "pure" races in the human species. Perhaps less well known is the fact that there exist several racial stocks, such as the African Bushmen and the Polynesians of the South Pacific, that do not fit any one racial classification but have characteristics of several races. Finally, although the average person may not be aware of it, and may even prefer to think otherwise, the greatest differences among human groups are not those of biology or race, but of culture.

Linking Expressions Within Paragraphs

In developing paragraphs of reasons, it is important to guide the reader from the topic statement through the specifics by means of **linking,** or **connecting,** words and expressions. First you must identify your key words in the topic statement. Then you must make sure that references to these key words are repeated throughout the paragraph.

1. Analyzing Linking Words and Expressions

a. Look at the topic statement in paragraph **c** in the preceding section. A key term in that sentence would answer the question, "What do physical anthropologists study?" The answer would be nonhuman primates. Look at the first reason given for the research. The phrase *these animals,* which refers to *nonhuman primates,* links the first reason to the topic statement.

Consider the second reason given. What words link that reason to the topic statement? _____

_____

Consider the third reason given. What words link that reason to the topic statement? _____

_____

b. In paragraph **d,** the writer suggests that a certain term is not useful for classifying human groups. What is that key term? Where does that term next appear?

_____

In the second reason given in paragraph **d,** that term appears twice in an adjective–noun combination; locate these phrases.

In the third reason, the key term is used again as a synonym for another word in the sentence. Locate that repetition. If both words mean the same thing, why do you think the writer used them both?

_____

_____

Signal Words for Listing Reasons

Review the four paragraphs in the section labeled "Topic Development by Reasons." Which words signal you that a new reason is being offered? These words are called **signal,** or **directional, words** because they tell the reader the direction in which the paragraph is going to continue.

> *first, second, third, finally* (followed by a comma)
> *in addition, additionally, furthermore* (followed by a comma)
> *besides* [this], *in addition to* [that] (followed by a comma)
> *also* (followed by a comma when it is the first word in the sentence)
> *one/another reason is* + *that* clause
> *one/another reason is* + *the* + *noun*

Logical Order of Reasons

When you develop a paragraph by providing reasons to support your topic statement, it is important to put your reasons into **logical order.** Three kinds of logical order for reasons are as follows:

> from most to least important
> from least to most important
> from most obvious or familiar to least obvious or familiar

1. *Paragraph Analysis: Order*

Examine the paragraphs in "Topic Development by Reasons" carefully to determine which logical order is being used. Underscore the words or expressions that signal that order to you.

a. In paragraph **a,** the order is _____

_____

b. In paragraph **b,** the order is _____

_____

c. In paragraph **c,** the order is _____

_____

d. In paragraph **d,** the order is _____

_____

From Paragraph to Essay: Development by Reasons

The visual outline of a paragraph of reasons might look like the following:

> *Topic statement:* **Humans can only develop their full human potential as members of a human culture.**

> *Reason 1:* **Communication in a specific language requires specific cultural training.**

> *Reason 2:* **Developing human personality traits requires human contact.**

> *Reason 3:* **Becoming physically human is possible only in a fully human context.**

> *Conclusion:* **Human culture has many forms; people become human in specific cultural ways.**

For longer essay development by reasons, each of the previously stated reasons would become a paragraph subtopic developed by explanation, descriptive or chronological details, historical facts, statistics, examples, and/ or illustrations in varying combinations. The visual outline of an essay developed by reasons might look like this:

> *Introduction paragraph—overall topic statement:* **Human beings can only develop their full potential as members of a human culture.**

> *Paragraph 1—main idea:* **Communication in a specific language requires specific cultural training.**
>
>> *Detail 1:* **communication based on shared verbal meaning**
>>
>> *Detail 2:* **myth, literature, history of a culture preserved in specific language**
>>
>> *Detail 3:* . . .

> *Paragraph 2—main idea:* **Developing human personality traits requires human contact.**
>
>> *Detail 1:* **sense of humor** . . .
>>
>> *Detail 2:* . . .
>>
>> *Detail 3:* . . .

Paragraph 3—main idea: Becoming fully physically human is possible only in a human context.

Detail 1: walking upright . . .

Detail 2: example of Indian wolf-children . . .

Concluding paragraph—restate main idea: Discuss importance of studying different cultures to understand similarity of human traits beneath surface layer of variety.

1. Brainstorming an Outline for an Essay of Persuasion

The essay of persuasion, or the argumentative essay, is a frequent assignment in academic and professional writing. Your opinions for or against a particular point of view must be informed and well reasoned if they are to gain support from others. The composition of your argument need not be long, but it should be well formed, with clear, fully developed reasons for your assertions or ideas.

With your class, brainstorm the following topic: *the superiority/inferiority of natural fabrics (such as wool, cotton, linen, silk, leather) versus synthetic fabrics (such as nylon, polyester, rayon, plastic)*

List every advantage and disadvantage you can think of for each of the two subtopics; these will be written on the chalkboard. Cluster the brainstormed items into several main categories. These will be your main paragraphs. Arrange the items within each category into logical order. Choose a point of view and compose a sample topic statement for your outline. (Your instructor may ask you to continue your outline by choosing two or three categories that you might discuss and making a brief note outline of each with reasons, details, and examples.

2. Composing Outlines for Persuasive Essays

Examine the following topics and choose one to outline. Decide which point of view you would take in your essay. Write an introductory topic statement for your outline. Then think about two or three main categories that you will use to support your topic statement. Outline these categories by stating some details, reasons, and/or examples in brief note form.

a. Your college has received a $10,000 gift. Should it be used to install video games and a television set in the student cafeteria or lounge, to buy plants, paintings, and sculptures to place throughout the college, or for some other purpose (you specify)?

b. Discuss the advantage or disadvantage of a climate with four separate seasons versus a climate that is consistently warm or mild.

c. Discuss the superiority or inferiority of film (video, movies, television) versus print (books, magazines, newspapers) as a means of communication, entertainment, education.

d. Argue for or against the sharing of household chores and child care by the male member(s) of a family.

e. Support or refute the argument that sex education should be offered as part of the junior high or high school curriculum.

Composition Topics

1. In today's increasingly technological society, many students think that college courses in the liberal arts (art, music, philosophy, literature) are a waste of time. Do you agree or disagree? Write an essay in which you present two or three well-developed reasons why liberal arts courses should/should not be required for a college degree.

2. In times of economic difficulty, school systems often eliminate the study of art, music, sports, and foreign language from the curriculum as "frills" or nonessential subjects. Do you agree or disagree with this policy? State your reasons for your point of view in well-developed paragraphs that include details and examples.

Gender Roles in a Cross-Cultural Perspective

Professional restaurant chefs have traditionally been men, while women cooked at home for their families. Today, however, many women, like the student on the right, are pursuing careers in fields that were formerly reserved for men.

Freewrite

Choose one male and one female name from the telephone book. Imagine who they might be. Create a story or dialogue about these two people interacting with each other. Share your Freewrite and discuss any gender-role patterns that seem to appear.

Vocabulary in Context

You will need to know the meaning of the following words to fully comprehend the reading passage. Use your dictionary as necessary.

Verbs	Nouns	Adjectives	Adverbs
initiate	shrewdness	altruistic	
liberate	aesthetics	mundane	
diminish	repertoire	frivolous	
incorporate	aspiration	affluent	
	bias		

Synonyms
Match each word in column A with its synonym in column B.

A	B
altruistic _____	**1.** informative
repertoire _____	**2.** study of beauty
	3. ambitions
initiate _____	**4.** begin
aesthetics _____	**5.** study of morality
	6. nurturing
affluent _____	**7.** variety of skills
aspirations _____	**8.** wealthy
	9. a multicolored pattern
bias _____	**10.** prejudice

Antonyms
Match the vocabulary words in column A with their opposites in column B. Then fill in the blanks of the following sentences with either the appropriate vocabulary word or its antonym.

A		**B**
a. liberate	_____	**1.** increase
b. diminish	_____	**2.** radically
		3. ignorance
c. incorporate	_____	**4.** oppress
d. shrewdness	_____	**5.** exclude
		6. serious
e. mundane	_____	**7.** cultivate
f. frivolous	_____	**8.** biologically
		9. noble
		10. subconscious

g. According to socialist thinker Friedrich Engels, society must _____ women from their domestic role so they can take full part in public service and productive work.

h. As child-care and homemaking services for women _____ , women have more opportunity for education and careers.

i. Many American teachers unconsciously _____ sexist stereotypes into their teaching methods.

j. _____ in business is a valuable trait generally associated in the United States with men.

k. In the United States, personal adornment and home decorations are usually considered _____ aesthetic activities associated with women.

l. There is no logical reason why husbands should not share the daily _____ tasks of housekeeping, cooking, and laundry with their working wives.

Reading: Gender Roles in a Cross-Cultural Perspective

Key Concepts
- *Gender*
- *Male and female roles*
- *Gender identity*
- *Stereotypes*
- *Direct/unconscious gender instruction*

[1]   Sex refers to the *biological* differences between males and females, especially the visible differences in the sexual organs and the related differences in the role each sex plays in the reproductive process. Gender refers to the *social* classification of masculine and feminine. Every society recognizes the sexual division of the species into male and female, but cultures differ in terms of what they consider masculine and feminine. However, some male/female differences in behavior appear to be quite widespread. For example, males have been observed in various cultures to be more likely to **initiate** activity. Females have been observed to be more **altruistic,** that is, more helpful to others, than males. Again, however, we must be careful about assuming that most of the qualities typically associated with either men or women are "natural," that is, biologically based and universal. In American culture, for example, it is assumed that men are more "naturally" objective than women, that they can look at problems logically, without emotions distorting their views. Thus, it is argued, men are the "natural" sex to be scientists, lawyers, or historians, because they are comfortable dealing with "facts," with "objective reality." On the other hand, women in the United States are frequently perceived of as "naturally" subjective, emotional, and illogical, relying on their feelings to solve problems and handle difficulties in the "real world," as they supposedly do in their "natural" sphere of the home. Women are considered "naturally" vain about their appearance and "naturally" possessed with a maternal instinct, the inclination to nurture and protect children. In fact, there is nothing at all natural and universal about these stereotyped, sex-linked characteristics. They are, as are so many other deeply ingrained traits, the product of a specific cultural upbringing.

[2]   An important study of the relationship between sex and gender was carried out by anthropologist Margaret Mead in New Guinea. Mead studied three different cultures and found that male and female roles were patterned differently in each. For example, among the Arapesh, *both* men and women were expected to act in ways Americans consider "naturally" feminine: Both sexes were concerned with taking care of children, with nurturing in general. Neither sex was expected to be aggressive. In the second culture, the Mundugamor, *both* sexes were what Americans would call masculine—aggressive, violent, and with little interest in children. In the third society, the Tchambuli, the personalities of males and females were different from each other, but they were opposite to the American stereotyped conceptions of masculine and feminine. Women had the major economic role, showed common sense and business **shrewdness,** and carried out the **mundane** tasks. Men were interested in **aesthetics** and spent much time in decorating themselves, gossiping, and other **"frivolous"** activities. The men also had easily hurt feelings and sulked a lot.

[3]   Mead's study showed that the entire **repertoire** of behavior,

emotions, and interests that constitute being masculine and feminine is patterned by culture. In the process of growing up, each child learns hundreds of culturally patterned details of behavior that become **incorporated** into its gender identity. Some of this learning takes place directly, that is, the child is *told* by others how to act in appropriately   50 feminine or masculine ways. Other details of gender behavior are taught unconsciously, or indirectly, as the culture provides different images, **aspirations,** and adult models for girls and boys.

[4]   For example, a recent study of American public schools showed there is a cultural **bias** in education that favors boys over girls.   55 The bias is unintentional and unconscious, the researchers stated, but it is there nevertheless, and it is influencing the lives of millions of schoolchildren every year. Doctors David and Myra Sadker videotaped classroom teachers to study sex-related bias in education and reported that many teachers who thought they were nonsexist were amazed to   60 see how biased they appeared on videotape. From nursery school to postgraduate courses, teachers were shown to call on males in class far more than on female students. This behavior has a tremendous impact on the learning process, for in general, those students who become active classroom participants develop more positive attitudes and go on to   65 higher achievement. It may be added here, parenthetically, that in the late 1960s, when many of the fine all-women's colleges in the northeastern United States opened their doors to male students, it was observed by professors and women students alike that the boys were "taking over" the classroom discussions and that active participation by   70 women students had noticeably **diminished.** A similar subordination of female to male students has been observed in law and medical school classrooms in recent years.

[5]   The research done by the Sadkers showed that sometimes teachers, unknowingly, actually prevent girls from participating as actively as boys in class by assigning them different tasks in accordance   75 with stereotyped gender roles. For instance, one teacher conducting a scientific "experiment" with nursery school youngsters continually had the little boys perform the experiment while the girls were given the task of putting the materials away. Since working "hands on" with classroom materials is an important aspect of early education, the girls were   80 being deprived of a vital learning experience that would affect their entire lives.

[6]   Another dimension of sex-biased education is the typical American teacher's assumption that boys will do better in the "hard,"   85 "masculine" subjects of math and science, whereas girls are expected to have better verbal and reading skills. And in an example of self-fulfilling prophecy, American boys do, indeed, develop reading problems, whereas girls, who are superior to boys in math up to the age of nine, fall behind from then on. But, these patterns are cultural, not genetic.   90

In Germany, for example, *all* studies are considered "masculine," and it is girls who develop reading problems. And in Japan, where early education at least appears to be nonsexist, both girls and boys do equally well in reading.

[7]   The different attitudes that accompany the educational process for girls and boys begin at home. For example, one study showed that when preschoolers were asked to look at a picture of a house and tell how far from the house they were permitted to go, the boys indicated a much wider perimeter than the girls, who generally pointed out a limited area close to the home. Instead of being encouraged to develop intellectual curiosity and physical skills that are useful in dealing with the "outside" world, as boys are, girls are instilled with fears of the world outside the home and with the desire to be approved of for their "goodness" and obedience to rules. These lessons carry over from the home to the classroom, where girls are generally observed to be more dependent on the teacher, more concerned with the form and neatness of their work than with its content, and more anxious about being "right" in their answers than in being intellectually independent, analytical, or original. Thus through the educational process that occupies most of the child's waking hours, society reinforces its established values and develops each sex in its traditional and expected mold.

[8]   Male-female differences in behavior and personality have generally been explained in terms of biological differences. Only women can bear children, and only women can nurse them. This intimate connection between women and children has given women the major responsibilities for child care, although there is some cultural variability in the degree to which men also take care of their young offspring. Some theorists assume that biological factors will always prevent women from moving outside their traditional sexual-biological roles into economic or political roles outside the family. They state that even in the changing family structure of modernized societies, made possible by safe, easy contraception and bottle feeding, the role that will bring most fulfillment to women is the maternal–housekeeping one. These social scientists claim that the woman's role has always been essential in transmitting cultural values from one generation to the next and that this conservative function is a key to social stability. Its form will perhaps change somewhat, but in its most important aspects, it will remain what it has been in almost every culture for thousands of years.

[9]   Of course, even in today's **affluent** countries and in socialist countries that have tried to **liberate** women from domestic duties by providing large-scale day care, the primary female tasks are still childbearing, child rearing, and housekeeping. Certainly, there are examples of cultures in which women do more of the "outside" work than men: For instance, in many West African tribes and in Vietnam, women are the traders, at least on the local market level. In Russia, more women

95

100

105

110

115

120

125

130

135

than men are in the medical profession, and even in the affluent
United States, more than one-half of married women work outside the
home. Yet, one can hardly say that women's roles have changed radically. In many countries, the educational base has not really widened
sufficiently to include women, especially above the secondary levels.   140
And even where women have moved into the employment market on
a technical, business, or professional level, it has mainly been in areas
such as nursing, teaching, or clerical work, which represent an extension of traditional maternal–housekeeping roles. In the final analysis,
whether we are speaking of a Vietnamese market woman or an Amer-   145
ican nurse, the working woman is still universally burdened with the
responsibility for the home, the husband's welfare, and the children's
upbringing in addition to her labor outside the home. For most women,
the altruistic, nurturing qualities that are so deeply ingrained as to be
almost symbolic of womanhood are the basis of their identities and   150
the essence of their roles. Whether women on a large scale and not
just in scattered exceptional groups will be able to overcome eons of
social training to develop a new repertoire of psychological attitudes,
whether men will cultivate "feminine" qualities to a significant degree,
and whether men and women can be liberated from traditional role   155
and identity stereotypes are questions that demand our deepest consideration. But what does appear certain is that the basic biological
tendencies characteristic of one sex or the other are responsive to
every extreme of cultural conditioning.

Reading Comprehension

1. True–False

After each statement write *T* for true, *F* for false, or *NI* for no information,
according to the information given in the reading passage.

a. Gender is a term that refers to the physical or biological differences
between men and women. _____

b. American culture views women as emotional, irrational, and person-
centered. _____

c. According to anthropologist Margaret Mead, men in every New Guinea
culture are aggressive and violent. _____

d. The research of Doctors David and Myra Sadker demonstrated that
American schoolteachers have a bias in favor of male students.
_____

e. Boys are born with better abilities in math and science than girls.
_____

f. Throughout the world, females have a longer life span than males.
_____

g. Safe, easy birth control and bottle feeding of babies have had little influence on the lifestyle of modern women. _____

h. West Africa and Southeast Asia are similar in that women there play an important role in trading at local markets. _____

i. Increasingly, women have been entering such traditional male fields of work as dentistry and engineering. _____

2. *Short Essay Questions*

On a separate sheet of paper, write brief but complete answers to the following short essay questions. Use the reading as your base of information.

a. State the main conclusion Margaret Mead drew from her New Guinea study. On what evidence did she base her conclusion?

b. Describe at least two sex-biased aspects of American education as revealed by the Sadkers' study. Explain the extent to which the teachers were aware of their biased methods.

c. Contrast the different attitudes or behavior patterns that are characteristic of American preschool boys and girls as described in the reading.

d. Explain why the author considers bottle feeding of babies and safe, easy contraception as important developments for women. Explain why you agree or disagree.

e. The author states that female employment has been "mainly in areas *such as nursing, teaching, or clerical work, which represent an extension of traditional maternal—housekeeping roles.*" What is meant by the italicized part of the statement? Does the author view the increasing employment of women in these areas as a true role change for women? Explain your answer.

f. In the last paragraph, the author asks whether men will cultivate "feminine" qualities. What are the feminine qualities being referred to? To what extent do you think men can or should cultivate (develop) them?

3. *Analyzing the Text*

Circle the number of the best response to each given statement.

a. In paragraph [1], the author states, "However, some male/female differences in behavior appear to be quite widespread." *However* signals that this sentence

      (1) contradicts the idea previously stated.
      (2) continues the idea previously stated.
      (3) results from the idea previously stated.
      (4) agrees with the idea previously stated.

b. The main idea of paragraph [1] is that
      (1) women are naturally more emotional than men.
      (2) men are naturally fitted to be lawyers and scientists.
      (3) some sex-linked characteristics are developed by culture.
      (4) some sex-linked characteristics are universal.

c. Mundugamor men and women both had violent, aggressive personalities and little interest in children. In this context, *interest* means
      (1) extra income earned from savings.
      (2) special concern or affection.
      (3) a legal share or title in something.
      (4) a prejudice or bias in favor of something.

d. In the Tchambuli culture, women had the major economic role and showed common sense and business shrewdness. *Common sense* is a trait that the author
      (1) probably considers immature.
      (2) probably dislikes.
      (3) probably considers to be masculine.
      (4) probably doesn't understand.

e. The purpose of Mead's study described in paragraph [2] was to
      (1) provide socioeconomic information about three different New Guinea tribes.
      (2) contrast male-female behavior in the area of aesthetic values.
      (3) explore how gender identity is patterned by culture.
      (4) prove that sex-linked behavior is genetic.

f. According to the Sadkers' study,
      (1) American education contains some unconscious sexist bias.
      (2) class participation is closely related to future academic achievement.
      (3) American schoolgirls show superior math ability to boys in the early grades.
      (4) all of the above

g. According to paragraph [8], which aspect of culture derived from the biological differences between men and women?
      (1) control over property
      (2) relationship between women and children
      (3) use of contraception
      (4) political inferiority of women

h. Paragraph [8] describes a social theory that could best be described as
      (1) radical.
      (2) conservative.
      (3) futuristic.
      (4) evolutionary.

   i. Paragraph [9]'s statement that "one can hardly say that women's roles have changed radically" is supported by

      (1) one personal anecdote.

      (2) four reasons.

      (3) two brief illustrations.

      (4) no specifics at all.

   j. Which of the following does the author consider important to the new gender roles possible for women today and in the future?

      (1) an increase in altruism among males

      (2) safe contraception methods and bottle feeding of babies

      (3) more anthropological studies of gender roles

      (4) increased presentation of feminine gender roles in the media

   k. The primary aim of this chapter's reading is to

      (1) show that violence and aggression are inborn male characteristics.

      (2) show that biology is the main influence on gender roles.

      (3) present information on the cultures of New Guinea.

      (4) examine cultural influences on gender-role development.

4. *Applying Concepts from Reading*

▪ **Gender Roles in Your Culture.** Roles are the parts we play in our social group. They may be assigned to us on the basis of our sex, our position in the family, our economic and social status, or our age. In this chapter we are primarily concerned with gender roles (the assignment of roles by sex). Study the following role situations. Be prepared to state whether in your culture a male, female, or a person of either sex would be most likely to take the given role.

   a. Cook the dinner daily.

   b. Wash the dinner dishes.

   c. Wash the windows.

   d. Do the laundry.

   e. Handle money for ordinary expenses.

   f. Purchase the tickets for family travel.

   g. Check the family into a hotel.

   h. Buy wine or liquor for family consumption or for guests.

   i. Visit a child's teacher.

   j. Take a child to the doctor.

   k. Make coffee or tea for visitors.

   l. Serve alcoholic beverages to visitors.

   m. Go to lunch in a restaurant with a friend of the same sex.

   n. Conduct religious services.

   o. Teach elementary school.

What do you think is the reason for the masculine or feminine association with each of these acts within your culture: physical strength, nonworking

In the past, only exceptional women, such as former slave Harriet Tubman (left), broke away from traditional women's roles. During the American Civil War, Tubman fought with Northern troops and led many slaves to freedom. Today, many women, such as this telephone repair person (right), are entering traditionally male occupations. Is this true in your native culture?

time available, "natural" interest or personality traits of one sex or the other, economic factors, biological/sexual factors?

- **How Gender Identity Is Taught.** The reading states that gender identity is taught both directly and indirectly, or unconsciously. Respond to the following items either orally or in writing, as directed by your instructor. Some examples are provided.

   a.   State one explicit, or direct, instruction given to boys in your culture that helps to form their masculine gender identity. (Example: American boys are told not to cry when they are physically hurt.)

   b.   State one explicit, or direct, instruction given to girls in your culture that helps to form their feminine gender identity.

   c. An English nursery rhyme says that boys are made of "snakes and snails and puppy dogs' tails," while girls are made of "sugar and spice and everything nice." What indirect, or unconscious, gender identity instruction is being given through this rhyme? Can you give examples of similar rhymes or proverbs in your language or culture? What indirect gender identity instruction do they provide?

   d. What are some traditional toys given to boys in your culture? What kind of activity or behavior do they encourage? What kind of toys do girls normally receive in your culture? What kind of activity or behavior do they encourage? (Example: American boys are often given a baseball or football to play with, which encourages physical activities such as throwing, catching, and running.)

   e. Who are some of the most famous popular figures or adult models in your culture? What are their most prominent characteristics? What do you think they teach about gender identity?

   f. Bring to class an American newspaper or magazine advertisement or describe a television commercial that features a male, a female, or a couple. What do you think these advertisements unconsciously teach about sex roles and gender identity?

Vocabulary Study

1. Word Meaning in Context

Use your dictionary as necessary to decide if the italicized word is employed correctly in the sentence where it appears. Write *C* if it is correct. If it is not correct, write *NC* and revise the sentence to demonstrate the correct use of the italicized word. Use separate paper for your new sentences.

   a. Doctors, lawyers, and engineers are taught to approach problems *logically*. _____

   b. The instructor gave her students an *objective* multiple-choice examination as a final. _____

   c. Men and women may *impact* differently to the same situation because their social training is different. _____

   d. It is a *stereotyped* view of women to believe that they cannot perform hard physical labor. _____

   e. The exercise of power and the quality of *subordination* are characteristic of those who control the lives of other people. _____

   f. The audience showed its *assumption* of the pianist by applauding loudly for five minutes. _____

g. You gain an added *dimension* to your life when you participate in local or national politics. _____

h. The two aspirins I just took have *reinforced* my headache. _____

i. *Theorists* claim that they commit crimes such as bank robbery or hijacking for political reasons. _____

j. The position of women has changed *radically* in the past 100 years. _____

2. *Word Form Table*

Fill in the following table with the appropriate forms of the given words. Some nouns or adjectives may have two forms.

	Verbs	Nouns	Adjectives	Adverbs
a.	sulk	_____	_____	_____
b.	initiate	_____	_____	_____
c.	_____	universality	_____	_____
d.	xxx	shrewdness	_____	_____
e.	_____	_____	characteristic	_____

Use the correct form from each lettered line to complete the same lettered sentence below.

a. A _____ child who always wants his or her own way is not a pleasant playmate.

b. Some people's _____ reaction to new or unusual foods is to refuse to taste them.

c. Gender roles in children _____ develop at an early age.

d. Women are considered to be _____ traders in many parts of Asia and Africa.

e. One should not _____ all women as maternal or altruistic; that would be stereotyping the female sex.

3. *Word Formation*

Suffix *ic:* frequent adjective ending signifying "of the nature of," "consisting of," "characterized by," or "belonging to"; often used for ethnic or regional adjectives.

angelic	characteristic (of)	classic
dramatic	altruistic	historic
frantic	romantic	comic/tragic
Nordic, Slavic	fantastic	volcanic

Use as many of the following words as you can in a brief paragraph on the broad topic of gender roles and identity. You may change the word forms (part of speech; singular/plural) of any word with an asterisk (*), but do not change the others.

altruistic	domestic	initiate*
analytic	fantastic	responsibility*
artistic	frivolous*	romantic
characteristic	genetic	universal*

Writing Exercises

Structures for Comparison and Contrast

A frequent requirement in academic and technical writing is comparison or contrast of data. In **comparing** subjects, the focus is on their similarities or likenesses. In **contrasting** subjects, the emphasis is on their differences or dissimilarities.

Adjectives and Adverbs

[1] **Adjectives in the Comparative Form.** This form is used to compare two subjects.

One-syllable adjectives: Add *er* or *r* to the base (*smart* becomes *smarter*).
Two-syllable adjectives ending in *y:* Drop the *y* and add *ier* (*pretty* becomes *prettier*).
Most other two- and three-syllable adjectives form the comparative with *more* or *less* (*more altruistic, less affluent*).

[2] **Adjectives in the Superlative Form.** Adjectives in this form are used to compare three or more subjects.

The *er* form of adjective becomes *est* (*smarter* becomes *smartest*).
The *ier* form of adjective becomes *iest* (*prettier* becomes *prettiest*).
More or *less* preceding the adjective becomes *(the) most, (the) least* (*[the] most altruistic, [the] least affluent*).

[3] **Irregular Adjectives.** The most common irregular adjectives take the following comparative and superlative forms.

good—better—best
bad—worse—worst
much, many—more—most
little—less—least

1. Sentence Composition with Comparative Adjectives

Column A contains a list of paired sentence subjects. Column B contains a list of adjectives. Use a separate sheet of paper to compose ten sentences of comparison using any of the paired subjects with any one of the given adjectives.

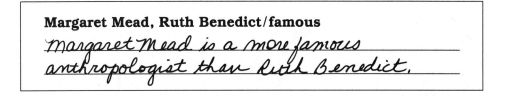

Margaret Mead, Ruth Benedict/famous

Margaret Mead is a more famous anthropologist than Ruth Benedict.

A	B
preschool boys, preschool girls	busy
young people, old people	skeptical
participants, nonparticipants	sociable
teenage boys, teenage girls	independent
the United States, China	lazy
urban, rural	radical
philosophy, botany	traditional
women, men	altruistic
businesswomen, homemakers	sophisticated
computer science, art history	smart
brother (sister, cousin), friend	aggressive
	abstract
	easy

2. Sentence Construction with Superlative Adjectives

Change the given adjective in each item to its superlative form. Then use the given items in any order to construct sentences with superlative adjectives. Study the examples as a guide.

> **aggressive: Semai   people   world**
>
> **The Semai people of Malaysia are among the *least aggressive* of the world.**
>
> **bad: poverty   humanity   problem**
>
> **Poverty and illiteracy are two of humanity's *worst problems*.**

a. important: culture   aspect   development
b. dark: December   afternoons   year
c. altruistic: universally   women
d. little: Sam   energy   on the team
e. radical: young people   political writers   the United States
f. lively: two-year-olds   group   day care center
g. high: intelligence test scores   middle class
h. bad: Asians   reaction   dairy products
i. lonely: studies   rural women   American population
j. lazy: sloth(n.)   one of the   animal kingdom

[4] Adverbs in the Comparative Form. These adverbs are used to compare the ways in which verb action is performed by two subjects.

One-syllable adverbs: Add *er* to the base form (walks *faster*).
Two- or more syllable adverbs form the comparative with *more* or *less* (speaks *more slowly*, acts *less quickly*).

[5] Adverbs in the Superlative Form. Superlative adverbs are used to compare the ways in which verb action is performed by three or more subjects.

The *er* form of the adverb becomes *est* (*faster* becomes *fastest*).
More and *less* become *(the) most* and *(the) least* (talks *[the] most rapidly*, drives *[the] least carefully*).

[6] Irregular Adverbs. The most common irregular adverbs take the following comparative and superlative forms.

well — better — best
badly — worse — worst
much — more — most
little — less — least

1. *Paragraph Completion*

Each of the following sentences is a main idea statement. Write three or four sentences to complete the paragraph. Give some specific information that includes comparison of adjectives and adverbs. The first one has been partly done.

a. Boys and girls behave differently in school.

Boys volunteer more than girls do and are stronger in their opinions. Girls do neater work in general and have larger vocabularies than boys.

b. I prefer reading a newspaper to watching the news on TV.

_____

_____

_____

_____

c. Dancing is a different kind of exercise than (name sport).

_____

_____

_____

_____

d. My personality is different from my sister's (cousin's, friend's).

_____

_____

_____

_____

e. My culture's New Year's celebration (or some other holiday) is different from the way most Americans celebrate the New Year.

_____

_____

_____

_____

Gender-specialized activities occur in all cultures, although they prevail more in some culture areas, such as the Middle East, than in others. Here, an exclusively male group of Arab falconers prepares for a game-bird hunting expedition. Discuss some exclusively male social activities in your culture. What are some social activities in which only females participate?

f.   There are more advantages (or disadvantages) to living in a large city than in a small town (suburb, rural area).

_____

_____

_____

_____

_____

_____

_____

_____

_____

Signals of Comparison and Contrast

[1]   **Signal Expressions of Comparison.**   These suggest relationships of similarity between subjects. They may be used in different structural patterns.

Generalizations of Comparison

> American working women *share many common traits*
> *have characteristics in common*
> *have features in common*
>
> with working women all over the world.
>
> American working women *are similar to* working women *resemble* *are like*
>
> all over the world in many ways.

Specific Comparisons

> American working women carry the double burden of a job and housework. *Similarly,* working women all over the world carry this double burden.
>
> Working women all over the world *also* carry this double burden.
>
> Working women all over the world carry this double burden *also.* *too.*

> *Both* American working women and working women all over the world carry the double burden of a job and housework.
>
> The *conditions* of working women *are as hard as* those of men. Women *work as fast as* men.

[2]   **Signal Expressions of Contrast.**   These emphasize the difference between subjects. They may be used in different structural patterns.

Generalizations of Contrast

Boys and girls *differ from each other* in behavior at school.
are different from each other.
behave differently from (you can substitute
                       any verb, for
                       example, *function*).

Boys *have different* behavior patterns in school than girls.
(You can substitute any object.)

Specifics Contrasted

Boys are quite active in classroom discussions;

on the other hand, girls are generally more passive.
however,
in contrast,

Boys are quite active in classroom discussions, *but* girls are generally passive.

Boys, *in contrast to* girls, are quite active in classroom
         unlike

discussions.

Although/Whereas boys are quite active in classroom discussion, girls are generally more passive.

---

1. Scanning for Statements of Contrast

Quickly read paragraphs [4] and [5] of the reading selection. Underscore the signals of contrast that you find. Then as a class, discuss the statements of contrast signaled by these expressions.

2. Sentence Completion

Use structurally appropriate signals of comparison or contrast to complete the sentences. Use information from the reading selection or your own experience and knowledge for the content of your answers. The first one is done for you.

a. Educated women throughout the world _*share*_ _*many*_ _*common*_ _*traits*_ .

b. Men in the Arapesh tribe are "masculine" in the American sense, _____ Tchambuli men act in ways that Americans consider feminine.

c. _____ the Arapesh men and the Mundugamor men of New Guinea demonstrate aggressive, violent behavior.

d. Margaret Mead's ideas about culturally patterned gender roles _____ _____ _____ my own.

e. American educators try to be free of sexual bias in their teaching; _____ , their videotaped lessons show sex-linked stereotyping.

f. In Japan, _____ the United States, education appears to be nonsexist in the early grades.

g. _____ boys and girls in Japan do equally well in reading. In Germany, _____ _____ _____ the United States, boys read well _____ girls have reading problems.

h. The home and the school have _____ _____ _____ _____ regarding the education of boys and girls. The home teaches girls to be passive and restrained, and the school does _____ .

i. _____ some social scientists take a conservative view of women's roles in the future, others see radical changes taking place.

j. In Russia and in China there are many women doctors. This _____ _____ the situation in the United States, where most women medical workers are nurses or technicians.

k. Where two _____ jobs are done by men and women, the   women   should   receive   the _____ pay _____ the men.

l. Political and social freedom often occur at the _____ time.

m. It is true that a few jobs in today's world require physical strength beyond that of the average woman. _____ , technology has equalized most jobs so that women can perform most of the _____ work _____ men.

3. *Sentence Expansion*

Expand the given statements by adding a clause (or new sentence) of contrast or comparison using any of the expressions from the preceding examples. Rewrite your new sentences on a separate sheet of paper.

> **The single, official language of the United States is English.**
>
> **The single, official language of the United States is English; *however,* in Canada, English and French are both official languages.**

a. American schools place great importance on individual expression.
b. Americans place a high value on punctuality.
c. In America, people usually eat their biggest meal in the evening.
d. More than one-half of American women work outside the home.
e. Television is an important influence in American life.
f. Most suburban American youngsters learn to drive at the age of sixteen.
g. Many American high school students smoke cigarettes and drink alcohol.

4. *Paragraph Construction*

The expressions of comparison and contrast in the following paragraph provide clues for the completion of the sentences. Add as many words or sentences in the blank spaces as you need to express your thoughts.

Mothers who work outside the home and those who are homemakers are similar to each other in several aspects. They both _____

_____

Similarly, they may _____

_____

The mother who works outside the home, in the same way as the house-keeping mother, _____

_____

But there are some important differences in the _____

_____

Mothers who work outside the home _____

but housekeeping mothers _____

In contrast to mothers who work outside the home, housekeeping mothers _____

_____

Although mothers who work outside the home must _____

_____

housekeeping mothers _____

Small Group Assignment

Discussion of a Literary Passage

Margaret Mead's gender study in New Guinea demonstrated that the entire repertoire of behavior, emotions, and interests that comprise being masculine and feminine are patterned by culture. In the process of growing up, each child learns hundreds of culturally patterned details of behavior that become incorporated into its gender identity. Literature, as well as life, supports Mead's view. Read the following translated passage from Anatole France's novel, *The Crime of Sylvester Bonnard*,* in which Bonnard, now an old man, remembers an incident from his childhood.

I recall my desires as a child. . . . I can see once more, with astonishing vividness, a certain doll which, when I was eight years old, used to be displayed in the window of an ugly little shop of the Rue de la Seine. I cannot tell you how it happened that this doll attracted me. I was very proud of being a boy; I despised little girls; and I longed impatiently for the day (which alas! has come) when a strong white beard should bristle

The Crime of Sylvester Bonnard by Anatole France, trans. by Lafcadio Hearn, 1918. Reprinted by permission of Harper & Row Publishers, Inc.

on my chin. I played at being soldier; and under the pretext of getting
my horse something to eat, I used to make a sad wreck of the plants my
poor mother kept on her windowsill. Those were manly amusements, I
should say. And nevertheless, I was consumed with longing for a
doll. . . . Was the one I had fallen in love with at all beautiful? No. I can
see her now. She had a splotch of vermillion on either cheek, short soft
arms, horrible wooden hands, and long sprawling legs. Her flowered
petticoat was fastened at the waist with two pins. . . . But I loved her in
spite of all; I loved her just for her coarseness; I loved her only; I wanted
her. My soldiers and my drums had become nothing in my eyes. That
doll was all the world to me.

I was unhappy. An unreasoning but irresistible shame prevented me
from telling my mother about the object of my love. Thus all my
sufferings. For many days that doll, incessantly present in my
imagination, danced before my eyes, stared fixedly at me, opened her
arms to me, assuming in my imagination a sort of life which made her
appear at once mysterious and weird, and thereby all the more charming
and desirable.

Finally, one day—a day I shall never forget—my uncle, Captain
Victor, invited me to breakfast. I admired my uncle very much, because
he had fired the last French shot at the Battle of Waterloo. My uncle
Victor also inspired me with much respect by his military coat, and still
more, by his way of turning the whole house upside down from the
moment he came into it. . . . My uncle put on his frogged coat and we
went down into the street. When we came to the Rue de la Seine, the
idea of my doll suddenly returned to my mind and excited me in an
extraordinary way. My head was on fire. I resolved upon a desperate
expedient. We were passing before the window. She was there, behind
the glass, with her red cheeks, her flowered petticoat, and her long legs.

"Uncle," I said, with a great effort, "will you buy that doll for me?"
And I waited.

"Buy a doll for a boy—*sacré bleu!*"* cried my uncle, in a voice of
thunder. "Do you wish to dishonor yourself? And is it that old ugly doll
there that you want! Well, I must compliment you, my young friend. If
you grow up with such tastes as that, you will never have any pleasure in
life; and your comrades will call you a precious fool. If you asked me for
a sword or a gun, my boy, I would buy them for you with the last silver
crown of my pension. But to buy a doll for you—a thousand thunders!—
to disgrace you! Never in the world! Why, if I were ever to see you
playing with a puppet dressed up like that, I would disown you for my
nephew though you are my sister's son!"

On hearing these words, I felt my heart so wrung that nothing but
pride—a diabolic pride—kept me from crying. . . . I felt an unspeakable

Sacré bleu is a French oath, equivalent to "oh my God!"

shame. My resolve was quickly made. I promised myself never to disgrace myself—I firmly and forever renounced that red-cheeked doll.

Discuss the following questions with your group. Prepare brief but complete written answers to the questions and then share them with your class.

1. In what way was young Sylvester Bonnard typical of little boys in your culture? In what ways was he different?
2. What kind of a role model was Uncle Victor for young Sylvester?
3. Young Sylvester had "mixed feelings" about the doll. Describe the different emotions he felt toward it and explain their source where possible.
4. Why did Uncle Victor refuse to buy the doll for his nephew? To what extent was his response the result of cultural training? What are some of the key words that indicate culture's role in forming Uncle Victor's gender identity?
5. What lesson did young Sylvester learn from this experience?

Composing: Recalling a Lesson in Gender Roles

Think about an incident in your life when an older relative, friend, or teacher tried to teach you a lesson in appropriate gender behavior. How did you feel about this lesson?

Composition Development

Comparison and Contrast

Comparisons are explanations of *similarities,* or likenesses, of two or more related subjects. Things compared are not identical, but they share substantial similarities. **Contrasts** explore the *differences* of two or more related subjects. Things contrasted have some point of similarity, or a contrast would be meaningless (as a contrast between tennis and poetry would be), but the emphasis in development is on their differences.

An essay of comparison or contrast must have (1) a clearly stated *topic,* (2) a logical *purpose,* (3) meaningful *types* to illustrate the topic, (4) significant *points* about the topic, and (5) concrete *details* about the points and types discussed.

Developing Compositions of Contrast: Two Approaches

[1] **Point Approach.**   In the point approach, the body of a paper is organized *by choosing important points for discussion* and illustrating each

point by contrasting types. Examine the following outline of the reading from Chapter Five for the point approach to contrast.

Topic sentence: Perceptions of time are different in different cultures, and these perceptions are culturally patterned.
Point 1: keeping track of time
Types: Americans concerned with being *on time*
Sioux have no word for "late"
Point 2: sense of future
Types: Americans oriented toward foreseeable future
Navajo skeptical about any future
Hindus conceive of indefinite future
Point 3: time as a commodity
Types: nonindustrial people allow time for sociability
Americans view time as money

In the point approach, **expressions of contrast** are continually needed *to link together the contrasting types.*

[2] Type (Block) Approach. In the type (block) approach, the body of the paper is organized by *choosing target types and discussing each type separately* in terms of several points. Examine the following outline of the reading from Chapter Three for the type approach to contrast.

Topic sentence: All aspects of sexual life are patterned and regulated by culture. A study of two cultures, the Irish of Inis Beag and the Polynesians of Mangaia, makes clear the role of culture in this area of life.
Type 1: Inis Beag
Point 1: sexually naive
Point 2: no discussions of sex at home
Point 3: nudity abhorred; no sexual jokes
Point 4: no premarital sex
Type 2: Mangaians
Point 1: sex a major interest of life
Point 2: sexual information transmitted by elders
Point 3: continual public reference to sex
Point 4: premarital relations common

In the type approach, **a transitional sentence** is needed *to introduce the second type* after discussion of the first type is completed.

1. *Sentence Reordering: Paragraph of Contrast*

Your instructor will divide the class in half. One-half of the class, either individually or in small groups, will reorder the following sentences into one paragraph of contrast using the point approach. The other half of the class will reorder the sentences into one paragraph of contrast using the type approach. Rewrite the sentences according to the assigned approach. Before beginning, read the introductory topic statement.

Japanese adults readily accept dependency needs in themselves and in others, whereas Americans place a high value on independence in themselves and in those with whom they have close relationships. Infant-care attitudes appear to be significant in the development of these two different types of personality development.

a. American infants sleep from twelve to sixteen hours a day.
b. Japanese infants are usually passive when awake.
c. Japanese mothers have close physical and emotional attachments to their children.
d. American mothers spend about four hours a day feeding, dressing, and diapering their infants.
e. Japanese mothers often soothe and quiet their babies.
f. American mothers spend a great deal of time positioning their babies' limbs and talking to them.
g. Japanese infants spend close to four hours a day being fed, dressed, and diapered.
h. American babies spend most of their waking time in an active manner, playing with their limbs and toys.
i. Japanese babies sleep approximately fourteen hours a day.
j. American mothers encourage their infants' physical and vocal responsiveness.
k. Japanese mothers spend a lot of time rocking, lulling, and carrying their babies.
l. American mothers view their babies as separate persons.

Have you noticed that some of the points about the Japanese and Americans are similar? Which points are these? Would you put these points of comparison at the beginning or the end of the paragraph? Why?

Now, individually or in groups, as directed by your instructor, turn your reordered sentences into a coherent paragraph by providing expressions of comparison or contrast or transitional sentences where needed.

2. *Constructing an Essay of Contrast: Point Approach*

The information in the following columns is derived from a magazine article that contrasts the Japanese and American systems of schooling. The data are listed in logical order. Some of the data compare the two countries or systems, but most contrast the two countries or systems. Use the following directions to compose your essay.

a. Carefully read the given data. In the blank space, write *Comp.* if the information about the United States and Japan is similar; write *Contr.* if the information is different.

b. Decide on two subtopics that would include the given data in two paragraphs of the body of your essay. You will be using the point approach, in which you combine information about the two contrasted subjects in one paragraph.

c. Study the given introduction, which makes a connection between education and successful industrialization.

d. Then proceed to construct an essay of contrast that incorporates all or most of the given data in any logical order you wish into a two-paragraph body. Pay particular attention to the use of signals of contrast as you move from statements about Japan to statements about the United States.

Today, Japan, like the United States, is a highly industrialized nation with a democratic political system. However, according to many observers, Japan is moving ahead of the United States educationally—which promises a brighter economic future for Japan. What are some of the differences between Japan and the United States that are giving Japan its current edge?

A. Japan	**B. The United States**
(1) currently experiencing great industrial growth	industrially based economy since 1940s
(2) belief that success in school equals success in job	belief that success in school equals success in life
(3) universal education through ninth grade	universal education through age sixteen or end of high school
(4) homogeneous society with few non-Japanese subcultures	heterogeneous society with many subcultures
(5) small, densely populated island	large nation; some isolated rural areas
(6) affluent urban centers	many low-economic inner cities

(7)   key values: obedience, industry, conformity, stability

key values: personal liberty, material comfort, mobility

_____

(8)   male-dominated society; few wives work outside the home

increasing female participation in all social, political, and economic areas

_____

(9)   mostly two-parent and extended families

many single-parent families; few extended families

_____

(10)   centralized schools; standardized courses and texts

decentralized schools; local governments decide all aspects of system

_____

(11)   school funding distributed fairly evenly through all districts

affluent school districts have more funding than poor ones

_____

(12)   teachers: high prestige, great authority over children

teachers: medium status, little authority over students

_____

(13)   large classes: forty to forty-five

medium classes: twenty-five to thirty-five

_____

(14)   students stay with same teacher two years

students stay with same teacher six months to one year

_____

(15)   students rotate responsibility for school maintenance: cleaning rooms and halls, gardening, cafeteria

students only minimally participate in school maintenance

_____

(16)   instruction is mostly rote memorization

variety of instructional methods; individual and group work; discussion

_____

(17)	little attention to exceptionally bright or slow students	many different classes for bright and slow students
		_____
(18)	low drop-out rate	high drop-out rate
		_____
(19)	all mothers active in PTA	few mothers active in PTA
		_____
(20)	national testing for ninth-grade exit	no national testing in public education
		_____
(21)	college entrance quite restricted	wide opportunities for variety of post-high school education
		_____

Write your own conclusion to your essay.

3. *Expanding a Paragraph into a Comparative or Contrastive Essay*

The following paragraph was written by a student about the current condition of women in his nation, Somalia, which is on the east coast of Africa. Read the paragraph and edit it as directed by the guide.

(1) Nowadays, women in Somalia are independent and self-determined. (2) They have maintained getting their complete rights by the supportance of the new government. (3) It's very easy for them to obtain the highest degree in education. (4) Schools are banded all over the country, and men have lost their priority in education. (5) Anyway, men have been familiar in seeing women working in all the fields. (6) They have gained the opportunities of being doctors, engineers, and officers in the military service. (7) All I have mentioned wasn't the real battle the women had for their self-determination. (8) The more complicated point they have faced was getting independent from their families. (9) It wasn't easy for the parents to see their daughters living in other apartments before getting married. (10) I still remember an argument I have had with a girlfriend while were were discussing women's rights in our country. (11) She said, "Men's empire has been broken."

a. This composition is basically a unified, coherent paragraph with a clear topic statement, three separate main points or aspects of the topic, and a conclusion. Identify each of these elements.

b. There are some vocabulary difficulties that obscure meaning or sound nonidiomatic. Edit the following: *maintained getting; supportance* (sentence 2); *are banded* (sentence 4); *have been familiar in seeing* (sentence 5); *getting independent* (sentence 8).

c. What signal word or expression is needed to indicate the relationship between sentences 6 and 7?

d. The present perfect tense should be used for actions begun in the past and continuing to the present. The simple past should be used for actions completed in the past. Check the uses of the present perfect tense in sentences 2, 4, 5, 6, 7, 8, 10, and 11. Which might you change for clearer communication?

e. Does the concluding quotation enrich or confuse the writer's main idea? How could you utilize the writer's conclusion as a transition to the opening of your paragraph about women's status in your culture?

Now think about the current conditions of women in your culture. Are they similar to or different from those described for Somalian women? Use the type (block) approach to expand the preceding paragraph into a full-length essay in which you add a paragraph that compares or contrasts the women in your culture with the Somalian women. Be sure to refer to the same points of comparison or contrast that are made in the student's paragraph. Write an appropriate brief introduction and conclusion to your essay.

4. *Block Approach Contrast*

The following paragraph has been written in the type (block) approach to contrast two different types of clothing worn by rural peasants in Latin America. Underscore the transitional sentence that moves the paragraph from a description of one type of clothing to the description of the other.

Latin American peasant clothing for daily use differs significantly from that worn on special occasions. Everyday clothing is sturdy and comfortable. It is frequently made of undyed, homespun, coarsely woven cotton that is relatively inexpensive to make or buy. The decoration, if any, is quite simple, and it uses only one or two colors of thread. On the other hand, clothing for special use is quite elaborate. Although such special clothing has the comfortable shape of everyday garments, it is woven of more finely spun cotton or even silk. Special shawls may be so fine that they can be drawn through a finger ring. The embroidery on festive garments may be heavy and intricate and employ many different colored threads. Such garments may be worn only a few times a year, and they are passed on to one's children.

Now consider whether clothing is or is not different depending on its daily or special use in your culture. Write an essay with two paragraphs for the body into which you incorporate some of the information about Latin American peasant clothing. You may write an essay of comparison or contrast in either the point or type (block) approach. Write an appropriate brief introduction and conclusion to your essay. Be precise in your use of signal words for comparison or contrast.

5. *Paragraph Combining*

The following sentences derive from a student essay on the topic of working mothers. Combine the sentence elements to form a well-developed paragraph. Make whatever changes are necessary for sentence correctness. Add appropriate signal words of addition, reversal of thought, cause-effect, example, comparison/contrast, condition, and time order.

Rewrite your new paragraph on a separate sheet of paper. The complete main idea sentence is given to you in (1).

(1) Today more women are working than ever before.

(2) Some have their own businesses.
(3) Others have jobs.

(4) They want to work outside the home.
(5) This is in the society.
(6) This is just as men do.
(7) This is for many reasons.

(8) They believe that working is good for women.
(9) They believe that working women are good.
(10) The goodness is for the economy.

(11) This may be true.
(12) Mothers who work outside the home are not good for children.
(13) These children need care.
(14) The care is by their mothers.

(15) My mother is working in a factory.
(16) My mother is studying at school.
(17) This school is at night.

(18) My mother wants to work.
(19) The reason is to have more money.
(20) This is for the family.

(21) My mother wants to study.
(22) The reason is to gain more knowledge.
(23) The reason is to have more experiences.

(24) Every day my mother goes out at 8:00 A.M.
(25) Every day my mother comes back at 10:00 P.M.
(26) This is a situation.
(27) This is not good for me.
(28) This is not good for my brothers.

(29) My brothers go to school.
(30) I go to school.

(31) We don't eat lunches at home.
(32) We don't eat dinners at home.

(33) We see my parents.
(34) This is in the morning.
(35) This is for a few minutes.
(36) This is the only time.

(37) I don't like to come home for dinner.
(38) No one is home.
(39) I spend a lot of time with friends.
(40) I study at the library.

(41) Home is a lonely place.
(42) Mothers work long hours.
(43) Mothers also study.

(44) Mothers can't spend time with their children.
(45) The time is enough.

(46) The children will have lives.
(47) The lives will be their own.
(48) Their lives will be different from their parents' lives.

(49) That is too bad.
(50) Mothers should be an influence.
(51) The influence should be the biggest.
(52) The influence should be in lives.
(53) The lives are of their children.

Composition Topics

1. It is true that working mothers bring some advantages to themselves and their families. However, it is also true that the families of working mothers suffer many disadvantages. Therefore, some claim, mothers

should make every effort not to work until their children are fully grown.

Do you agree or disagree? Support your point of view with explanations, reasons, and examples from your reading and life experience.

2. Several recent court decisions have given the care of children in divorce cases to the father rather than the mother. The judges believe that fathers can provide equally good parenting as mothers.

Do you agree or disagree with this point of view? Discuss this issue, supporting your opinions with facts, reasons, and illustrations.

9

Emotion and Motion:
A Cross-Cultural View

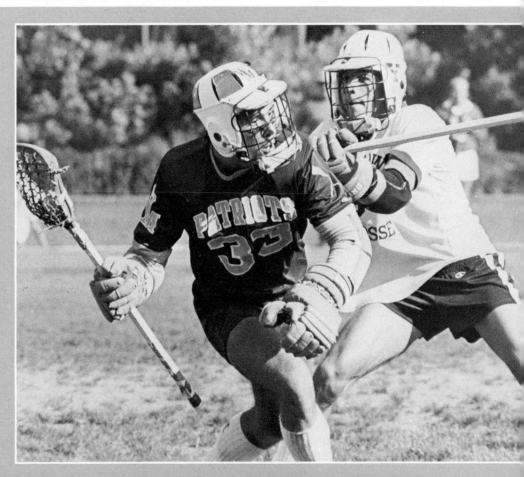

Participation in sports like lacrosse, shown here, develops eye-hand coordination, speed, and dexterity of body and limb movement. The physical movements and team spirit associated with these sports can heavily influence the motor patterns and emotional traits of adult life. What physical skills and emotional patterns are associated with sports in your culture? Are these the same for men and for women? Explain.

Freewrite

Closely observe people in some busy place, such as at a street crossing or on a train. Note their physical movements and gestures. What emotional or mental states does their behavior suggest to you?

Vocabulary in Context

Verbs	**Nouns**	**Adjectives**	**Adverbs**
confront	hostility	relevant	
predominate	contempt	inevitable	
accentuate	compensation	perfunctory	
convey			
derive			

Guessing Meaning from Context

Read the following passage. As you come to each italicized word, note down a definition or synonym of your own *without* using a dictionary. When you have finished the passage, consult a dictionary to check your definitions. How correct were you? Where you were not correct, did you misunderstand the statement at that point?

Some current research is trying to *confront* the increasing problem of mental illness in American life. Many studies convey the surprising information that mental illness is on the rise faster in small town and rural populations than in the large cities. Emotional pressure may *derive* from such stressful urban situations as subway rush hours. But it seems that such stressful situations have less of an *impact* on the mental and emotional health of big city residents than might be expected. Long-term residents of large cities seem to develop nearly *instinctual* stimuli-reducing mechanisms that protect them from feeling stress in certain habitual conditions. The media *accentuate* the impersonality, *hostility,* or just plain "craziness" that *inevitably* characterizes much of urban public life. But although such aspects of city life might prove stressful to the visitor, in fact, many urban residents have learned to ignore them or *compensate* for them in various ways. Urban residents usually have *perfunctory* relationships with their neighbors and coworkers, which may indeed lead to feelings of isolation. But again, isolation is at least as *relevant* to rural or even suburban life as it is to city life. In large cities, people often have kin, friends, or at least professional therapists to whom they can turn in times of depression, whereas rural residents may be physically as well as emotionally isolated. Especially among women, alienation, loneliness, and *self-contempt* seem to *predominate* in rural rather than urban populations.

Reading: Emotion and Motion: A Cross-Cultural View

Key Concepts

- *Culture-specific emotions and motor habits*
- *Gender-specific motor habits*
- *"Human nature"*
- *Communicative function of gesture and motor habits*

[1]   The range and quality of human emotions are potentially the same for all human groups. In the course of growing up in a particular culture, the range narrows and becomes shaped into a pattern. Fear, love, anger, **hostility,** shame, guilt, grief, joy, or indifference become channeled by culture so that they appear in different situations, against 5 different objects and persons, or hardly appear at all. Each culture selects, elaborates, and emphasizes certain feelings about the self, others, and the world as appropriate or not. This is communicated in direct and indirect ways, verbally and nonverbally. For example, a boy who learns not to cry may have been told that crying is only for girls, but he is also 10 surrounded by males who do not cry. Both experiences help pattern his inner responses to situations.

[2]   Because human emotions are felt to be "natural," part of "human nature," they are sometimes believed to be the same in every human society. We have lost sight of the tremendous role culture plays 15 in shaping our emotions. For instance, Americans consider it natural for a mother to love her child, for an individual to be jealous of another's success, for people to be sad when someone dies. Americans project these emotions, which they have been *trained* to feel, onto people in other cultures. The "naturalness" of these emotions leads Americans to 20 see them as inevitable causes for certain kinds of behavior. Americans explain war by humanity's natural aggression, view marriage as the natural result of romantic love, see motherhood as the natural expression of the maternal instinct, and free enterprise and capitalism as the **inevitable** expression of a natural desire to get ahead in the world. Amer- 25 icans consider these emotional responses as natural and responses that differ as unnatural.

[3]   In fact, however, every culture has different expectations about emotion, when and why certain emotions should be felt, and how they should be acted out. For example, it may be hard for Americans 30 to understand why several women married to the same man are not jealous of each other or why a mother may neglect her child's health and permit it to die, or even kill it. Yet these emotional patterns exist in numerous strong, satisfying cultures. In American culture, children are taught that it is not good to "carry a grudge," to store up anger or 35 hatred against a person who has hurt them. But in cultures where blood

feuds exist, as among the Pathans of the northwest frontier of Pakistan, an individual is not only allowed to feel the desire for revenge, but his or her very honor depends on it. A man who does not avenge a hurt shames himself and his whole group of kin. 40

[4]   As one looks over human history, one kind of emotional behavior does seem to stand out: violence, aggression, and destructiveness. Because of the seeming universality of this human trait, many people have sought to explain it biologically. "Humans," they say, "are inherently aggressive." Yet aggression, like other emotional patterns, differs 45 so among cultures that we must include it among the habits and capacities acquired by people as a result of their membership in a specific human society. In fact, in numerous societies practically no physical aggression occurs. Some of these societies, like that of the Pygmies of the Ituri forest in Africa, are hunting and gathering societies. Another society in 50 which there is no physical aggression is that of the Semai of the Malay Peninsula. The Semai consider themselves, and are considered by others, a nonviolent people. They believe that anger is bad, and it has been observed that they rarely become angry. However, Semai life is not without conflict, which usually occurs over the sexual favors of 55 women. But when one individual is offended by another, the Semai believe that the offended person will become the victim of an accident if he or she stays angry. In addition, if a person feels offended by another, he or she can ask for **compensation** for the distress. If the offender admits the offense, he or she will pay the compensation. If not, hostility 60 simmers, leading to insults and the spreading of rumors, but not to physical assault. No murder has ever been recorded in Semai society. Given the existence of such nonviolent cultures as the Pygmies and the Semai, we must examine very carefully the theory that humans are by nature aggressive and warlike. We cannot overlook the fact that humans 65 have the capacity for making peace as well as war, for cooperation as well as for deadly competition.

[5]   Closely related to the concept of emotion are such aspects of human behavior as facial expression, gesture, and movement patterns, all of which are so deeply ingrained that they appear "natural" until 70 they are subjected to closer investigation. Again, whereas every culture employs these nonverbal means of social interaction, each culture has its specific forms of these motor habits, which are organically integrated with the culture's entire system of values. The expression of such emotions as anger, fear, disgust, surprise, sadness, and happiness differ from 75 culture to culture. The question of whether the facial expressions used to convey these emotions are universal or culture specific is still open. To date, out of the multitude of communicative body movements and gestures, only the smile has been found to carry a universal message, that of pleasure, interest, and receptivity. The universality of this facial 80 expression suggests that it may have a biological basis. At the same time,

however, it is equally clear that culture and experience have a strong
effect on the shaping of facial expressions that **convey** emotions. Some
emotions, such as **contempt,** for example, seem to be culturally specific
in their expression. And if a culture values the masking of emotions,   85
facial movement will be affected, especially in public. For instance, in
Japan, where people are taught to be polite and sensitive to the feelings
of others, negative feelings are not demonstrated by facial expressions,
as they are in the United States. Americans find that the Japanese smile
far more than they do, and they may do so in situations in which a smile   90
seems inappropriate to Americans. But to the Japanese and other Asian
peoples, Americans often appear rudely blunt, showing emotion where
it would be more polite to hide it.

[6] Cultural patterning is also seen in the body movements of
different peoples, the way they stand, sit, and carry themselves. The   95
anthropologist Margaret Mead has said of the Balinese, for example,
that in the act of picking up a pin they will only use those muscles
immediately **relevant** to the act and leave the rest of the body un-
disturbed. Such activity is in contrast to Americans, for instance, who
will involve almost every muscle in their bodies to perform such a   100
simple action. The Balinese are economical in their motor habits.
When they perform a specific action, they will not draw all the muscles
into a unified act but will move only the units involved, perhaps the
fingers alone, or the hands and forearm alone, or the eyes alone, as
in the characteristic Balinese habit of moving the eyes to one side   105
without turning the head.

[7] Like perceptions of time and space, specific motor habits become established early, and because they are deeply ingrained, they
are difficult to change. The cultural patterning of motor habits shows
up in many different arenas of behavior. Melville Hershkovitz, an an-   110
thropologist well known for his work in West Africa, reports that a
European contractor working in Ghana was constantly **confronted** with
the problem of the local laborers digging curved rather than straight
trenches. The contractor would lay out a straight line between two points
for the workers to follow, but the result was always a curved trench.   115
The laborers came from an area in Ghana in which circular forms **predominate** in construction, and this pattern was carried over into their
new activities. A similar example of deeply ingrained culturally patterned motor habits may be observed among the Trobriand Islanders,
who when introduced to the British game of cricket, imposed their native   120
pattern of spear throwing on the new activity of batting.

[8] Many people have noted the graceful walk of women who
traditionally carry burdens on their heads. That this grace is learned
and not "natural" is shown by the fact that American women who go to
charm schools are taught to walk with books on their heads to give them   125
this "natural" grace. Motor habits not only differ among cultures but

also among subcultures* in complex societies and between men and women. In describing the "male warrior role" in black urban ghettos, the anthropologist Herbert Ellis mentions stance and movement as important aspects of this role. The "hip"** position consists of "either 130 standing with the knees bent so that a convex impression is formed in the knee of the trousers, or flexing the calf muscles, leg thrust backward, so as to accentuate the musculature of the leg." Part of this role also consists of a special walk, in which there is a "smooth, bobbing, up and down movement, with the body carried slightly to one side." Ellis's 135 informants insisted that they could tell a "hip" male even at the beach by the way he stood and walked. These body movements are intended to convey personal characteristics that are valued in that subculture: "coolness" and confidence.

[9]   The motor habits of males and females are somewhat differ- 140 ent, just as certain emotions are viewed as either typically male or female. Gender-related movements arise partly because of the different kinds of work men and women have traditionally performed and partly because of cultural images of what is "proper" for each gender. For example, the walk of the middle-class American male is usually brisk 145 and confident, with the arms held away from the body, often swinging. American females, whether walking or sitting, tend to have their arms closer to their bodies, and their thighs are closer together than men's are, suggesting a different cluster of cultural traits. Most preening (courting) gestures are gender specific, that is, they are characteristic of either 150 the male or the female. For instance, recent investigation in the field of body movement and gesture have shown that a flirting woman will lift her hand to push back her hair from her face or rearrange it above her ears, whereas a man's preening gesture involves adjusting his tie or straightening the creases of his pants.   155

[10]   It is because culture is a system of shared symbols and meanings that culturally patterned body movements or gestures can be used to communicate special emotional messages. Depending on culture, gender, or context, the same body movement may convey different messages. Kissing, for example, is body language that may communicate a 160 variety of messages. Kissing may be a ritualized gesture, such as the **perfunctory** goodbye kiss between husband and wife or the greeting kiss of two women. Or kissing may be erotic, a preliminary to sexual relations. The origin of human kissing is not known, but it may **derive** from the passing of food from mouth to mouth, a practice common in 165 the bird kingdom and among such primates as gorillas and chimpanzees.

---

*A system of perceptions, values, beliefs, and customs that are significantly different from those of the dominant culture.

**An American slang expression for behavior that is current and fashionable.

Kissing is also employed in some tribal societies in which parents chew and predigest food and then pass it by mouth to their children. It is the intent to communicate and the purpose of the communication that may make two identical body movements vastly different. For example, con- 170 sider a twitch and a wink. A *twitch,* an involuntary rapid blink of the eye, is not intended to convey a message. But a wink, which is also a rapid eye blink, does have culture-specific communicative intent. In America, at least, it serves as a signal, a message of interest or agreement to friends or allies. Such shared meanings are only possible when both 175 parties have had the same cultural instruction.

Reading Comprehension

1. True—False

After each statement write *T* for true, *F* for false, or *NI* for no information, according to the information given in the reading passage.

a. Telling a boy not to cry because only girls cry is an example of nonverbal social instruction. _____

b. It is not natural and instinctive for all human beings to feel a competitive need to win over others. _____

c. Feelings of revenge and retribution are considered honorable in American society. _____

d. Pygmy and Semai cultures demonstrate that violence and aggression are learned behaviors. _____

e. Among the inhabitants of the British Isles it is considered polite to hide one's feelings. _____

f. The Japanese smile more than Americans because they have happier lives. _____

g. The Balinese "economy of motor habits" means they spend less on transportation than other people do. _____

h. Women and men have different patterns of movement chiefly because of their different physical characteristics. _____

i. The purpose of a gesture such as an eye blink or a kiss will determine its emotional message. _____

2. *Reading Review*

In oral discussion or in writing, answer the following questions based on information in the reading passage.

a. According to paragraph [1], how does culture influence human emotions?

b. Briefly explain the meaning of the following sentence: "[All people] project [their] emotions, which they have been trained to feel, onto people in other cultures."

c. What does it mean to "carry a grudge"? What does it mean to "avenge a hurt"? How were you taught to handle the emotion of anger, hostility, or hurt caused by another person's behavior to you?

d. In paragraph [4], what is the author's purpose in describing the Pygmy and Semai cultures?

e. What is paragraph [5]'s central idea about the smile?

f. Explain what is meant by the expression "masking of emotions." Of which culture(s) is this typical, according to the reading? To what extent is this concept typical of your culture?

g. Why might it be said, according to the information in paragraph [6], that the Balinese are "economical" in their movements whereas the Americans are not?

h. What idea is supported by the illustration of the Ghanaian laborers and the example of the Trobriand Islanders in paragraph [7]?

i. What is the central idea of paragraph [8]?

j. What is implied about American female personality traits by their typical body movements, according to paragraph [9]? Is the contrast between men's and women's personalities and postures as described in this paragraph true of your culture as well? Explain.

3. *Analyzing the Text*

Respond to the following items as appropriate.

a. In paragraph [1], the fifth sentence begins "This is communicated . . . " To what does "this" refer?

b. In paragraph [2], sentence 1, what is the thought relationship between the first two clauses? Which word signals the relationship to you?

c. From which point of view is the author writing paragraph [2]: first-person singular or plural, second-person, third-person singular or plural? Which pronouns signal that point of view?

d. In paragraph [3], what method of support for the main idea is used: chronological details, explanatory details, an extended illustration, examples, or reasons?

e. In paragraph [4], the first sentence uses the word *seem,* the second sentence the word *seeming.* Are these words intended to strengthen or weaken the author's assertion?

f. In paragraph [4], the fifth sentence includes the expression "in fact" to signal
   (1) a contradiction of a previously stated fact.
   (2) a reason for a stated result.
   (3) an example from real life.
   (4) emphasis of a point.

g. Give three examples of conditional sentences in paragraph [4]. Which word signals the relationship of condition?

_____

_____

h. In paragraph [5], the second sentence includes the phrases "these non-verbal means" and "these motor habits." Why is the word *these* used in each?

i. In paragraph [6], *for example* is used in the second sentence. What is the example?

j. In paragraph [6], sentence 2 includes the words "muscles immediately relevant to the act. . . . " What act?

k. The word *units* in sentence 5 in paragraph [6] is the equivalent of which other word in paragraph [6]?

l. To whom does the word *local* refer in sentence 3 of paragraph [7]?

m. In paragraph [7], which of the following signal expressions would be most appropriate in the third sentence?
   (1) Therefore, **(2)** Finally, **(3)** For example, **(4)** On the other hand,

n. Sentence 5 of paragraph [7] may be divided into two main statements:
   - Circular forms predominated in the area from which the Ghanaian workers came.
   - This pattern was carried over into the workers' new construction activities.
   Which of the following expressions would most logically link these two statements together? Why?
   (1) For instance, **(2)** Consequently, **(3)** In contrast, **(4)** Nevertheless,

o. In paragraph [8], the sixth sentence begins "Part of this role. . . . " What role is being referred to?

p. In paragraph [9], sentence 2, to what does the word *gender* refer?

q. In paragraph [9], sentence 4, the word *courting* follows the word *preening*
   (1) because it is opposite in meaning.
   (2) as an explanation.
   (3) as a reason.
   (4) as an example.

r. In paragraph [10], which of the following expressions has a meaning equivalent to "It is because . . . " in sentence 1?
   (1) Even though
   (2) Since

(3) As a result
(4) In comparison

s. In paragraph [10], sentence 6, which word is referred to by the first pronoun *it*? Which word is referred to by the pronoun *it* in sentence 7?

t. In paragraph [5], sentence 5, the expression "to date" implies that
(1) all the research on the subject has been completed.
(2) male and female pairs carried out the research.
(3) no other research needs to be done in this area.
(4) this research will probably be continued in the future.

4. Applying Key Concepts

- **Analyzing Movement Patterns**
Analyze the body movements and gestures of one character in a television program that takes place in a contemporary American setting. Describe five of the specific movements and gestures that you find and tell what message you believe they are meant to convey. Identify the program and the character's role before beginning your discussion.

- **Talking with Your Body**
Show and discuss various body movements, gestures, and facial expressions you would use to convey the following messages.

a. that you don't understand
b. that you don't agree
c. that you do agree
d. that you are angry
e. that you have contempt for someone
f. that you think someone has done something shameful

- **Dialogues.** Choose a partner and then together study the following situations and decide which emotions are involved in each. Choose one situation and write a dialogue for the persons involved. If time permits, role play your dialogue for the class, using appropriate facial expressions and gestures.

a. A school principal informs a parent that his or her child has just passed the examination for a specialized school with high standards of achievement.
b. A teacher informs a student that a classmate has just been seriously injured in an accident.
c. A professor takes away the examination paper of a student believed to be cheating.
d. A college student informs her boyfriend that she is transferring to an out-of-town college for two years.
e. Two best friends learn that only one of them has been accepted to the college of their choice.

    f. A parent wants his or her child to go to college, but the child, who has just graduated from high school, wishes to take a year off for work and travel.

Vocabulary Study

1. Synonyms and Parts of Speech

Many English words keep the same form while being used as different parts of speech. The italicized words in the following sets of sentences are used as different parts of speech, and in some cases their pronunciation differs (follow your instructor's pronunciation as a guide). The meanings of the pairs are different, and each paired word requires a different synonym. First, label the part of speech for each italicized word. Then substitute an appropriate synonym for each.

    a. **(1)** The river cut a deep *channel* in the land.
           (2) If you *channel* your anger constructively, you may overcome certain difficulties in daily life.
    b. **(1)** The instructor did not take the time to *elaborate* on every point in the lecture.
           (2) In every culture, *elaborate* meals are served on religious or national holidays.
    c. **(1)** Several housing *projects* in the city have been poorly constructed.
           (2) The principal *projects* next year's school population at 900 children.
    d. **(1)** A charge of *neglect* may be issued against parents who do not clothe their children properly in cold weather.
           (2) In examining the subject of human emotions, we should not *neglect* the role played by culture.
    e. **(1)** In most foreign cities, the *train* station is in the center of the city.
           (2) Directly and indirectly, all cultures *train* boys and girls to behave in different manners.

Write an original sentence for each of the following words on a separate sheet of paper. Use each word first as a noun and then as a verb. The first one has been done.

    f. experiences   **g.** patterns   **h.** desires   **i.** mask   **j.** fear

noun: We had many interesting experiences on our vacation. verb: A person experiences many failures before succeeding in life.

2. Word Form Table

Fill in the following table with the appropriate forms of the given words. Some nouns or adjectives may have two forms.

Verb	Noun	Adjective	Adverb
a. _____	hostility_____	_____	_____
b. _____	_____	_____	violently_____
c. _____	_____	predominant__	_____
d. _____	_____	_____	rudely_____
e. _____	_____	identical_____	_____

Use the correct form from each lettered line to complete the same lettered sentence below.

a. Your arguments will be more persuasive if they are presented rationally rather than _____.

b. Non_____ resistance to unjust authority was the key political tactic of Mahatma Gandhi and Dr. Martin Luther King, Jr.

c. Right-handedness appears to _____ in all of the cultures of the world.

d. To many foreigners, Americans seem quite tolerant of _____ behavior in their children.

e. Can you _____ some similarities between baseball and cricket?

3. Word Formation

Suffix *ness;* a common noun ending signifying "condition," "quality," or "state"; usually attached to the adjective form.

aggressiveness	helpfulness	politeness
carefulness	kindness	responsiveness
goodness	narrowness	thoughtfulness
happiness	naturalness	

a. Without using your dictionary, write a word that means the opposite of each of the words listed in the preceding section. Most but not all of these antonyms also end in *ness.*

b. Choose one of the words listed in the preceding section or its antonym as the appropriate quality that describes the following conditions.

  (1) The opening of a door for an older person: _____

  (2) The appearance of someone wearing a great deal of makeup:

_____

(3) The hard-hitting, competitive quality of a successful football player:

_____

(4) The reaction of a baby who smiles and laughs often:

_____

(5) The "wild boy's" (Chapter One) lack of interest in the human social life he was introduced to: _____

(6) The type of action taking place when a group of children make fun of one child: _____

Writing Exercises

Principles of Coordination and Subordination

Coordination

Coordination means the linking together of many two-sentence elements that are parallel in form, logically related, and equal in importance. **Coordinating conjunctions** are used to join coordinated elements as follows:

[1] And connects two sentence elements that *add* information.

Dance is a form of movement that is purposeful and rhythmic.
(coordinated adjectives)

Dance and music communicate without language.
(coordinated noun subjects)

---

[2] But connects two sentence elements that contrast with each other.

Dance appears in every culture, *but it takes* different
(coordinated independent clauses: a compound sentence)

forms.

Disco dancing is *exhilarating but exhausting*.
(coordinated adjectives)

---

[3] Or connects two sentence elements that *offer alternatives*.

> **Dancing may be done *for entertainment or for religious***
> (coordinated prepositional phrases)
>
> ***purposes.***

Any two sentence elements may be coordinated:

a. Coordinated subjects: *Dance and music* may stir up intense feelings.

b. Coordinated verbs: Dancing *teaches and reinforces* rhythmic movement.

c. Coordinated direct objects: Dancing may redirect *sexual energy and tension.*

d. Coordinated independent clauses: *Dance appears* in every culture, *but it takes* different forms in each.

e. Coordinated dependent clauses: In some cultures, *when battle is near or when social disaster strikes,* ritual dances are performed.

f. Coordinated prepositional phrases: Feelings of *love or of aggression* may be stirred by dance.

g. Coordinated adjectives: Dance movements are *purposeful and rhythmic.*

h. Coordinated adverbs: Dance movements are performed *purposefully and rhythmically.*

1. *Identifying Coordinated Elements*

Divide a piece of paper into two columns. As you read the following paragraph, underscore each set of coordinated elements you find. Write the first element of the set in the left-hand column and the second element in the right-hand column. (Where the coordinated elements are clauses, write only the subject-verb combinations in the columns.)

> **Dance is a form of human behavior that is purposeful and intentionally rhythmical.**
>
> **purposeful | rhythmical**

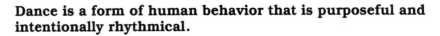

Dance is a form of human behavior that is composed of artistic and rhythmic body movements and gestures. Dance appears in every human culture, in which it is universally combined with other kinds of media—music and song, for example. Dance often involves adding materials to the human body, such as costume and decoration. Like the other arts, dance is also symbolic behavior. In human societies, dance is used to communicate a variety of ideas and emotions. Because of its physical nature and because of its ability to stir intense emotions, dance is often associated with special events in the lives of individuals or groups. Dance and music can be and often are used to deal more effectively with the environment or cope with specific social problems. War dances, for example, may rouse men to the pitch of excitement and confidence necessary to do well in battle.

2. *Sentence Composition*

On a separate sheet of paper, compose complete sentences according to the directions.

   a. Use coordinated nouns to name two sports that women in your culture enjoy playing.
   b. Use coordinated infinitives to describe two benefits of a specific athletic activity.
   c. Use coordinated independent clauses to describe how different parts of your body feel after you've done a hard day's work.
   d. Use coordinated *that* clauses to state two aspects about daily exercise that you realize are beneficial.
   e. Use coordinated dependent clauses with *when* to describe a situation in which you shake hands with someone.
   f. Use coordinated independent clauses to describe two different tasks performed by men and women in your culture.

3. *Paragraph Completion with Coordinated Elements*

Use coordinated elements to complete the sentences in the following paragraph. Your coordinated elements should be parallel in form and related in content to each other. (In some cases, one part of the coordinated set has already been added.) The first one has been done.

In some countries of the world (1) ___*cricket*___ or (2)

_____ are among the most popular spectator sports. But

in the United States, football reigns supreme. One anthropologist has

suggested that this fact is true because football reflects the

(3) _____ and characteristics that predominate in the life

of American males. The athletic skills required in football, such as (4)

_____ and (5) _____, would not seem to

have much relevance to everyday life. But apparently, the teamwork and

specialization that are the essence of football provide a model for Amer-

ican males in many (6) _____ and occupations. Every

weekend, in every American (7) _____ and (8)

_____, millions of men sit down by their radios or (9) _____ to listen to or (10) _____ a college or professional football game. Women are largely excluded from the football scene; they may occasionally (11) _____ or cheer, but they almost never play the game. Is it that football is too physically (12) _____ and (13) _____ for women to play? Or is it that most women, who have been trained to be (14) _____ and (15) _____, are repelled by the sport's violent, aggressive nature?

4. *Paragraph Composition with Coordinated Elements*

Write a paragraph in which you describe a favorite art (painting, music, sculpture), craft (woodworking, knitting, sewing, repairing objects), sport (baseball, dancing, running), or other leisure-time activity (watching films, reading, baking) that brings you physical, mental, aesthetic, or emotional pleasure. Use coordinated structures as appropriate to convey your ideas and feelings to your reader.

Subordinate Structures
Subordinate structures can be used to shift the relative weight of sentence elements. In the following examples, note how weak, wordy coordinate sentences can be improved by subordinating the less important elements.

[1] Subordinate Verb Phrases. A weak coordinate sentence can

> **The Balinese perform a specific action and will not draw all the muscles into a unified act.**

be improved by a subordinate participial phrase:

> **The Balinese *performing a specific action* will not draw all the muscles into a unified act.**

The sentence can be still improved further by a subordinate infinitive phrase of purpose:

> **The Balinese will not draw all the muscles into a unified act *to perform a specific action.***

[2]   Subordinate Dependent Clauses.   A weak coordinate sentence

> **Ghanaian workers were accustomed to circular patterns, and they carried these over into new activities.**

can be improved by a subordinate adjective clause:

> **Ghanaian workers, *who were accustomed to circular patterns,* carried these over into new activities.**

And the sentence can be improved still further by a subordinate adverbial clause (dependent clauses of time, cause, contrast, condition):

> ***Because Ghanaian workers were accustomed to circular patterns,* they carried these over into new activities.**

[3]   Subordinate Descriptive Structures.   A weak coordinate sentence

> **Usually American women cross their legs, and their thighs are close together.**

can be improved by a subordinate prepositional phrase:

> **Usually American women cross their legs *with their thighs close together.***

A weak coordinate sentence

> **Melville Hershkovitz is a well-known anthropologist, and he has studied African and black American motor habits.**

can be improved by a subordinate appositive:

> **Melville Hershkovitz, *a well-known anthropologist*, has studied African and black American motor habits.**

1. *Sentence Combining*

On a separate piece of paper, combine the statements in each item into one sentence using subordination techniques. Make all changes necessary for fluency. Remember that the information you want to emphasize or give importance to should go in the independent clause. Consult the following list for appropriate subordinators:

who, which	participial phrases
where	prepositional phrases
when, before, after	appositives
although, whereas	infinitive phrases
because, since	
if	

a. (1) Yoga originated in India.
  (2) There are now thousands of Americans studying yoga.
b. (1) These Americans are of all ages and physical types.
  (2) They have found yoga exercises of great benefit to them.
c. (1) Americans have discovered that yoga provides a practical approach to physical fitness.
  (2) They are willing to reorient their minds and bodies to its requirements.
d. (1) Yoga stabilizes the emotions.
  (2) Yoga elevates one's mental attitudes.
  (3) Yoga is a total approach to well-being.
e. (1) Yoga systems were designed by ancient religious masters.
  (2) Yoga systems have been practiced for centuries.
  (3) Yoga systems are a means of cultivating human potential.
f. (1) There are vast cultural differences between India and the United States.

      (2) Americans in large numbers are practicing yoga.

      (3) They are enriching their personal lives.

g. **(1)** You may be surprised to learn that the first yoga technique requires no movement at all.

      (2) You may be interested to learn that the first yoga technique requires no gestures at all.

h. **(1)** In fact, you become passive, quiet, and motionless.

      (2) Then you will derive the greatest benefits.

i. **(1)** Yoga is different from quick, forceful exercises.

      (2) These exercises are called calisthenics.

      (3) Calisthenics are used to attain physical fitness by many Americans.

j. **(1)** Americans are not accustomed to moving slowly.

      (2) Americans find yoga difficult at first.

k. **(1)** Americans forget the breathing patterns.

      (2) The breathing patterns are necessary for the yoga exercises.

l. **(1)** Americans carry brisk movement into their yoga activities at first.

      (2) Then they form the new motor habits required.

m. **(1)** Most Americans do not adopt yoga motor patterns in their daily life.

      (2) Americans do find yoga perfect for meditation and relaxation.

Small Group Assignment

Teaching a Motor Pattern

Form pairs or groups of three. Decide on the motor pattern that your group would like to teach. Some motor patterns to consider are an exercise, a popular or folk-dance step, an athletic task such as kicking a soccer ball, or using chopsticks.

    After your group has decided on a motor pattern, compose one paragraph that provides detailed, step-by-step instructions of how to do your chosen motor activity. Begin your paragraph with an introduction about the task: the larger activity to which it belongs, its context in that activity, its culture or gender specificity, if any. When you have finished your paragraph and have proofread it for errors, be prepared to teach your activity to another group or to the class, as directed by your instructor.

    As a model of your task, your instructor will teach the class the following exercise. Note the step-by-step directions.

This yoga exercise is called the Side Bend. It will improve the contour of the figure and help remove excess inches from the waist. First, stand up straight with your heels together. Gracefully raise your arms overhead, keeping them parallel. Turn your palms to face each other. Rest your left ear on your left shoulder. Very slowly, bend your raised arms, your trunk, and your head to the left a few inches. Keep your elbows straight and your fingers close together and outstretched. Hold this position for a count of ten. Then slowly straighten to your original upright position. Now do the same thing to the right. Finally, slowly lower your arms to your sides, wiggle your fingers, and relax.

Composition Development

Writing for Academic and Career Purposes

In English composition classes, much of the assigned writing is personal and expressive in nature. Students are asked to narrate personal experiences, describe places they have personally visited, and/or express personal opinions on subjects of general interest. The support for assertions in such papers is usually drawn from personal experiences, the experiences of people the writer knows, or from general knowledge recalled from reading books or media articles or watching television. In these personal essays, the reader does not primarily look for profound treatments of complex issues. If the paper focuses on the subject, is logically organized, and moves developmentally between valid generalizations and concrete supporting details, it will satisfy the requirements.

Personal, expressive writing is an important mode for you to master, but it is only the first step on the ladder of composing activities. As a college student with the potential for entering a profession or career in the technical, social, scientific, or commercial worlds, a different kind of writing will be required of you. This writing demands that you focus closely on a specific subject without digressing, or going off the topic; it demands serious consideration of a subject from a variety of viewpoints; and it holds you to account for the accuracy and completeness of your factual statements and the interpretations and conclusions you derive from specific, text-based information. Your supporting evidence in this kind of writing may include personal illustration, quotations of proverbs or popular sayings, and/or figures of speech to help your reader visualize your abstract thoughts. But, these supporting devices are the minor, not the major types of support for your ideas. Your most important developmental methods in this type of writing are as follows.

(1) Citation of accurate statistics and facts
(2) Careful paraphrasing of the work of authorities in the field
(3) Apt references to the texts you are interpreting
(4) Logically reasoned statements that lead to justifiable conclusions.

Complete comprehension of the question or task assigned, an understanding of the material you have read on the subject, a substantial yet flexible outline, mastery of English signal words and expressions, and firm control over paragraph development are necessary for the successful accomplishment of such writing tasks that you will encounter in your academic, vocational, and civic lives.

Terms for Critical Thinking

Your academic or career course writing assignments may take the form of essay examination questions or research papers. In your civic life or in your occupation, you may have such writing assignments as reports, summaries, analyses, budget narratives, or numerous other types of compositions. The following list presents some helpful terms for approaching your subject or responding to a given assignment.

Enumerate or List:	To write points, one by one, making them as concise as possible.
Trace:	To follow the course or trail of something; to give a description of progress from one point in time to another.
Define:	To give the meaning of a term or theory, often with an illustration to clarify the term or theory.
State:	To answer briefly and to the point, usually omitting details, examples, and illustrations.
Summarize:	To present in condensed form principles, facts, ideas, or explanations, often omitting details, examples, and illustrations.
Illustrate:	To clarify an idea by presenting a diagram, figure, or statistics.
Explain:	To make clear; to give reasons for conditions or results; to tell how something works.
Analyze:	To examine separately the component parts of a work, situation, or object.
Relate:	To show relationships by emphasizing how ideas, conditions, or people connect; to show how one thing causes or is caused by another; to show how things are alike or different.
Compare:	To show differences but emphasize similarities among objects, people, events, or ideas.
Contrast:	To emphasize differences among objects, people, events, or ideas.
Criticize, Judge, Evaluate:	To express a personal judgment of objects, works, issues, or ideas, giving weight to both positive and negative points.

**Discuss, Consider,
Describe:**   To write a full and detailed answer, examining the
                   subject from different perspectives and presenting
                   both sides of any argument.

Justify: To give reasons that support an idea, condition, or
                   point of view.

1. *Choosing Suitable Writing Approaches*

Read the following list of writing tasks. Then consult the list of terms for
critical thinking and choose the one that you think offers the best approach
to each item. Write the name of that approach in the blank space provided.
A term may be used more than once. The first one has been done.

a. *Summarize* ___ Briefly present the basic ideas about language
learning expressed in Wilga Rivers's new book on English as a second
language.

b. _____ Show how the first and second editions of Serena
Nanda's *Cultural Anthropology* differ from each other.

c. _____ Present a paper to your Parent-Teachers Association telling why you dislike a newly adopted history textbook.

d. _____ Write the director of your school's computer section a brief memo suggesting that computer use be extended to evening
hours.

e. _____ Show by the narration of important events how
the program for gifted children in your neighborhood elementary school
developed to its present condition.

f. _____ Produce statistics, facts, and details showing that
despite different brand names, two different types of equipment in your
field are basically similar.

g. _____ Present a paper in which you point out the connections between the condition of the American economy and the style
of American women's clothing.

h. _____ Write a report for your company on the possible
effects of flexible working hours (flextime) in your firm.

i. _____ Use a passage from William Shakespeare's play

Romeo and Juliet to support your point of view that Shakespeare was the world's greatest playwright.

j. _____ Using actual case studies, support your view that a fare increase for public transportation would be disastrous for working people in your city.

k. _____ As a plant manager, write a report explaining why your recommendation to close a certain section of the plant's operations was the correct decision.

l. _____ Briefly state five different functions of the human brain.

2. *Topic Statement Analysis: Comparison or Contrast?*

Read each of the following topic statements and decide if they suggest a paragraph of comparison or contrast. Underscore the key words that explain your choice. Remember that in complex sentences, the main idea is carried by the independent clause.

a. Although human groups have differences in physical or genetic makeup, all humans alive today belong to a single species, *Homo sapiens.*

b. The extensive research on American health care indicates that there is a difference in such services depending on social class and ethnic background.

c. Anthropologist Ruth Benedict examined three Native American and one South Pacific society and showed how a different cultural core predominated in each group.

d. Although the Australian Arunta and the Alaskan Eskimo would not seem to be similar in any respect, they do, in fact, share one significant feature: an environment characterized by open, undifferentiated space.

e. American culture has been characterized as containing major discontinuities between what is expected of children and what is expected of adults.

f. Anthropologist Francis Hsu has theorized that the adult personalities of the Chinese, the Hindu, and the American are each formed around a different central relationship: The central tie in Chinese culture is that of father-son; in Hindu culture, mother-son; and in American culture, the relationship between peers, or equals.

g. How do different language systems cope with the real events in nature that are observed by human beings? Benjamin L. Whorf tended to divide languages into groups that focus on *things* and those that focus on *events.*

h. Haiti in the twentieth century and France in the nineteenth century may seem like very different places. Yet I can recall an incident that happened in which the attitudes of my brother and my father were similar to those of Sylvester Bonnard and his uncle Victor.

State the *topic* of each of the preceding statements on a separate sheet of paper. In **c, d, f,** and **g,** the *types* are identified. Circle them.

3. *Proposition Analysis*

Frequently in academic writing tasks, you will be given a proposition to examine critically or criticize (see the list of terms for critical thinking). Before beginning to write, you must fully understand the terms and limits of the given proposition. Careful reading of each of the following assignments and discussing the related questions with your class will help you analyze future writing assignments.

a. You have been asked to examine critically the criteria for becoming president of the United States. You have learned that although there are no legal restrictions about the race, sex, or religion of the person who becomes the president, there are two legal requirements that he or she must meet. First, he or she must be a native-born American citizen; and second, he or she must be above thirty-five years of age. In criticizing these criteria,

    (1) Should your essay contain a paragraph on the subject that no woman has ever been a United States president? Explain your answer.

    (2) Would it be relevant in your essay to discuss the example of President John F. Kennedy as the first Catholic president? Explain your answer.

    (3) Would it be useful to discuss some of the typical accomplishments of a thirty-five-year-old, middle-class, well-educated American?

b. Today, many private citizens want to own handguns for their own protection. American law permits citizens to own handguns if they follow certain registration procedures. Do you agree or disagree that it should be legal for private citizens to own handguns? You will present your opinion at your neighborhood's community meeting.

    (1) Should your essay refer at length to hunting rifles and shotguns? Why or why not?

    (2) Would it be relevant to include the pros and cons of whether police officers should carry guns? Explain your answer.

    (3) Would an example of a drugstore owner who keeps the store open until 11:30 P.M. be relevant in this essay? Why or why not?

c. In a text on marriage and the family, a psychologist has stated that drafting married women into the army would increase the strain on married life so severely that there would be a tremendous increase in the divorce rate. For this reason, the psychologist advises against drafting married women. You are asked to justify the psychologist's point of view.

(1) You have read a newspaper article about an eighteen-year-old unmarried girl who became a skilled technician through enlisting in and studying in the armed forces. Would this example be relevant for your essay? Explain your answer.

(2) In principle, you are a pacifist, that is, you believe that no one should be drafted to fight. Should you discuss your pacifistic beliefs? Explain your reasoning.

Composition Topics

Answering Text-Based Essay Questions

Essay questions on examinations are intended to test your understanding of the topic and your ability to apply your knowledge. The following guidelines will help you respond to assigned topics on essay examinations.

- **Get right to the point.** Do not use time on elaborate introductions. You may take it for granted that the reader (instructor) is familiar with the background of the subject.
- **Look for clue words in the question,** such as those in the list of terms for critical thinking (pages 241–242) and number expressions such as "one major aspect," "three significant differences," "several dominant characteristics," and so on.
- If it is an open book exam, or if you are given passages to read, **mark the key concepts and most important points** as you go along. Limit your responses to the assigned material.
- **Follow the developmental form of assertion, explanation, and specific examples** as closely as possible. Make your supporting material as concrete and specific as you can.
- Where you are asked for a personal opinion, **make sure it is clearly distinguished from the objective, or factual parts,** of your response.

1. Read the following passages and review paragraph [4] of the reading selection. Then discuss in an essay the following quotation with reference to these passages and other material you have read on the subject.

   Conflict is universally human, but the bursting out of conflict into violent behavior is not. Violence and physical aggression against others is something humans are trained into, and it is something they can be trained out of.

Passage A

An important aspect of child rearing among the Khalapur Rajputs of India is that aggression and assertiveness are inhibited in small children. But, there is a dual feeling about the expression of these traits. The family system requires that an individual be submissive to those above him or her in status, yet he or she must be dominant over those below him or her. Furthermore, as a warrior caste, the Rajput men feel that they have a strong masculine image to maintain. The value they give to bravery and physical assertiveness on the battlefield is partly contradicted by the value they give to peaceful cooperation in their domestic lives.

Passage B

Whereas war in most societies is an intermittent event, in some cultures, feuding and warfare seem to be constant. For example, among the Yanomamo of South America, intertribal hostility and warfare are almost a way of life. Yanomamo villages organize and conduct war parties against each other not for land but to steal each other's women. In a Yanomamo raid, as many men as possible are killed and as many women as possible are captured. Fighting often breaks out among individuals, and the villages may divide into hostile camps. To survive, members of the village adopt a hostile and aggressive stance toward other villages. Yanomamo aggressiveness is encouraged and reinforced by deeply ingrained cultural patterns.

2. Review Chapter One's reading selection for the descriptions of Victor, the "wild boy," and the "wolf-children" of India. Describe the nonhumanlike qualities of these children. What conclusions does the author draw from the case studies? To what extent do you agree or disagree with the author's conclusions?

The joyous emotions of friendship are expressed in smiles, physical closeness, and kissing. Discuss some emotions, gestures, facial expressions, and body movements that express friendship and affection in your social group.

10

Pluralism in Action: The Caribbean

The Rastafari are one of the many different religious groups that are found in the multicultural region known as the Caribbean. Rastifarianism combines Jewish, Christian, and African beliefs and symbols, as we can see in this depiction of "The Last Supper," an incident from the New Testament, which is painted on a food stall in Barbados, West Indies.

Freewrite

Freewrite an informal ethnic survey of a familiar place such as your classroom, entertainment center, apartment building, workplace, or health facility. What different factors indicate ethnicity to you: physical appearance? language? dress? family behavior? food patterns? economic patterns?

Vocabulary in Context

You will need to know the meanings of the following words in order to fully comprehend the reading passage. Use your dictionary as necessary.

Verbs	**Nouns**	**Adjectives**	**Adverbs**
encounter	abolition	communal	
prosper	conquest	indigenous	
comprise	divinity	conventional	
absorb	dominion	subsistence	
	colonists	impoverished	
	mosaic		

Replace each italicized word in the following paragraph with an appropriate synonym from the above lists. Nouns and verbs may require changes in number or tense.

The history of human development *includes* many *meetings* between different cultural groups. Through military *victory,* one ethnic group may gain economic and political *authority* over another, but the conquering society may then adopt the *gods,* clothing, and dietary customs of the *native* people whom they have brought under their rule. When the Manchurians conquered the Chinese in the sixteenth century, for example, they *incorporated* customs of the Chinese culture into their own lifestyle, just as the Romans enriched their society with the culture of their Greek slaves. Usually, in a nation's colonial possessions, it is the *settlers from the mother country* who *grow wealthy* from the land while the local people exist at a *very low* level as workers, not owners of the soil. The *elimination* of native customs and ceremonies, the rejection of native *cooperative* values, and the restriction of educational opportunities all serve to keep the native population *poor* and dependent. Thus, while it is *customary* to describe a pluralistic society as a "melting pot" or a *multicolored design,* in fact, most such societies have certain groups at the top and others at the bottom.

Reading: Pluralism in Action: The Caribbean

Key Concepts
- *Ethnic diversity/pluralism*
- *Colonialism*
- *Capitalism*
- *Communal ideals*

[1]   The Caribbean, a region of subtropical islands lying between the continents of North and South America, is the home of an extraordinarily diverse population. The area was named after the Carib Indian peoples whom Christopher Columbus **encountered** on his second voyage to the "New World." However, both the Caribs and another **indigenous** group called the Arawaks were either eliminated or **absorbed** by the Spanish conquerors in the first years of the sixteenth century. The ethnic pluralism that characterizes the Caribbean today is chiefly a result of the **conquest,** colonialism, and slaveholding in the region by various European nations.

[2]   The French, Dutch, Danish, and English invasions of the Spanish Caribbean domains were at first limited to the islands of Barbados and St. Christopher, but these European nations afterward spread their **dominion** over all of the Caribbean islands. Thus Puerto Rico, Cuba, and the Dominican Republic, for example, are Spanish-speaking and share many cultural values inherited from Spain, while Haiti and Martinique are French-speaking and share a French cultural heritage. Barbados and Jamaica are English-speaking and retain some British characteristics; St. John and St. Thomas retain some Danish influence from those European **colonists;** and the Dutch presence of former times is still apparent linguistically and architecturally in St. Maartens, Aruba, and Curaçao.

[3]   The major impact on the ethnicity of the Caribbean islands was not, however, the various European settlers. By the early eighteenth century, the Europeans had introduced African slaves to work the vast sugar plantations that were the mainstay of the Caribbean economy, and it is their descendants whose ethnic presence dominates nearly all of the Caribbean region. Even on such islands as Cuba or Puerto Rico, where the introduction of slavery was severely restricted, or in the Dutch islands where agriculture never **prospered,** the African heritage is evident in the music, language, and religious culture of the people.

[4]   In addition to the African groups, the Caribbean population **comprises** significant numbers of other ethnic minorities as well. The Chinese were imported in the nineteenth century to such islands as Cuba and Jamaica to build roads and later cut sugarcane. But the Chinese rapidly left the rural areas to enter the small business world of the urban

centers, and it is still in the role of small entrepreneur that one finds the many thousands of Chinese in the Caribbean today. After the **abolition** of slavery in the West Indies, laborers were imported under five- and ten-year contracts from such **impoverished** European regions as the Madeira Islands of Portugal and the Canary Islands of Spain. Additionally, many thousands of East Indians, both Hindu and Moslem, were imported into the Caribbean right up into the twentieth century. Today their descendants are found all over the region, but particularly in Trinidad, where about one-third of the population is East Indian. 45

[5]   Religious practices in the Caribbean are as diverse as the ethnicity of its populations: Hinduism, Islam, Buddhism, Judaism, and various forms of Christianity coexist throughout the region. The latter religion, brought in by the European colonists, was adapted and transformed by the descendants of the African slaves into such distinct belief 50 systems as Voudou in Haiti and Rastafarianism in Jamaica. The Rastafari are a small subcultural group, sometimes called a religious sect, that began in Jamaica in the 1930s. They merit our close attention because of the way in which they have integrated the economic, social, political, and religious aspects of their lifestyle, and because, in their 55 blending of beliefs and activities from a variety of cultures, they are representative of the pluralistic society that is the Caribbean.

[6]   Since the beginnings of the Rasta movement in Jamaica, the Rasta system of belief has spread throughout the Caribbean, into parts of the African nations of Kenya and Ethiopia, and into urban centers in 60 the United States, England, and Canada. The Rasta are easily recognized by their "dreads," or long, twisted locks of hair, and their clothing is often ablaze with the green, gold, and red of African patriotism. Probably their best-known but least-understood characteristic is their use of "ganja" or marijuana as part of their religious beliefs. Rastafarians pro- 65 claim the **divinity** of Haile Selassie, late emperor of Ethiopia, and use texts of the Bible to justify their lifestyle. Repatriation to Africa is also a key ideal in Rasta belief.

[7]   Rasta philosophy condemns modern society with its "boss-and-worker" wage-earning mentality and favors a **communal** identity. 70 Urban Rasta earn a living by bonding together and forming small-scale cooperative enterprises such as eateries, clothing stores, and craft markets. All these enterprises are based on extended family-like networks. Rural Rasta communities engage in family-based **subsistence** agriculture with only a minimum of involvement in the region's money 75 economy. According to anthropologist William Lewis, a noted authority on the Rastafarians, the wearing of dreadlocks is related to the Rasta rejection of mainstream wage labor, for this hairstyle is not acceptable to many **conventional** employers. Other ways in which the Rasta separate themselves from the economic and social life of mainstream society 80

40

is through their linguistic inventions, such as new words and suffixes and prefixes that change the meaning of existing English words, and their prohibitions on Rasta women and children mixing with non-Rasta populations. In drawing boundaries around themselves with their distinctive dress and hairstyle, in rejecting mainstream authority figures, in utilizing an illegal substance in their religious system, and in striving to be independent of the capitalistic economy, the Rastafarians contribute their own unique and colorful pieces to the pluralistic **mosaic** of Caribbean life.

85

Reading Comprehension

1. True–False

After each statement write *T* for true, *F* for false, or *NI* for no information, according to the information given in the reading passage.

a. Christopher Columbus and his sailors were the first people in the subtropical islands called the Caribbean. _____

b. Colonial settlement of the Caribbean was limited to the French and Spanish nations. _____

c. Cuba and the Dominican Republic share a similar European heritage. _____

d. European influence in the Caribbean today is found only in the architecture of the island towns. _____

e. The majority of slaves imported to the Caribbean came from West Africa. _____

f. The Caribbean region includes only people of European and African descent. _____

g. Rastafari "dreadlocks" suggest a rejection of the capitalistic values of modern Western society. _____

h. The Rastafari use of marijuana in their religious system is currently illegal. _____

i. The Rasta ideal is emigration to Canada and the United States, where they can improve their standard of living. _____

j. Rastafarians cannot communicate in English with other English-speaking Caribbean people. _____

2. *Reading Review*

Orally or in writing, answer the following questions based on information in the reading passage.

a. What happened to the indigenous peoples whom Columbus encountered on the Caribbean islands?

b. What factors are primarily responsible for the ethnic diversity of the Caribbean?

c. What is the cultural similarity among Cuba, Puerto Rico, and the Dominican Republic? How is this group of islands different culturally from Martinique and Haiti?

d. Would a native of Aruba and a native of Jamaica speak the same language? Explain.

e. What originally brought the Chinese to the Caribbean? What role do the Chinese fill today in the Caribbean area?

f. What do the religions of Voudou and Rastafarianism have in common?

g. List one or more key beliefs of the Rastafarian religion.

h. In what ways do the Rastafari separate themselves from the mainstream population among whom they live?

i. What does the phrase *"boss-and-worker" wage-earning mentality* mean? What alternative economic system do the Rastafarians engage in?

j. Repatriation, or return to Africa, is a Rastafarian ideal. What problems might Caribbean Rastafarians encounter if they were actually to return to an African country such as Ethiopia?

3. *Analyzing the Text*

Respond to the following items as appropriate.

a. In the first sentence of paragraph [1], which of the following phrases could correctly precede the words "a region"?
(1) *because it is*
(2) *while it is*
(3) *which is*
(4) none of the above

b. In the second sentence of paragraph [1], the word *whom* refers to
(1) the area.
(2) the Carib Indian peoples.
(3) Christopher Columbus.
(4) the "New World."
In the same sentence, why is the expression "New World" in quotation marks?

   c. In the last sentence of paragraph [1], the expression "that characterizes" refers to

     (1) European conquest.
     (2) European settlement.
     (3) Caribbean islands.
     (4) ethnic pluralism.

   d. Paragraph [2] contains one signal of contrast, one signal of result, and one signal of specific instance. List these signals.

   e. The first sentence in paragraph [3] uses the word *however*. What two items are being contrasted by this signal?

   f. Which expression in the first sentence of paragraph [4] means the same as *also?*

   g. The last sentence of paragraph [4] includes a description of Trinidad. What is the clause marker for that description?

   h. In the second sentence of paragraph [5], to what does the phrase "the latter religion" refer?

   i. The last sentence in paragraph [5] is a reason-result statement. Underline the clause of result and the signal expression of reason.

   j. In the first sentence of paragraph [6], the word *Since* signals

     (1) a reason.
     (2) a time clause.
     (3) a conditional clause.
     (4) an addition of description.

   k. In the fourth sentence of Paragraph [7], the word *for* is a connector that means

     (1) although.
     (2) so.
     (3) because.
     (4) while.

4. *Paraphrasing*

In the writing style of a particular author, we sometimes find an idiomatic use of language, figures of speech, or phrases that are not stated in the plainest way, but in a more decorative or elaborate way. Paraphrasing, or putting these phrases into your own words, is a good way to ensure that you understand the writer's meaning. Paraphrase the italicized phrases in the following statements.

     a. . . . these European nations afterward *spread their dominion over* all of the Caribbean islands.

     b. . . . the Dutch presence of former times *is still apparent linguistically and architecturally* in St. Maartens, Aruba, and Curaçao.

     c. . . . the vast sugar plantations . . . were *the mainstay* of the Caribbean economy. . . .

d.   . . . it is still *in the role of small entrepreneur* that one finds the many thousands of Chinese in the Caribbean today.

e.   [The Rastafari] clothing *is often ablaze* with the green, gold, and red of *African patriotism.*

f.   Rastafarians *proclaim the divinity* of Haile Selassie. . . .

Vocabulary Study

1. Prefixes and Roots

Prefixes and roots are important clues to the general meaning of English words. Use your dictionary to find the meaning of the words in column A whose prefixes and roots are defined for you. Then, try to state the meanings of the related words in column B, based on the prefix and root associations. Use your dictionary as necessary.

A		**B**
(1) proclaim	*pro*: before *claim*: call out	propose; a claimant
(2) coexist	*co*: together *exist*: live, be	cooperate; Existentialism
(3) invasion	*in*: in/into *vade*: go	intrude; evade
(4) impoverished	*im*: in *pover*: poor	immersed; poverty
(5) repatriation	*re*: again *patria*: country	review; patriotism

2. Word Form Table

Fill in the following table with the appropriate forms of the given words. Some nouns or adjectives may have two forms.

	Verbs	**Nouns**	**Adjectives**	**Adverbs**
a.	condemn	_____	_____	xxx
b.	_____	_____	significant	_____
c.	_____	influence	_____	_____
d.	_____	_____	_____	prosperously
e.	_____	ideal	_____	_____

Use the correct form from each lettered line to complete the same lettered sentence below.

a. Do you agree with the _____ of modern society as materialistic, corrupt, and violent?

b. Some _____ aspects of Rastafarianism are its blend of Christianity with African religious belief and its rejection of capitalism.

c. European colonialism has had a major _____ on the lives of people in the Caribbean area.

d. In order to become _____ in a capitalistic society, one must have an ambitious and competitive character.

e. The Rastafari view communal African patterns of economic life as the _____ .

3. *Word Formation*

Prefix *trans:* syllable attached to the front of a word meaning "across."

> transact
> transcribe
> transfer
> transform
> transgress
> transmit
> transport

a. Write a noun form for each of the preceding verbs. Write a meaningful sentence for each word, using either the verb or noun form.

b. Explain the meaning of each of the italicized words in the following sentences:

(1) Mr. Jones's residence in California was of a *transitory* nature.

(2) The United States Constitution provides for a peaceful *transition* between presidents.

(3) My typewriter is very *transportable* because it weighs only 15 pounds.

(4) The *transcontinental* railway stretched from New York to California.

(5) It is not easy to *transcend* the linguistic, economic, and social problems faced by most immigrants to a new country.

Writing Exercises

Editing for Sentence-Level Consistency

Consistency in writing refers to the agreement of related sentence elements in number, point of view, and/or structure. Consistency is important for sentence-level correctness in English, yet it is often neglected by student writers. Editing for consistency should be done by reading aloud the prefinal draft of a paper, pencil in hand, to catch and correct errors with the ear as well as the eye. It is useful to edit homework assignments in this way several hours or one day after you have written them. Some common trouble spots in consistency are discussed in this section. Keep alert for these as you edit your own work.

   [1] Subject + Verb Agreement: Separated Elements. In any English clause, the subject must agree with its verb. That is, a singular subject takes a singular verb; a plural subject takes a plural verb. Disagreement between subject and verb frequently occurs when the subject and verb are separated by a prepositional phrase or an adjective (relative) clause.

One of the main **purposes of art** *is* the communication of
(sing. subject)   (prep. phrase)   (sing. verb)

emotion.

Frequently, *Western artists,* who are accustomed to
           (pl. subject)   (pl. verb)   (adjective clause)

freedom of imagination and expression, *have* difficulty
                                                   (pl. verb)

adjusting to political constraints.

Note that *each, either,* and *neither* take singular nouns and that *one* and *everyone* are singular subjects. Verb agreement is shown in active verbs in the simple present, present continuous, past continuous, and present perfect tenses. Passive verbs in all tenses except future and past perfect show agreement.

1. *Sentence Completion for Consistency*

Read the following paragraph. Then determine the simple subject of each clause and note whether it is singular or plural. Fill in the blank spaces with the consistent form of the verb in parentheses. Choose the correct verb tense based on the context of the material.

A number of anthropologists (to study) (1) _____ mental perceptions in different human groups. One interesting aspect of these studies (to be) (2) _____ their discovery of different kinds of perceptual ability based on the demands of the physical environment and the culture. For example, the Temne, an African tribe that (to inhabit) (3) _____ a heavily vegetated area, (to require: negative) (4) _____ strong spatial perception skills to survive. The Temne environment, which (to include) (5) _____ many multicolored plants, thus (to provide) (6) _____ many easily identifiable landmarks for the traveler. Furthermore, each of the Temne communities (to be) (7) _____ a self-contained farming unit, so going outside the village for food (to be) (8) _____ not necessary. Every parent and authority figure in the Temne community (to enforce) (9) _____ strict discipline on the children. Obedience to adult authorities (to instill: passive) (10) _____ in Temne children from their infancy. Independence of movement and imagination (to encourage: passive, negative) (11) _____ among the Temne. Either a Temne elder, a parent, or even an older sibling closely (to supervise) (12) _____ the Temne child at all times. These Temne patterns of child rearing (to develop: negative) (13) _____ the individualistic imagination that we (to associate) (14) _____ with the Western artist. Thus, if Temne art (to judge: passive) (15) _____ by Western standards, it might appear to us as craftwork rather than as true art. Such cross-cultural differences, which (to distinguish) (16) _____ most traditional societies from our own, (to be) (17) _____ important factors in appreciating artistic forms.

[2] Agreement Between Nouns and Referents. Pronouns, words that substitute for nouns in the same or subsequent sentences, must agree in number (and sometimes in gender) with their nouns.

> *Museum visitors* should know what cultural values lie
> (pl. subject)
>
> behind *their* response to a work of art.
> (pl. object pronoun)

Verbs in the adjective clause must agree in number with the noun that immediately precedes them.

> There are many *symbols* in this painting that *relate* to
> (pl. subject)   (pl. verb)
>
> American cultural values.

Possessive adjectives and demonstratives *(this, these, that, those)* must agree in number with their referents.

> *Motivation, training, and talent* are important for success
> (pl. subject)
>
> in the field of illustration. *These* factors must all be
> (pl. demonstrative adjective)
>
> considered in entering that field.
> (sing. demonstrative adjective)

Logically related nouns in a sentence must agree with each other in number.

> *Art students* who want *jobs* in today's market need
> (pl. subject)   (pl. referent)
>
> appropriate college *degrees* in addition to *their* artistic
> (pl. referent)   (pl. referent)
>
> talents.

1. Agreement in Number

Read the following paragraph. On a separate sheet of paper, revise it by changing all the italicized noun phrases to the plural. Change all related verbs and noun referents to the plural and make whatever additional changes are necessary for correctness.

(1) *The Kpelle tribe* lives in Liberia, West Africa. (2) *A cultural conflict* exists between the Kpelle learning *style* and that of the scientific Western world. (3) Traditionally, *the Kpelle learning pattern* has been based on the unquestioning acceptance of authority and rote learning. (4) *A Kpelle adult* sees the world as a mystery and accepts his or her *world view* as it is handed down by tribal elders. (5) *The Kpelle individual* does not perceive a rational pattern to the operation of the universe, nor does *he or she* comprehend a *law of nature* that regulates its workings. (6) *The Kpelle child or adult* does not look for patterns in visual stimuli or in language the way a Westerner does. (7) In addition, among the Kpelle, *a number* does not exist abstractly; it must always be linked to a specific noun. (8) There is no *Kpelle word* for "one" or "two" on its own. (9) *A Kpelle person* must say "one of this" or "two of that." (10) *Such a cognitive style* presents difficulties in learning the multiplication table, for example. (11) Currently, *the Kpelle school* is still trying to teach its pupils new concepts in science through *the traditional method*. (12) *This method* is not working well, because it does not develop the skills of abstract thinking and intellectual curiosity that underlie Western scientific education. (13) *The Kpelle teacher* must learn a new mode of instruction to help *the Kpelle child* cross from his or her old world to the new technological one.

2. *Noun-Pronoun Consistency*

Circle each of the pronouns in the following paragraph and draw an arrow to the noun that is its referent. Mark the noun singular or plural. The first one has been done.

(1) Every culture has its own traditional constraints for dress and behavior at places of religious worship. (2) When tourists visit such sites, they should wear modest attire and conduct themselves in a restrained way. (3) Many religions have dress codes for women; these usually request females to cover their bodies. (4) For example, women visiting Catholic churches or Islamic mosques are often requested not to wear dresses that bare their arms or their backs. (5) A woman's skirt that bares her knees or a blouse that reveals her chest is not considered sufficiently modest to wear inside an active place of worship. (6) Although women may generally wear pants, tight jeans that reveal their figures are considered disrespectful. (7) Neither men nor women are permitted to wear shorts on their visits to religious sites

in many countries. (8) In many Catholic churches, women must cover their heads and men remove their hats. (9) But in orthodox Jewish synagogues, it is the opposite: A man wears his hat and a woman removes hers. (10) One way we can show our respect for foreign cultures is to learn their codes of dress and behavior and follow them to a reasonable extent.

3. *Sentence Construction*

The following items are based on the information given in the preceding paragraph. Use all the given words in the given order to construct complete, correct English sentences by adding words before and after those provided. The first one has been done.

a. culture   traditional   dress and behavior   religious

Each culture has a traditional way of dress and behavior for visiting religious sites.

b. tourists   religious sites   wear   clothing   bodies

_____

_____

c. woman's skirt   knees   visits   temple   church

_____

_____

d. women   not   jeans   reveal   figures

_____

_____

e. men   shorts   visit   holy places   countries

_____

_____

f. church   women   heads   men   uncover

_____

_____

[3]   Point of View: Consistency.   The point of view of a piece of writing refers to the person from whose eyes the topic is being seen or discussed. **First-person point of view** is used to relate the writer's own experiences. It uses the pronouns *I, me, my, mine, myself*. **Second-person point of view** addresses the reader directly, as if the writer were in conversation with the reader. It uses the pronouns *you, your, yours, yourself, yourselves*.

Third-person singular point of view discusses a topic or relates opinions not in reference to the writer or the reader but to a third person. It uses the pronouns *he* or *she, his* or *her, his* or *hers, himself* or *herself*.

Third-person plural point of view refers to third persons in general, that is, two or more persons. It uses the pronouns *they, them, their, theirs, themselves*.

First person:	**As a motivated student, I prepare thoroughly for all my exams.**
Second person:	**If you are a motivated student, you will prepare thoroughly for all your exams.**
Third-person singular:	**A motivated student will prepare thoroughly for all of his or her exams.**
Third-person plural:	**Motivated students will prepare thoroughly for all of their exams.**

The point of view with which you begin your paper must govern the point of view all the way through. You may change from third-person singular to third-person plural in different sentences to give your paper some variety, but basically, the same point of view should be used consistently.

1. *Paragraph Writing: Point-of-View Consistency*

Choose one of the statements in the preceding boxed example as the topic sentence for a paragraph that describes the process by which a motivated student prepares for an exam. Write for fifteen minutes. Do not edit for grammatical correctness while writing. At your instructor's signal, stop writing and read your paragraph quietly aloud, pencil in hand, to check for point-of-view consistency. Also pay attention to noun-referent and subject-verb agreement. Your instructor may copy one or two paragraphs on the board for peer correction. Look at these for consistency.

2. *Composing Complex Sentences: Point-of-View Consistency*

Use each pair of given items to compose a complex sentence that demonstrates point-of-view consistency. Vary the points of view. The first one has been done.

a. eat junk food/become ill

If I eat a lot of junk food, I may become seriously ill.

b. cook rabbit/like it

c. take vitamins/improve health

d. save money/bring lunch

e. find uses for seaweed/decrease famine

f. bake pastry/follow a recipe

g. learn about diet/take a course

h. be overweight/avoid fattening foods

_____

_____

i. become a good cook/practice

_____

_____

j. invite guests/serve food

_____

_____

3. *Editing for Point-of-View Consistency*

A person who has intelligent eating patterns is likely to be a healthy, energetic person. Write for fifteen minutes about intelligent patterns of buying, preparing, or consuming food. Choose the point of view from which you will write before you start. At your instructor's signal, stop writing and edit your paper for point-of-view consistency.

Editing for Correct Verb Forms

Confusion between the simple present or simple past tense on the one hand and continuous present or continuous past tense on the other may give your compositions a nonnative sound. Review the "Verb Summary" in Appendix B and then complete the following exercises.

1. *Simple Present or Present Continuous*

- **Sentence Completion.** In China, emotional attachment to a scenic place is quite strong. In the following paragraph by a Chinese student about the Green Lake Park in his city, blank spaces have been left for the verb form. Use either the simple present or the present continuous of the verb in parentheses as appropriate.

Every Sunday I (stroll) (1) _____ through beautiful Green

Lake Park in the heart of my city. On that day, when most people (work:

negative) (2) _____, they (visit) (3) _____

the park in great numbers to enjoy the activities there. Then the park (present) (4) _____ a fascinating spectacle of colorfully dressed couples, families, and young people. Here, in the sunshine, on the bank of the lake, a child (feed) (5) _____ the ducks that (swim) (6) _____ in the cool water. There, in a shady arbor, where the sun (intrude: negative) (7) _____, old men (play) (8) _____ cards while their spouses (knit) (9) _____ sweaters for the grandchildren. On two sides of the stream that (divide) (10) _____ the park, peasant men and women (sing) (11) _____ to each other in a country dialect of which I (understand) (12) _____ only a little. Until well after midnight, when the moon (rise) (13) _____, our beautiful Green Lake Park (attracts) (14) _____ visitors. I (know) (15) _____ that if I ever (leave) (16) _____ my city, the memory of Sundays in Green Lake Park will remain fresh in my mind.

- **Paragraph Writing.** Write a similar paragraph that describes an activity you customarily enjoy in your free time.

2. *Past Continuous Tense: Paragraph Reconstruction*

Read the following paragraph as many times as you can in three minutes. The scene is that of a writer's arrival at the airport in Kingston, Jamaica. People's activities are described in the past continuous tense. After you have read the paragraph, reconstruct it as close to the original as you can by following the subject-verb chart of its sentences, which your instructor will put on the board. Close your text and use only the chart for reference.

(1) When I first arrived at the Kingston airport in May, the temperature was 94°.* (2) A light breeze was blowing, and an enormous moon was shining above the airport towers. (3) Although it was 2:00 A.M., many people were moving about. (4) Some families were saying goodbye to relatives who were going abroad; other people were greeting relatives and friends who had just arrived. (5) Everyone was carrying something: flowers, fruit, suitcases, crying babies. (6) There were several scenes of deep emotion. (7) Men were shaking hands warmly with each other; men,

---

*This temperature is in Fahrenheit; the Celsius equivalent is about 34°.

women, and children were kissing each other and embracing. (8) Despite the heat and the late hour, it was a lively scene.

	Subject	**Main Verb (Infinitive Form)**
1.	I	to arrive
	the temperature	to be
2.	breeze	to blow
	moon	to shine
3.	it	to be
	people	to move
4.	families	to say
	relatives	to go
	people	to greet
	relatives and friends	to arrive
5.	everyone	to carry
6.	There	to be
7.	Men	to shake
	men, women, and children	to kiss
		to embrace
8.	it	to be

3. *Simple Past and Past Continuous: Paragraph Writing*

Reflect for three minutes on a scene of arrival at a busy place (for example, your arrival in the United States, a party, college registration) that you have experienced. In brief note form, list as many activities as you can recall that other people were doing. Also list various details of the environment. Use these details as the basis for a paragraph.

Editing for Sentence Boundaries

A prefinal draft of your essays should always be read aloud (softly, if you are in class) to make sure you have used punctuation correctly to mark your phrase, clause, and sentence boundaries. Review the material on sentences and punctuation in Appendix B. Then work on the following exercises, reading each item aloud with a pencil in your hand to insert or revise your punctuation as necessary.

1. *Comma Use*

The comma represents a *brief* pause. It is used to separate essential or main clause information from nonessential information, extra description, or dependent clauses. The comma is also used to separate items in a series. Edit the following sentences for meaningful comma use.

a. Although many of the Caribbean islands such as Jamaica and Barbados are English-speaking others such as Martinique and Haiti use French or a French-based Creole to communicate.

b. Haitian Creole which is a blending of French and African language elements is a fascinating language to study. In some American cities such as New York where there is a large Haitian population the Haitian newspapers which are written primarily in French also include some columns in the Creole language.

c. Puerto Rico which has commonwealth status with the United States is currently undergoing examination of its political structure. Some Puerto Ricans favor maintaining the commonwealth status others desire full statehood and still others want full independence from the United States.

d. In many of the Caribbean nations with their limited raw materials and natural resources tourism is the mainstay of the economy. Therefore according to some observers it is in the best economic interests of these nations to maintain a stable political and social environment that will encourage vacationers to visit.

e. Judaism Buddhism Islam Hinduism and various forms of Christianity are among the many religions practiced throughout the Caribbean. Jewish synagogues Catholic and Protestant churches Hindu temples and Islamic mosques may be found on various islands of the region.

2. *Periods and Semicolons*

Periods and semicolons mark off independent clauses that can stand on their own as complete sentences. Semicolons are generally used to separate short independent clauses that have a close relationship to each other. Mark off the sentence boundaries in the following passage with periods or semicolons as appropriate.

Marie Galante is a small Caribbean island that is part of the French Antilles the island is one of the few in the Caribbean that has not been invaded by mass tourism so it retains its authentic local flavor Christopher Columbus landed in Marie Galante in 1493 and named the island "Marie the Gracious" after the name of his ship the island was later settled by French colonists and the African slaves they brought in to work on the sugarcane plantations the island still retains French and French Creole as its languages the only remains of the original Indian population is an ancient Carib Indian site at Les Galieres many of the people on Marie Galante are farmers everywhere throughout the countryside you can see men working in the fields swinging their machetes and women in plaid cotton dresses and broad-brimmed hats carrying baskets and bundles on their heads just as 200 years ago sugarcane is the dominant commercial crop interesting visits can be made

Many people have emigrated from the West Indies, or Caribbean, to the large cities of the United States. Yet they continue to maintain their cultural traditions. Here a young Caribbean woman, elaborately costumed, marches in the annual West Indian Day parade in New York.

to the old sugar mills and newer rum distilleries that lie in the middle of the island

Composition Development

Developing Central Ideas: Concept-Detail Outlines

Whether you are responding spontaneously to an essay question on an examination or preparing a research paper that will take the entire semester to complete, the most effective response to the subject is to make a prewriting plan. Once you have analyzed the assignment and formulated your overall central idea, it is useful to box outline two or three of the most significant concepts related to the theme. Depending on the length of the assignment, jot down two, three, or more details to develop your concepts. Study the following examples. Note the revision that takes place after the first draft of the outline.

Original Outline

> **Assignment:** Discuss one predominant characteristic of American culture and describe and illustrate its effect on American life.
>
> > **Introductory paragraph notes:** American culture places a high value on *individuality,* and Americans of all ages
> > (topic)
> >
> > are encouraged to "do their own thing." (Expand definition of individuality.) This cultural value clearly can be seen in *American family life,* in which it has both
> > (limit on
> >
> > *negative and positive effects.*
> > central idea)

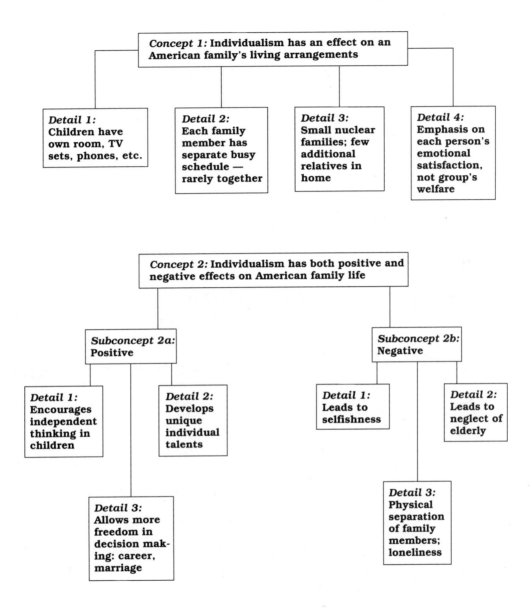

Concept 1: Individualism has an effect on an American family's living arrangements

Detail 1: Children have own room, TV sets, phones, etc.

Detail 2: Each family member has separate busy schedule — rarely together

Detail 3: Small nuclear families; few additional relatives in home

Detail 4: Emphasis on each person's emotional satisfaction, not group's welfare

Concept 2: Individualism has both positive and negative effects on American family life

Subconcept 2a: Positive

Subconcept 2b: Negative

Detail 1: Encourages independent thinking in children

Detail 2: Develops unique individual talents

Detail 1: Leads to selfishness

Detail 2: Leads to neglect of elderly

Detail 3: Allows more freedom in decision making: career, marriage

Detail 3: Physical separation of family members; loneliness

Revised Outline

Move concept 1, detail 4 to a new position as concept 3 with its own developmental details. Renumber subsequent concepts.

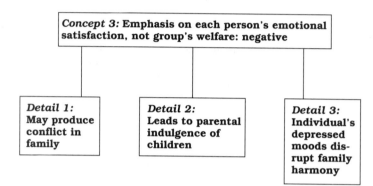

```
┌─────────────────────────────────────────────────────┐
│ Concept 3: Emphasis on each person's emotional        │
│ satisfaction, not group's welfare: negative           │
└─────────────────────────────────────────────────────┘
```

| Detail 1: May produce conflict in family | Detail 2: Leads to parental indulgence of children | Detail 3: Individual's depressed moods disrupt family harmony |

1. *Developing Concept-Detail Outlines*

Complete the following box outlines with appropriate choices from the list of items on the right.

a. Introduction: Forty years ago, American publisher Henry Luce wrote that this era would be and should be known as the "American Century." And in fact, American culture is sweeping the globe today.

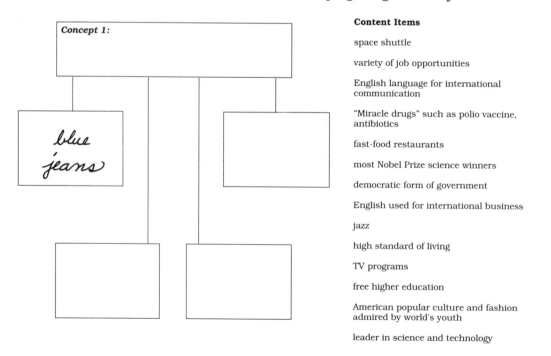

Concept 1:

blue jeans

Content Items

space shuttle

variety of job opportunities

English language for international communication

"Miracle drugs" such as polio vaccine, antibiotics

fast-food restaurants

most Nobel Prize science winners

democratic form of government

English used for international business

jazz

high standard of living

TV programs

free higher education

American popular culture and fashion admired by world's youth

leader in science and technology

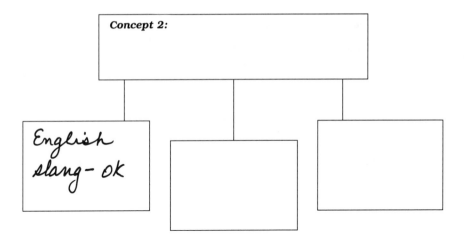

Concept 2:

English slang – ok

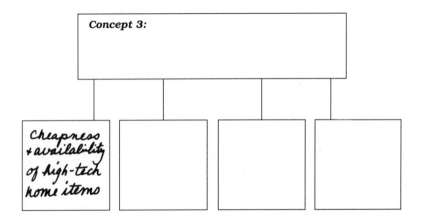

Concept 3:

Cheapness + availability of high-tech home items

Concept 4:

U.S. most desired country for immigrants

2. *From Outline to Essay*

From the example of the concept-detail outline about individualism and the American family, compose a complete essay using the given structure. You may add or change details if you wish.

3. *Talking About Writing*

In round-robin fashion, with your class discuss the type of writing assignments you have had in your courses. Try to recall the topic and requirements of the assignments as precisely as possible. Have someone put these topics/requirements on the board. Continue the class discussion by answering some of the following questions.

   a. How did you choose your final topic? By what process did you narrow it down?

   b. What kind of prewriting plan, if any, did you use? How closely did you follow your plan? If you made major changes, what were they?

   c. Did you need to consult any reading materials for your paper? If so, what kind? How did you take notes on your reading material?

   d. What was the hardest part of completing your paper? Did you need any help with your paper? If so, what kind?

4. *Outlining*

Individually, as a group, or as a class, create a box concept-detail outline for a composition about how to write a college essay or term paper.

Writing Introductions

An introductory paragraph of an essay has three related main purposes: (1) to alert the reader to the topic in an interesting way, (2) to acquaint the reader with the writer's purpose, and (3) to present the writer's controlling point of view about the topic. The introductory paragraph should be proportionate to the body of the essay; in a paper of any length, the introduction and conclusion together should not equal more than about one-quarter of the total number of words.

You can introduce any given topic in a number of different ways. Suppose that the following topic is assigned:

The religious and cultural systems of some groups include practices that are illegal according to American laws. (Examples of some religious or cultural practices that are currently judged illegal in the United States would be the Pennsylvania Dutch [Amish] refusal to send their children to school, the Rastafari use of marijuana, and the practice of polygamy by some Mormon groups.) The members of these groups claim that the United States

Constitution protects their religious and cultural freedom and the government should not interfere, even if their practices are against current American laws. Do you agree or disagree with these claimants? Support your point of view with data from your reading and life experience.

Following are five different ways of introducing an essay on this topic.

Useful Introductory Techniques

[1] **Anecdotes.**   Beginning an essay with a brief anecdote, narrative, that is related to your central idea is one way to engage your reader's interest. But, illustrative introductory anecdotes must have a clear focus and lead into your controlling idea without confusion.

> *(Example of anecdote)* **Recently I saw a Rastafarian man being searched on the street by two police. The police were searching under his hat and in his dreadlocks, probably to find marijuana. Since the police know that the Rasta use marijuana in their religion, they probably thought they would find marijuana on him.** *(Controlling idea:)* **But in my opinion, this search was unfair. If the Rasta use marijuana for religious purposes, and are not caught selling it to other people, why should the police care. Religious freedom is an important right in the United States.**

[2] **Proverbs or References to Popular Literature, Historical Events, or Legends.**   Quoting popular proverbs or traditional stories gives a rich, culture-specific tone to an introduction. In making such references, you must be accurate both in paraphrasing the content and naming the source.

> *(Example of proverb)* **There is an American saying: "If you want to play, you've got to pay." I think this applies to all people living in the United States. If you want to stay here and enjoy the benefits of our country, you have to obey the laws.** *(Controlling idea:)* **No religious or cultural custom is an excuse for breaking American laws. If religious groups don't like our laws, they should try to change them or move somewhere else.**

[3] Extended Definition of Key Concepts. Some essay questions include a key word or phrase that is general or abstract. People may interpret this concept in different ways. One good way to begin an essay about such a topic is to define and explain the key concept in a way that leads to your main idea.

> *(Example of extended definition)* The word *illegal* means "against the law." But who made the law? Laws are made by powerful groups of people, and they are often unfair to minority groups without power. *(Controlling idea:)* Personal faith and conscience are higher laws than the laws made by other humans. I believe people ought to be able to practice their religion even if it includes some "illegal" activities, as long as they do not harm others.

[4] Statements About the Current Importance of the Topic. This type of introduction is suitable when the topic is one that affects modern life and has been widely reported by the media or is commonly experienced by people.

> *(Example of statement of current importance of the topic)* Today in pluralistic countries like the United States, there is a lot of discussion about cultural practices that do not fit into the American mainstream. The newspapers are constantly reporting about different cultural groups who have done something illegal because it is part of their own social or religious background. *(Controlling idea:)* Because there are so many different ethnic groups in the United States today, we must examine this topic from all angles to see if we can find a solution. Different cases may call for different solutions.

[5] Statements of Concession. An introduction that uses this technique begins by stating several points that are opposite to those of the main idea that the writer intends to develop. Then, using a strong expression of contrast, the writer states the thesis. Concession is a useful way to begin a paper on a controversial subject.

> *(Example of concession: giving some facts for the opposite point of view)* It is true that the U.S. Constitution protects freedom of religion. Most Americans support the constitutional right of other Americans to practice their personal faith and follow their own cultural values. *(Controlling idea:)* But it is also true that we have laws in the United States for the protection of all the people. These laws keep us free and secure. No group, even a religious one, has the right to decide which laws they will obey and which ones they won't.

1. *Composing Introductions*

Choose one of the following essay topics (or more, as directed by your instructor) and compose an introduction, using one of the techniques illustrated above. Underscore your controlling idea in each introduction.

a. Racism used to be a strong and widespread characteristic of people all over the world. But today, with higher education and improved communication, racism has decreased significantly in every area of life. Do you agree or disagree?

b. Crime has increased so much in the large urban centers that our regular police force can no longer control it. Private groups or community volunteers are needed to help the police control crime. Do you agree or disagree?

c. The audible playing of radios on beaches, in parks, and on public transportation has been prohibited in many places. This is unfair to those for whom music is an important part of life. People should have the right to listen to their music wherever they wish. Do you agree or disagree?

d. Alcohol and tobacco are proven causes of disease and early death. Marijuana is no more dangerous than these two substances. If alcohol and tobacco are legal, marijuana should be, too. Do you agree or disagree?

e. In the United States, religious groups do not pay taxes on the property and businesses they own. This exemption from taxes puts a heavier burden on the ordinary taxpaying citizen and should be changed. Religious groups should pay their fair share of taxes like everyone else. Do you agree or disagree?

f. Currently, in the United States, public schools do not set aside any time for prayer or religious meditation. This is too bad, because religious prayer is a constructive, wholesome activity that our public institutions should support. Do you agree or disagree?

Composition Topics

1. Some people say that knowing how to write well is no longer an important skill. They claim that telephones, tape recorders, television, computers, and other forms of nonwritten communication have made good writing skills unnecessary. Do you agree or disagree? Support your viewpoint with rational arguments, concrete details, and examples from your life experience.
2. Every country in the world today is suffering from economic problems. Even wealthy countries cannot provide full employment and a good standard of living for all their people. Therefore, it is unfair to the citizens of a country to have to accept immigrants from other places. All immigration should be stopped until the economic situation of a country improves. Do you agree or disagree? Support your viewpoint with logical reasons, explanatory details, and illustrations from your reading and life experience.

Appendix A

The Composition Process

Just as each culture has its own language and cultural patterns, each also has its own style of composition. The composition style of English-speaking Western cultures emphasizes the logical, linear development of one main idea through a series of closely related paragraphs. Each paragraph is expected to contain a subtopic developed through main idea statements supported by facts, details, reasons, or examples. The English composition style requires that sentences follow each other in clearly related sequence and that directional words and expressions be used to indicate the relationships between sentences. The consistent use of verb tenses and pronouns, subject-verb agreement, and consistency of singular-plural reference are all important.

Composition Review Form

1. Introduction

Is your topic clearly stated and limited according to the given question? Is your opinion or point of view about the topic clear to the reader? Underscore the sentence or parts of the sentence that state your opinion or view about the topic.

2. Paragraph Structure

Each paragraph must have its own topic statement that expresses a main idea about one aspect of your overall main idea. Is it clear which subtopic or aspect of your main idea you are going to develop? Is your point of view or opinion clear? Do you begin a new paragraph for each new subtopic?

Consider the different details and examples in each paragraph that support the topic statement. Does each specific detail relate to the topic?

Are all the sentences about one detail or example together? Are they in logical sequence? Are there any details or examples that do not relate to the stated topic of the paragraph? Ask yourself if you should eliminate these. Or can you revise them to fit into the paragraph? Should you save them for another paragraph in the composition? Have you used appropriate signal words and expressions to guide your reader from sentence to sentence?

3. Development of the Composition

Does your introduction supply your readers with the information they need to understand your topic and main idea? Recheck it.

Do all your paragraphs develop the topic statement? Does each paragraph *support,* not contradict, your stated opinion? Are the paragraphs in logical order: most important to least important, similarities to differences, meaningful time order?

Are your verbs consistent and complementary throughout? Look at your first complete main verb. What is its tense? Look at several more complete main verbs. Check their tenses. Are they in agreement with or in appropriate relationship to the opening verb?

Did you begin your composition in the first-person singular *(I)*, second-person *(you),* third-person singular (noun, or *he, she,* or *one*), or third-person plural *(they)?* Do all your relevant nouns and pronouns continue this point of view?

Does your conclusion summarize the main points of your paper? Does the conclusion express the same opinion as the topic statement?

4. Editing for Correctness

Read each sentence aloud, beginning with the last and working backward. Does each sentence have a complete main verb? Are all the necessary parts of the verb included? Is the verb singular or plural? What is its subject? Do the verb and subject agree in number?

Have you used such words as *because, if, since, although, which, that, when* to introduce dependent clauses? Do these clauses have their own complete verbs? Are they connected to independent clauses to make a complete sentence?

Are your periods and commas clearly differentiated? Look at every period you used. Is the thought that comes before it completely finished? (Test it by making it a *yes* or *no* question.)

Look at every comma you used. Have you mistakenly used a comma to close off a complete thought? Should you change the comma to a period or a semicolon? Can you give a reason for every comma you used?

Your instructor will help you identify and correct errors you may have overlooked in your review.

Composition (Editing) Correction Symbols

ap.   apostrophe error *(Tonys parents are going to the Far East.)*

awk.   awkward expression; tangled syntax *(Everyone knows it is true many of the old people will cause many of inconvenient because of the sickness with them.)*

cap.   capitalization *(A visit to the brooklyn botanical gardens is a delightful experience.)*

carat ∧   something left out *(My neighbor was walking∧dog last night at 10:00.)*

frag.   fragment; incomplete sentence; dependent clause used as a sentence *(For example.; Many college students holding part-time jobs.; Although I like my neighborhood.)*

n.s.   number shift: change between number of noun and pronoun *(A student has to work hard to pass their courses.)*

omit ℒ   *(I received ~~the~~ good instruction in English at the University of California.)*

¶   Paragraph; begin new paragraph for a new topic.

pl.   Plural error; disagreement in number between plural nouns and related words *(There are many good reason for continuing your education.; Many students at our college want to become accountant.)*

p.s.   person shift: change in point of view *(If students work hard, you will succeed.)*

punct.   punctuation error: comma or semicolon incorrectly used *(Because, I have to work part-time, I can't study too much.; although it's raining; the game will go on.)*

RO   run on sentences: two independent clauses incorrectly joined by a comma *(I only watch the news on TV, everything else is junk.)*

sp.   spelling *(Do your two children have seperete rooms?)*

s–v   subject–verb disagreement *(The world of older people have changed a lot.)*

VF   verb form wrong *(I was lived in Hawaii for two years.)*

VT   verb tense wrong *(In the past people pay more attention to writing.; When I first left my native city it is very hard for me.)*

Vague   lack of a clear main idea or lack of clear supporting details

WF   wrong form of word: noun/adjective/adverb confusion *(Not having a car is very inconvenience for me.)*

WW   wrong word *(There are many attentive* (for attractive) *restaurants in most large cities.)*

Appendix B

Basic Terminology for English Language Study

Parts of Speech

Noun. A word that names a person, place, thing, quality, idea, or action.

> **John Jones, boy, city, desk, honesty**

Verb. A word that expresses an action performed by or on the subject (action verb) or that expresses a state of being or feeling experienced by the subject (linking verb).

> The students *answered* the questions correctly.
>
> The final exam *was taken* by all the students.
>
> I *feel* strange when I *am* in a new place.

Adjective. A word that defines, describes, or makes specific a noun or noun equivalent. Articles *(a, an, the)* are also adjectives. Adjectives precede the noun they describe. They do not have a plural form. In a series of adjectives that includes a nationality, the adjective of nationality is nearest the noun.

> I feel *strange* in a *new* place.
>
> The *tired American* businessman wanted a *fine French* meal as soon as he landed in Paris.

Articles

Indefinite Article: a, an. The indefinite article is placed before a singular countable noun when the noun is mentioned for the first time and represents no specific person or thing.

> **There is *a* cat in my backyard.**

It is used when the noun is an example of a class of things.

> ***A* bicycle has two wheels.**

It is used with a noun complement.

> **She is *an* interesting person.**

Definite Article: the. The definite article is placed before a singular or a plural noun when someone or something is mentioned a second time.

> **I saw a man in the park. *The* man was walking his dog.**

It is used when someone or something is made definite by the addition of a clause or a phrase.

> ***The* women that I met were friendly.**
> ***The* boy in the blue sweater is my son.**

It is used when there is only one of something.

> ***The* sky is blue. *The* weather is fine.**

It is used before names of seas, oceans, rivers, groups of islands, mountain ranges, and geographical areas.

> **She lives in *the* West near *the* Rocky Mountains.**

It is used before countries that represent a union.

> ***the* United States, *the* Netherlands, *the* Dominican Republic**

It is used before the superlative degree of adjectives.

> **Paul is *the* best student in the class.**

It is used before singular nouns that represent a class of objects.

> ***The* rose is a beautiful flower.**

Preposition. A word that generally has some meaning of position, direction, time, or other abstract relation to a noun. Prepositions frequently begin phrases that answer such questions as *where? in what place? when? how?*

> **The anthropology test *on* the table is *for* you.**
>
> ***In* some traditional countries, students rise *to* their feet when a teacher walks *into* the room.**

Conjunction. A word that joins together related clauses, phrases, or words that are parallel in form. *Compound* coordinators join structurally equal items or independent clauses: *and, or, but, yet, so.*

> **You may have ice cream *or* cake, *but* you can't have both.**

Adverb. A word that describes the extent of or way in which verb action is performed, describes an adjective, or tells how often an event occurs.

> **The dog barked** *loudly.*
>
> **My sister is** *unusually* **intelligent.**
>
> **We** *frequently* **visit our family.**

Adverbial Coordinator. A word that joins a dependent clause to an independent clause. Common adverbial coordinators are *because, since, although, if, where, before, after, while.*

> **The game was cut short** *after* **it started,** *because* **it began to rain.**

Phrases

A group of two or more words that forms a thought unit.
Prepositional Phrase. A phrase that begins with a preposition.

> **The politician spoke** *on television.*

Infinitive Phrase. A phrase that begins with an infinitive.

> **I asked the landlord** *to lower* **the rent.**

Present Participial Phrase. A phrase that begins with the "ing" form of a verb.

> *Singing softly,* **I walked home alone.**

Gerund Phrase. An "ing" form of a verb that acts as a noun (either subject or object). A gerund phrase is a phrase that begins with a gerund.

> *Writing good English* is important in college.
>
> Are you shy about *asking questions?*

Past Participial Phrase. A phrase that begins with the past participle form of a verb.

> The words *spoken by the president* reached millions of homes.

Clauses

A group of words with a subject and a complete main verb.

Independent Clause. A clause that can stand by itself as a completed thought. An independent (main) clause has *no* adverbial marker such as *if, because,* and so on.

> *I have attended* this college for two semesters. After I finish college, *I will work as a lab technician.*

Dependent Clause. A clause that cannot stand alone either because it begins with an adverbial marker such as *if, although,* or *because,* or because it begins with *which, who, whose, that, what,* or *where* to introduce additional information about the independent clause.

> I'm carrying an umbrella *because it's raining.*
>
> *Although I don't usually eat lunch out,* I'll join you today.
>
> A paper *that is neatly typed* makes a good impression.
>
> I like people *who help others.*
>
> I don't understand *what you mean.*
>
> It was clear *that you didn't understand* the question.
>
> The neighborhood *where I live* is lively and interesting.

Sentence Types

A complete sentence can be tested by turning it into a *yes* or *no* question.

Simple Sentence. One independent clause expressing one main thought.

> **New York City offers many pleasures to the adventuresome tourist. (Does New York City offer many pleasures to the adventuresome tourist?)**

Compound Sentence. Two independent clauses joined by a conjunction or a semicolon.

> **First I'm going to the museum, and then I'm stopping at the library. Watch the traffic lights; they change quickly.**

Complex Sentence. A sentence that includes one or more dependent clauses.

> **Although New York has many tourist sights, you need a**
> (dependent clause)
> **map to find them all.**
> **I met my brother at the airport when he came to the city**
> (dependent clause)
> **last week.**
> **People who come late to the theatre annoy others.**
> (dependent clause)

Useful Signal Expressions for Coherence

Thought Relationship	Signals Introducing Independent Clauses	Signals Introducing Dependent Clauses	In Phrases + Nouns
Time	Now, Later, Then, Next, Afterward,	Before/After/ When/While/ Since	On + day On + year At + time
Sequence	First, Second, etc. Finally, In conclusion		
Addition of Items	and (connector) In addition, Also, Moreover, Furthermore, too		as well as
Addition of Description (Adjective Clause)		who, which, that whose, where	
Contrast	but/yet (connector) However, Nevertheless In contrast, On the other hand,	Although/Even though While/Whereas	despite the in spite of
Reason		because, as, since whereas	as a result because of
Result	so (connector) Therefore, As a result, Thus, Consequently		
Condition		If/Whether/ Unless Until	
Example	For example, For instance,		such as
Emphasis	In fact, In other words, Of course,		
Choice	or (connector) otherwise		

Punctuation

Period. Closes a finished thought unit that can stand by itself as a complete sentence.

> **Although I don't agree with you, I believe in your right to speak. Stand up.**

Semicolon. Takes the place of a period between two independent clauses that are closely related in thought.

> **Mary and I used to be quite *close; she* was my best friend until high school.**

Comma. Closes a dependent clause that begins a sentence.

> **Although my daughter is a good driver, I still worry about her.**

Indicates *nonessential* descriptive phrases or dependent clauses.

> **My father, *who travels a lot,* just came back from Paris.**
>
> **José's brother, *the tall man in the middle of the photograph,* works in the city.**

Marks off signal words and expressions.

> **Cats are clean and quiet. Dogs, *however,* are more playful and affectionate.**

Separates parallel items in a series.

> ***Writing, figuring, and understanding* basic science are fundamental aspects of education.**
>
> **Most children would rather watch TV than *read, draw, play outdoors, or listen to music.***

Quotation Marks. Set off the names of television programs, book chapters, magazine articles, or poems (but not book, movie, or painting titles, which are in italic type or are underscored).

> **In his chapter "TV and Violence," in the textbook *Social Patterns in American Life*, Professor Pacheco discusses some interesting ideas.**

Set off direct speech, that is, the exact words spoken by someone.

> **Professor Jones stated, "If children are casually exposed to violence, they may accept it as a normal resolution of conflict."**

Verb Summary

Basic Form. Simple verb, no endings for person or tense.

> ***dance, sing***

Infinitive. "To" + basic form of verb.

> **I would like *to dance* with you.**

Present Participle. Stem of verb + "ing."

---

dance/ *dancing*

Past Participle. The past form of a verb used with a helping verb in perfect tenses, in passive voice, or used alone as an adjective.

I haven't *seen* you lately.

Sometimes angry words are *spoken* too quickly.

The *whipped* dog hung its head.

Tenses

Simple Present. Basic form of verb *except* for third-person singular, which adds *s.* Used for habitual or general action.

Every Sunday we *visit* my family.

History often *repeats* itself.

Present Continuous. *Am, is,* or *are* + present participle ("ing") of main verb. Used for actions that are taking place "right now."

Please don't bother me now; *I'm working.*

Also used for actions that communicate a sense of ongoing activity.

When my father *is reading* the paper, he doesn't like to be disturbed.

Simple Past. Basic form of verb + "ed," or irregular form. Used for actions that were completed in the past.

> **Yesterday I *spoke* with my mother on the phone.**
>
> **The attendance *was* poor because it *snowed* heavily.**

Past Continuous. *Was* or *were* + present participle ("ing") of main verb. Used for ongoing actions in the past.

> **My sister *was studying* every night last week.**

Also used for interrupted past actions, usually with another clause in the simple past.

> **I *was reading* last night when the lights went out.**

Present Perfect. *Has* or *have* + past participle of main verb. Used for actions that began in the past and have continued to the present. Also used for actions repeated in the past that may be repeated in the present. (Often used with time words *for* or *since*.)

> **My family *has lived* in the United States since 1968.**

Present Perfect Continuous. *Has been* or *have been* + present participle ("ing") of main verb. Used for actions that began in the past, are taking place presently, and will probably continue.

> **Professor Nanda *has been studying* Indian culture for many years.**

Past Perfect. *Had* + past participle of main verb. Used for one action in the past that happened earlier than another action in the past. Used with another clause in the simple past tense.

> **I *had studied* English for four years before I entered the United States.**

Past Perfect Continuous. *Had been* + present participle "ing" of main verb. Used for an ongoing action in the past that happened earlier than a completed action in the past.

> I *had been working* in a grocery store for three years before I decided to return to college.

Modals

Modal forms are used to express certain conditions of ability, possibility, probability, or advisement. The main verbs following the modal are always in the basic form.

Can. Present ability; possibility.

> I *can* drive a car well.
>
> I *can* do it later.

Could. Past ability (complementary clause in simple past).

> My father *could* swim well when he was young.

Will. Future certainty.

> I *will* meet you tomorrow at noon.

Would. Conditional probability (complementary clause in simple past).

> If I spoke French fluently, I *would* study in Paris for a year.

Should. Advisability; obligation; expectation.

> You *should* take three semesters of English.
>
> I *should* write a note of thanks to my hostess.
>
> She *should* be here soon.

Must. Necessity; strong probability.

> I *must* pay my rent by the tenth of each month.
>
> You *must* be tired after working so hard.

May. Possibility; probability; permission.

> I *may* go to California next summer.
>
> She is absent. She *may* be sick.
>
> *May* I leave now?

Might. Uncertain possibility.

> I *might* attend the concert tomorrow night.

Could have + past participle of main verb. Past ability; possibility not taken.

> We *could have driven* to California, but we preferred to fly.

Would have + past participle of main verb. Past conditional action not taken.

> I *would have gotten* tickets for the show, but the box office closed at 3:00 P.M.

Should have + past participle of main verb. Past obligation not fulfilled.

> I *should have written* my parents, but I called them instead.

May have + past participle of main verb. Past possibility.

> She *may have gone* already since her class ended at 3:00 P.M.

Must have + past participle of main verb. Deduction about a past event.

> The snow *must have fallen* during the night, as it covered all the cars on the street.

Conditional Patterns with Modals. The use of *if* in sentences suggests that the action depends on certain conditions being met.

> If I *can help* you, I *will.*
>
> If I *could buy* a new car, I *would get* a Dodge.
>
> If I *had gotten* my check yesterday, I *could have bought* my books.
>
> If you *will call* me tomorrow, I *will give* you the assignment.
>
> If you *would speak* to your instructor, she *would explain* the work.
>
> If you *had eaten* a better breakfast, you *would feel* better now.
>
> If you *had gotten* better seats, you *would have enjoyed* the show more.

Passive Voice

Appropriate form of *to be* + past participle of main verb. Used for statements in which the identity of the verb actor is not as important as the person or object *receiving* the verb action.

Simple Present.

> A great deal of furniture *is made* in the Philippines.

Present Continuous.

> Much of this furniture *is being sold* in the United States today.

Simple Past.

> The president's speech *was written* by a professional writer.

Past Continuous.

> The president *was being photographed* while he was speaking.

Present Perfect.

> The laws of the universe *have been known* for thousands of years.

Past Perfect.

> The exam *had been collected* before the bell rang.

Future.

> In the future, all fees *will be paid* at the bursar's office.

Modals.

> No credit *can be given* for dropped courses.
>
> Nothing *could be done* for the poor sick animal.
>
> What *could have happened* to cause such anger?

Appendix C

List of Common Irregular Verbs with Their Basic, Simple Past, and Past Participle Forms

be, am—is—are, was—
   were, been
beat, beat, beaten
become, became, become
begin, began, begun
bend, bent, bent
bet, bet, bet
blow, blew, blown
break, broke, broken
bring, brought, brought
build, built, built
buy, bought, bought
catch, caught, caught
choose, chose, chosen
come, came, come
cost, cost, cost
creep, crept, crept
cut, cut, cut
dig, dug, dug
dive, dove or dived,
   dived
do, did, done
draw, drew, drawn
drink, drank, drunk
drive, drove, driven
eat, ate, eaten

fall, fell, fallen
feed, fed, fed
feel, felt, felt
fight, fought, fought
find, found, found
fit, fit, fit
fly, flew, flown
forget, forgot, forgotten
freeze, froze, frozen
get, got, got or gotten
give, gave, given
go, went, gone
grow, grew, grown
hang, hung, hung
have, had, had
hear, heard, heard
hide, hid, hidden
hit, hit, hit
hold, held, held
hurt, hurt, hurt
keep, kept, kept
know, knew, known
lay, laid, laid
lead, led, led
leave, left, left
lend, lent, lent

let, let, let
lie, lay, lain
lose, lost, lost
make, made, made
mean, meant, meant
meet, met, met
pay, paid, paid
put, put, put
read, read, read
ride, rode, ridden
ring, rang, rung
rise, rose, risen
run, ran, run
say, said, said
see, saw, seen
sell, sold, sold
send, sent, sent
set, set, set
sew, sewed, sewn
shake, shook, shaken
shine, shone, shone
show, showed, shown
shoot, shot, shot
shut, shut, shut
sing, sang, sung
sink, sank, sunk

sit, sat, sat
sleep, slept, slept
speak, spoke, spoken
spend, spent, spent
spread, spread, spread
stand, stood, stood
steal, stole, stolen
stick, stuck, stuck
strike, struck, struck

swear, swore, sworn
sweep, swept, swept
swim, swam, swum
take, took, taken
teach, taught, taught
tear, tore, torn
tell, told, told
think, thought, thought

throw, threw, thrown
understand, understood,
    understood
wake, woke, waken
wear, wore, worn
win, won, won
wind, wound, wound
write, wrote, written

Reference Map

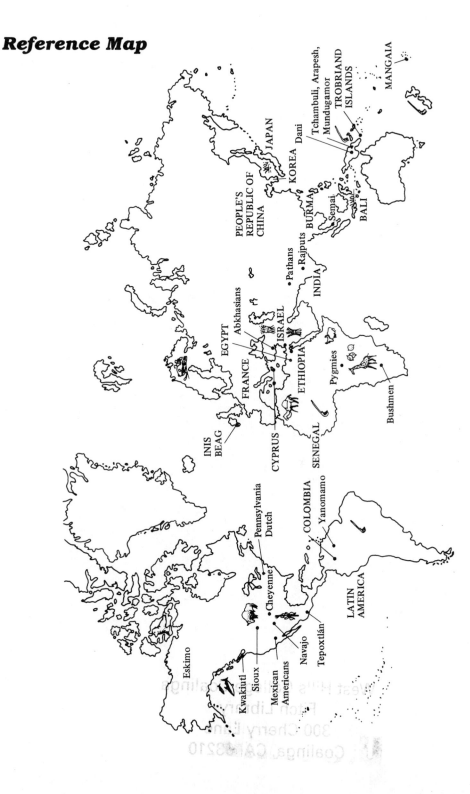

Communication and Culture: A read